Advanced Principles o
and Psychotherapy

Advanced Principles of Counseling and Psychotherapy covers advanced helping-skills topics, including inductive reasoning, Socratic questioning, working with double-binds, and creating second-order change. The ultimate expression of these is in the use of paradoxical interventions, including the use of humor. Professors and students alike will find that *Advanced Principles of Counseling and Psychotherapy* is not just a guide to training; it provides an in-depth understanding of material covered in introductory courses and supplements the material students will cover in practicum and internship.

Gerald J. Mozdzierz, PhD, is a professor in the Department of Psychiatry and Behavioral Neurosciences at Loyola University and also maintains a private practice.

Paul R. Peluso, PhD, is an associate professor and chair of the Department of Counselor Education at Florida Atlantic University. He is the coauthor of five books and author of numerous articles and book chapters.

Joseph Lisiecki, LCSW, has 32 years of clinical experience at Hines VA hospital in Illinois.

Advanced Principles of Counseling and Psychotherapy

Learning, Integrating, and Consolidating the Nonlinear Thinking of Master Practitioners

Gerald J. Mozdzierz, Paul R. Peluso, and Joseph Lisiecki

Routledge
Taylor & Francis Group

NEW YORK AND LONDON

First published 2014
by Routledge
711 Third Avenue, New York, NY 10017

and by Routledge
27 Church Road, Hove, East Sussex BN3 2FA

Routledge is an imprint of the Taylor & Francis Group, an informa business

© 2014 Gerald J. Mozdzierz, Paul R. Peluso, and Joseph Lisiecki

The right of Gerald J. Mozdzierz, Paul R. Peluso, and Joseph Lisiecki to be identified as authors of this work has been asserted by them in accordance with sections 77 and 78 of the Copyright, Designs and Patents Act 1988.

Library of Congress Cataloging-in-Publication Data

Mozdzierz, Gerald J., 1940–
Advanced principles of counseling and psychotherapy : learning, integrating, and consolidating the nonlinear thinking of master practitioners / by Gerald J. Mozdzierz, Paul R. Peluso, and Joseph Lisiecki.
    pages cm
Includes bibliographical references and index.
  1. Psychotherapy.   2. Counseling.   3. Counseling psychology.   I. Peluso, Paul R.
II. Lisiecki, Joseph.   III. Title.
  RC480.5.M688 2014
  616.89′14—dc23
  2013046439

ISBN: 978-0-415-70463-2 (hbk)
ISBN: 978-0-415-70465-6 (pbk)
ISBN: 978-0-203-76189-2 (ebk)

Typeset in Minion
by Apex CoVantage, LLC

GJM—This book is dedicated specifically to Felix and Genevieve Mozdzierz, whose devotion to parenting, guidance, and support provided the foundations for learning, hard work, and contributing; it is in general dedicated to those teachers and supervisors who served as mentors of great humanity, wisdom, and patience. In particular, I would like to acknowledge Drs. Paul Von Ebers, Bernard Shulman, Roy Brener, and Jeffrey Levy for their particularly encouraging mentorship. Finally, I would like to acknowledge Charlene Greco Mozdzierz, without whose cooperation none of my contributions to this work would have been possible. She gave of her time, supplied encouragement through long stretches at the computer, and, most of all, she gave understanding.

PRP—To Roy M. Kern, Augustus Y. Napier, Jon Carlson, John Gottman, and Paul Ekman, my teachers, my mentors, my colleagues, and my friends. Many thanks for all the lessons I have learned.

JL—To Jack Cowen, Kurt Adler, and all of our other mentors, colleagues, clients, friends, and family who inspired us.

Contents

Preface

This work represents a different way of conceptualizing what it takes to become a master practitioner. Among the defining characteristics of such a clinician are hard work, a thirst for learning and understanding at a profound level, and an insatiable curiosity. We have come to conclude—in this text and in our previous one, *Principles of Counseling and Psychotherapy: Learning the Essential Domains and Nonlinear Thinking of Master Practitioners,* 2nd edition (Mozdzierz, Peluso, & Lisiecki, 2014)—that at the core of such a practitioner is someone who thinks in profoundly different (nonlinear) ways about clients/patients, the work of therapy, and life in general. This takes the aspiring master practitioner on an incredible journey filled with unique personalities and often difficult narratives of struggling, suffering, and overcoming the adversities of what it is to be a human being. They know it is a privilege to have earned the trust to share in the intimate details of so many lives.

In both texts, we have attempted to describe how to think in nonlinear ways on the road to mastery. That nonlinear way takes into account the individual variability of those who consult us while simultaneously looking for the commonalities they share. It also takes into account that thinking in nonlinear ways allows for integrating seemingly disparate and incompatible understandings in a never-ending thirst to grow. Of course, it is not the destination of becoming a master practitioner but rather the journey of becoming that is the essential ingredient of career enjoyment. It is with that sentiment in mind that we hope you find this text instructional in your journey.

Acknowledgments

We would like to thank all of the people at Routledge but especially Ms. Anna Moore, our editor, on this project for her undoubting confidence in our ability to bring it to a successful conclusion. She has been gracious, fair, gentle, thoughtful, and honest in her helpfulness, and for that, we are most grateful. In addition, we would like to thank those individuals who made some of the unique features of this book possible, including "the Avengers" from the Alliance Lab at Florida Atlantic University, especially Ashley Luedke, Mike Norman, Raffaela Peter, Rob Freund, Patricia Diaz, and Vanessa Heine. Finally, we are indebted to Elizabeth Robey at Alexander Street Press who facilitated the inclusion of video material and helped make this edition really come alive.

We would like to express gratitude to mentors who throughout the years by their personal and professional behavior provided the implicit and explicit guidance necessary for professional growth and development to take place. We are also indebted to the countless patients, clients, and families with whom we have worked and who sparked our imaginations, stimulated our thinking, and in the end, promoted our development as better clinicians. These nameless individuals were the inspiration for the clinical case examples contained in the book.

Last, and most heartfelt, we could not have devoted the time, energy, and effort that a work such as this requires without the love and support of our families, especially our spouses, Charlene Mozdzierz, Jennifer Peluso, and Mary Ann Lisiecki. We also extend a specific loving acknowledgment to our children (Kimberly, Krista, Pamela, and Andrea Mozdzierz; Helen and Lucy Peluso; and Ann Marie, Joseph, Teresa, and Paul Lisiecki).

Introduction

"Pass on What You Have Learned . . ."

"When gone am I, the last of the Jedi, you will be." With that, Yoda, the Jedi master in the movie *Return of the Jedi*, passes the "mantle" of maintaining the Jedi order to Luke Skywalker. Two films earlier, in *Star Wars: A New Hope*, Luke's first Jedi master Obi Wan Kenobi explains what happened to the Jedi: "For a thousand generations, the Jedi Knights were the guardians of peace and justice in the Old Republic; before the dark time, before the Empire! Now the Jedi are all but extinct . . ." For many master therapists who remember it, the 1960s, 1970s, and part of the 1980s may represent the "golden era" of counseling and psychotherapy. During this time, practitioners were developing dynamic approaches to counseling and had a level of freedom in the practice of therapy and in training its new practitioners that was unparalleled. Then came the "dark time" of managed care and insurance panels; licensure regulation and strict accreditation standards, evidence-based practices and manualized treatments. While these developments created "order" and "stability" (and maybe even a dose of credibility and respectability) to a field that was once criticized as being too "loose" and "unscientific," these changes also came at a cost. For many practitioners, there was a sense of loss and disconnect as the creativity and artfulness of the profession were driven out in favor of precision and measurable outcomes. Today, many practitioners feel a sense of loss at the depth and wealth of knowledge from some of the best traditions of the past that have almost been forgotten in the modern-day training of clinicians. As some of the great master practitioners pass away, we feel that unless preserved, some of their secrets will pass away with them. As he is about to die, Yoda tells Luke: "Pass on what you have learned" to a new generation of Jedi. This is what we intend to do in this book.

The Three Dimensions of Learning to Be a Master Therapist

As in all professions, growth and maturity take place on the way from novice to journeyman to master practitioner. This book is part of a larger system of training individuals to become master practitioners, beginning with Mozdzierz, Peluso, and Lisiecki (2014) and concluding here. It is based in part on some of the oldest traditions in the field, as well as on some of the latest research in psychotherapy, neuroscience, and mastery training fields. This training system had three elements to it: (1) nonlinear thinking of master practitioners; (2) the seven domains of competence; and (3) a model for therapist development.

Nonlinear Thinking and Master Practitioners

Our first, basic conclusion about master practitioners is that they *think differently* than other practitioners. They seem to have the ability to evaluate a client's situation and know just what to say, when to say it, and how to say it in ways that most novice (and even experienced) clinicians don't (or seemingly can't). Nonlinear thinking means that a person sees beyond the facts to the patterns that emerge and realizes that there may be more to a situation than is presented on the surface. People who consult practitioners typically do so because they apply only personally linear, *reactive* (i.e., automatic, unreflective, unconscious, etc.) thinking in attempting to solve the dilemmas with which they are faced. Correspondingly, they begin to avoid, excuse, withdraw, become anxious, and generally become "stuck" in their life. As a solution, they attempt to do "more of the same" only to find that such solutions ineffective and typically worsening their circumstances. Nonlinear thinking is more *reflective* and finds meaning and possibilities that go beyond what is readily observable, or responses that are reflexive.

Of course, learning *how to think like a therapist* (i.e., the process of formulating a case conceptualization; understanding the double-binds in which a client may find himself or herself; realizing the purpose being served by certain symptomatic behavior; and devising a coherent plan about how to proceed that encompasses the relevant clinical findings and social circumstances of the person) is vastly different from telling someone *what* to think. Such *how* thinking maximizes therapist flexibility in dealing with the infinite variety that clients and their circumstances bring to the treatment setting. Teaching *what to think* would involve, for example, insisting that others learn a particular orientation (e.g., Freudian, Adlerian, or Jungian) and working only from that framework as the "truth" no matter what the problem or complaint of the client might be. Traditionally, psychotherapists are exposed to a particular theory of personality, a theory of therapy, specific protocols on how to treat particular conditions (e.g., anxiety, obsessive-compulsive disorder, or depression), or a set of micro-level skills that they then adopt as an operational model. It is our hypothesis that each novice adopts a particular theory (of personality or therapy) because of its "fit" with his or her own world-view (see Information Box I.1, "Theory Is for the Clinician; Therapy Is for the Client!"). The therapist then learns "how to think" from that particular frame of reference.

Information Box I.1: Theory Is for the Clinician; Therapy Is for the Client!

Clinicians who think in nonlinear ways and understand how to effectively utilize the common convergence factors (i.e., domains of competence) can have a greater likelihood of achieving maximally effective therapeutic outcomes. At the same time, those clinicians who have a firm grasp on their *own* theory of counseling or personality have a roadmap *for themselves* whereby they can understand and interpret the client and the problem, the process of therapy, and their own role in the change process. Consider the following metaphor to understand this point more fully.

Suppose you are putting together a jigsaw puzzle that has a picture on it. The box has the completed puzzle picture on it to give you an idea of what the puzzle will look like when finished. The client gives you information about himself or herself (the pieces), but you don't know in what order to place them. You know that there is a picture that the puzzle should make. Having a good grasp of theory is like having a completed puzzle box picture to let you know where the pieces should generally fit, and what the picture (i.e., the collection of all of the client's pieces) should look like. Although you can try to put together a 500- or 1,000-piece puzzle without the box, it will probably take a lot longer. The same is true with conducting therapy without a solid theoretical grounding. Clients may provide a great many "pieces of their puzzle," but to fully understand and appreciate what those pieces mean and what to do about them will take longer.

The amazing thing is that the research literature demonstrates that the particular theory or model of therapy (e.g., object relations, Adlerian, or Jungian) makes absolutely no difference in treatment outcome (see Duncan, Hubble, & Miller, 2000; Hubble, Duncan, & Miller, 1999; Lambert & Barley, 2002; Miller, Duncan, & Hubble, 1997; Norcross, 2002b; Walt, 2005). In fact, research from more than half a century ago (i.e., Fielder, 1950) revealed that experts with different theoretical orientations are much more similar than different in what they actually do with clients. Duncan (2010) has summarized this issue quite cogently:

Given a therapist who has an effective personality and who consistently adheres in his treatment to a system of concepts which he has mastered and which is in one significant way or another adapted to the problems of the sick personality, then it is of comparatively little consequence what particular method that therapist uses. It is . . . necessary to admit the more elementary consideration that in certain types of mental disturbances certain kinds of therapy are indicated as compared with certain others . . . the following considerations . . . apply in common to avowedly diverse methods of psychotherapy: (1) the operation of implicit, universalized factors, such as catharsis, and the as yet undefined effect of the personality of the good therapist; (2) the formal consistency of the therapeutic ideology as a basis for reintegration; (3) the alternative formulation of psychological events and the interdependence of personality organization as concepts which reduce the effectual importance of mooted differences between one form of psychotherapy and another.

(pp. 12–13)

So while theory is important for the clinician, we feel that in order to "operate" the "implicit universal factors of therapy" and to make an alternative "formulation of psychological events" requires nonlinear thinking.

This text focuses on the application of nonlinear thinking in general and paradoxical interventions in treatment as a domain. We will demonstrate that paradoxical interventions are ubiquitous in practice with clients; all classical and contemporary theories and orientations to therapy describe their own brand of paradoxical interventions. Each orientation has its own label or name for what they call nonlinear thinking and paradoxical interventions. It makes little difference as to what particular practitioners and theorists call an intervention when it is identical to what other practitioners and theorists do but call by another name. As Shakespeare once said, "A rose by any other name would smell as sweet." That's precisely why we have labeled such interventions as universal and transtheoretical. Thinking in *nonlinear/paradoxical* ways is an integrating principle of psychotherapeutic work. This applies to those researchers/practitioners who understand such things as the following:

- It is not techniques *but monitoring the client's sentiments about treatment and its perceived effectiveness* that is important (Lambert, 2010);
- It is the *relationship and therapeutic alliance* that is at the core of what is accomplished in treatment (Miller, Hubble, Duncan, & Wampold, 2010; Norcross, 2010);
- Paradoxically, not all clients coming for treatment are interested in change or if they are interested, they are not necessarily at the same level of preparedness for change (Prochaska, 1999; Prochaska & DiClemente, 1982, 2005);
- Eliciting feedback *from* clients is crucial to successfully reaching therapeutic success (Lambert, 2010; Lambert & Shimokawa, 2011); and
- Evidence-Based Practices ("EBPs") must always be put into a context before they are applied in mechanical, technical and "if *this* condition then apply *this* treatment."

We conclude that to learn about therapist nonlinear thinking, in combination with the factors that are known to increase a therapist's general effectiveness, from the earliest point of development seems to be the most appropriate way to train clinicians.

The Seven Essential Domains of Expertise

The second dimension of this system of training is drawn from the research on "common therapeutic factors," or what we term *domains of convergence*. A *domain* can be defined as the scope of a particular subject or a broad area or field of knowledge (Skovholt & Rivers, 2004). As a result, it is worth stressing that domains are *not* the same as skills or techniques—skills are applied within the context of a domain of knowledge (or field). As such, they represent a *refinement of one's thinking within a certain area* rather than an application of mechanical skills. The refinement of one's thinking within particular domains includes the thought processes behind skills, explanations, and theories regarding the topic, and research about the subject area. It represents an *understanding and discernment.* The skilled surgeon knows *how to operate,* whereas the wise surgeon knows not only *how* to operate but also *whether or not to operate* in a given instance. In other words, it includes both linear and nonlinear thinking!

The present text is devoted in large measure to the seventh domain, namely, paradoxical interventions and the nonlinear thinking behind it. As an orientation, we will discuss the first six domains briefly below. They are the following: connecting with and engaging a client; assessment; establishing a relationship; attending to what clients are thinking;

attending to what emotions clients are experiencing; and identifying and helping clients to resolve ambivalences that they experience (e.g., wanting one's cake and eating it too, choosing between the lesser of two evils, etc.). For a more thorough description and discussion of the first six domains, we recommend Mozdzierz et al. (2014).

Introducing the Seven Domains of Competence

1. *The domain of connecting with and engaging the client.* This domain includes both linear and nonlinear listening and responding to clients as primary vehicles for "connecting with and engaging" the client in the work of therapy. Linear listening and responding includes listening and responding to content (the "what" that is being said), and listening and responding to feelings (or the emotion behind what is being said). In addition, there are five categories of nonlinear listening and responding. They can be easily remembered using the acronym CAPIR (like "caper"). This stands for Congruence, Absence, Presence, Inference, and Resistance. Effectively connecting and engaging will increase the probability of clients becoming invested in the therapeutic process in the crucial first sessions.

2. *The domain of assessment of clients' symptoms, stages of change, needs, strengths, and resources; and the theme behind a client's narrative, therapeutic goals.* This domain describes the linear and nonlinear methods of assessing clients' presenting problems and concerns at multiple levels. That includes attending to clients' readiness for change (or stage of change) as well as their symptom patterns, diagnoses, strengths, and (untapped) resources that can be used in overcoming problems. In addition, the domain of assessment also includes actively eliciting client cooperation in the treatment-planning process and developing appropriate preliminary goals for treatment. Finally, we outlined seven broad themes that client problems generally fall into, including themes of helplessness, hopelessness, exhaustion, despair, etc.

3. *The domain of establishing and maintaining the therapeutic relationship and the therapeutic alliance.* This domain encompasses perhaps the central aspect of psychotherapy: developing a therapeutic alliance. An integral part of this domain concerns developing an understanding of what factors contribute toward building a trusting therapeutic relationship with a client in the service of establishing and maintaining the therapeutic alliance. Using the most recent research findings on the components (such as the alliance between client and therapist, empathy, goal consensus, collaboration) that have the greatest impact on the therapeutic relationship, as well as the methods of adapting the therapeutic relationship that are demonstrated to be effective, we describe what a good therapeutic relationship should look like and how a therapist can effectively create one.

4. *The domain of understanding clients' cognitive schemas.* This domain requires a clinician to have both linear and nonlinear understandings of clients' schematized view-of-self, view-of-others, and view-of-world around them. This domain deals with global concepts such as clients' internal response sets and belief systems that can be positive or negative, realistic or unrealistic, and rigid or flexible. These schema dynamics guide attitudes, thoughts, and behavior that can impact treatment. As such, it is important for clinicians to understand the nonlinear components of clients' schematized belief systems. It includes becoming proficient in working with the effects of clients' developmental (family-of-origin) dynamics on their perceptions. In addition, utilizing this

domain includes skills for helping clients challenge and alter distorted perceptions of the world around them using assimilation and accommodation to create first-order and second-order change.

5. *The domain of addressing and managing clients' emotional states.* This domain defines the nature of emotions in all of their complexity. In addition, it requires the clinician to have an understanding of the relationship between affective expressions, internal feelings, and emotional states, and their role in treatment progress (or lack thereof). Clinicians must learn the art of managing overwhelming emotions (e.g., grief and anger) that clients may express, allowing them to feel emotion in appropriate and productive ways. This includes using emotion-focused and mindfulness-based techniques that allow for the client to understand and appropriately express his or her emotions.

6. *The domain of addressing and resolving client ambivalence.* This domain deals with understanding the process of client "ambivalence" including the underlying dilemmas that drive it (approach-approach, avoidance-avoidance, etc.). In addition, effective strategies for dealing with ambivalence that borrow from Motivational Interviewing, Acceptance and Commitment Therapy, Dialectical Behavioral Therapy, Solution-Focused Therapy, and Narrative approaches demonstrate how to hold clients accountable and successfully help them maintain therapeutic focus.

These six domains (see Mozdzierz et al., 2014) merge together in a seamless way in their use of paradoxical thinking. This requires both linear and nonlinear thinking. The present work is focused on learning about master practitioners' use of a particular "domain," called *paradoxical/nonlinear thinking.* Figure I.1 demonstrates the relationship between the various domains and how they build upon one another. Notice that the domain on paradoxical/nonlinear thinking with humor included is at the top of the cone. In effect, it is in that location because it is the most elegant and sophisticated of the domains and requires the *integration of the other domains for its effectiveness.*

The seventh and final domain is *the domain of understanding nonlinear thought processes and utilizing paradoxical interventions.* This is the pinnacle of the therapeutic endeavor, and as mentioned above, the basis for this book. It is not a trick or technique, but a sophisticated method of nonlinear thinking that can be learned and used to quickly and efficiently help to facilitate some relief for clients' suffering and progress toward their therapeutic goals by neutralizing, energizing, tranquilizing, or challenging dysfunctional thought and behavioral patterns. It crystallizes the direct relationship between nonlinear thinking and the previous six domains. Nonlinear interventions are elegant, complex, and yet simple reflections of how human perception contends with reality on an everyday basis. Such interventions reflect a mature understanding of human communication, motivation, and positive influences in encouraging change.

These common factors, or domains, are so important because, according to Wampold (2010): "A model that emphasizes the common factors predicts that, with some qualifications all cogent treatments, embraced by therapists and client competently delivered to a client motivated to engage in the process are equally effective" (p. 56). Another way to metaphorically think about these domains is to think of them as the basic ingredients that consistently appear to be identified in the literature as vital to all effective therapy, regardless of one's theoretical orientation. By paying attention to these domains, master

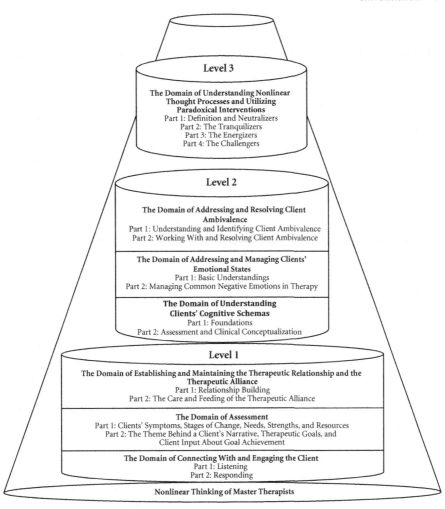

Figure I.1 The Seven Domains that Master Practitioners Attend to and Emphasize

practitioners greatly enhance their chances of having positive therapeutic impact, increasing client satisfaction, and sense of goal attainment, thereby shortening the treatment process. Knowing that these are the *key* areas to observe and concentrate on enhances their effectiveness because it makes for better choices as to how to intervene with clients.

Developmental Processes

The third dimension to our system of training is the developmental model described by Stoltenberg (1993, 1997) and his colleagues (Stoltenberg & Delworth, 1987, 1997; Stoltenberg & McNeill, 2009). Their model of therapist growth recognizes a three-level integrated-developmental model of counselor development. Defining the contours of therapist development is useful. It helps enhance a sense of the *typical* personal and professional issues confronted at various stages. Gauging their own professional performance, developing therapists are able to evaluate progress and determine professional areas (specific content domains) in need of improvement. Development and growth in professional skill, judgment, and competence, however, are not rigid concepts; they are quite vibrant, flexile, and dynamic since not all practitioners grow and develop in the same way. In order to put the advanced practitioner in a context, we begin our discussion with a brief sketch of "the beginner," their preoccupations, and typical focus of attention.

The Level 1 Practitioner

According to the Stoltenberg model, a "Level 1" therapist is characterized more by an internal focus, feeling anxious, requiring structure and oftentimes formulaic solutions (i.e., "techniques") for client ills. They may not be particularly insightful, and when looking for specific "techniques" with clients (i.e., "How do you deal with a woman who has been anxious all her life?"), they can "miss the forest for the trees." Their focus of attention has much more to do with such things as "not making mistakes with clients . . . how good a job am I doing . . . am I doing it right . . . why didn't this technique work . . . etc." rather than focusing on *the client.* This is important because *focusing on the client, their needs and goals, perception of the value of the treatment and sense of progress toward their goals* has been identified by Norcross (2010), Duncan, Miller, Wampold, and Hubble (2010), as well as others, as essential in eliciting maximal client satisfaction with the treatment outcome. Unfortunately, the Level 1 practitioner is often far from the psychological mindedness suggested by Norcross and Duncan et al. (For a more thorough clinical descriptive profile of the Level 1 and Level 2 counselor/therapist profile, see Mozdzierz et al., 2014.)

The Level 2 Practitioner

"Level 2" therapists have developed more confidence and are much more comfortable in the consultation room. Along with their increased confidence and comfortableness, the Level 2 clinician can more readily concentrate on a client's narrative as well as his or her cognitions and emotional state of mind. They understand and appreciate the value of the therapeutic relationship and alliance. At times, Level 2 practitioners may demonstrate overconfidence in their abilities as demonstrated in oversimplifying issues, agreeing to see clients with complex problems or multiple co-morbidities beyond their level of competence, losing professional objectivity, or becoming overinvolved emotionally with clients.

The Level 2 practitioner is on the way to learning how to think differently. Rather than being preoccupied with self, they are beginning to understand that empathy, the therapeutic relationship, and the therapeutic alliance must be a prime focus of attention for maximum client satisfaction with treatment and goal attainment. However, the Level 2 therapist's thinking has not thoroughly evolved thinking processes that are completely *nonlinear* in nature.

The Level 3 Practitioner

Level 3 practitioners understand that their chosen life's work continually evolves as a product of personal maturation and professional growth. Becoming a master practitioner is also fraught with disquiet, frustration, query, setbacks, and the like, as demonstrated in the feeling of sometimes taking two steps forward and one step back. This has been well expressed by master practitioner Scott Miller:

> I, on the other hand was plagued by doubt. Even later, as a fully *bona fide* treatment professional, seated opposite a particular client, I often felt like I had missed the one crucial day in graduate school—that one day when they taught you the secret handshake, the secret ingredient in the "Big Ma" of therapy.
>
> (Quoted in Walt, 2005, p. 1)

In a number of dimensions, master practitioners are much more "balanced" than practitioners at Levels 1 and 2. As discussed above, at the Levels 1 and 2, there is a measure of angst regarding being in professional settings, relating to clients, and a host of other concerns. In contrast, Level 3 is familiar with and comfortable in their surroundings (e.g., hospital, an outpatient clinic, private practice, or a counseling center), duties and responsibilities, support network available to them, etc. Likewise, Level 3 practitioners are equally comfortable in their professional role. Clearly, they experience a palpable sense of comfort with their ability while simultaneously remaining realistically aware of their limitations. For example, masters are sensitive to, humbled, and moved by many varieties of human suffering, but they do not allow themselves to be overwhelmed or immobilized by them. At the same time, being human, they understand that they can be vulnerable to the "first responders' syndrome" (i.e., secondary traumatization, emotional burnout, grief, etc.) and as a result engage in proper self-care. The Level 3 practitioner is intuitively compassionate and empathic with the anguish that his clients experience. Despite their intuitive empathic concern, Level 3 practitioners are ever mindful of a need to maintain professional boundaries and responsibilities. In that regard, the practitioner at this level is able to provide warmth, comfort, reassurance, and validation to troubled clients without violating appropriate boundaries. Master practitioners also maintain a muted sense of understanding that if some clients were not intransigent, irascible, and disquieting, they would have little need for being in a therapist's office. Under challenging conditions prompted by such client behavior, masters understand that maintaining a hopeful and realistic outlook and a positive therapeutic alliance are paramount. They also are continually mindful of the expression "It is *not the illness* that the person has but *the person that has the illness* that is important!" (Author unknown)

Operating within their frame of reference, Level 3 practitioners have a well-calibrated sense of the potential impact of their interventions. They also seek, accept, and integrate client feedback regarding the direction and fruitfulness of the treatment process or lack of such progress. Correspondingly, Level 3 practitioners are able to critique their interventions and use client feedback as "practice-based evidence" (Hubble, Duncan, Miller, & Wampold, 2010, p. 39). They incorporate client feedback into their work as an important source of information for making certain that the client's goals and their own therapeutic goals are in alignment. Miscues are taken in stride without a sense of guilt, immobilizing self-denigration, or feeling of failure. In keeping with the characteristics of "resilient" individuals, Level 3 practitioners do not define themselves according to therapeutic frustrations, reversals, adversities, or misfortunes. Rather, with the help of professional values, they ground themselves with a devotion to learning from such setbacks because they understand that they are building another dimension of clinical experience.

The irony is that once someone achieves true mastery of his or her province, the person seems to care less about being a master and more about bringing out the best in himself or herself. Paradoxically, master practitioners understand that although earlier aspirations (i.e., those described in our introductory volume as being at Levels 1 and 2) may have been driven by a desire to *be* a master, they now have little concern or preoccupation with such matters. They are more concerned with being themselves, relating in an authentic way, and being fully available to clients. They are continually involved in the process of *becoming* a master practitioner rather than an end-point of being one. They continue to strive and enjoy the process of striving. The reader will note that, throughout this introduction, there is an implied relationship between practicing at Level 3 and becoming a master practitioner. The reasoning for this interchangeability is that practicing one's profession at Level 3 is the gateway to becoming a master practitioner.

The Purpose of This Text

With the above considerations in mind, the purpose of this book is to focus on the seventh and final domain, the use of paradoxical interventions, which is characteristic of a Level 3 practitioner. In addition, we are expanding our discussion to include a more in-depth understanding of what we call *advanced nonlinear thinking*. This includes a thorough understanding of deductive and inductive reasoning, double-binds, using Socratic questioning, and first- and second-order change. We have expanded what we call "precursors" to the use of paradoxical interventions, which includes different aspects of reframing prescribing the symptom. Finally we will discuss the use of humor in therapy, how it requires advanced nonlinear thinking, and how it shares common characteristics with paradoxical interventions. Throughout the text, we will incorporate the tenets of deliberate practice, which according to researchers in the field, is necessary for achieving mastery in any field, as well as creating innovation within a discipline—a *must* for successfully utilizing paradoxical interventions.

Development of Mastery and "Deliberate Practice"

Chi (2006) described a number of characteristics that distinguish experts from nonexperts. First, they are able to generate the best solution for a given situation, and they can do this better than nonexperts. Second, they can detect and recognize features of a given situation that novices cannot, such as deeper concerns or structures in a given situation or problem. Third, experts seem to spend a lot of time analyzing a problem qualitatively, thus bringing in knowledge from both within and outside their given field to apply to a problem. Fourth, experts are also able to engage in self-monitoring, thereby evaluating their progress more accurately. Fifth, experts are "opportunistic": They make use of whatever information sources or resources are at their disposal and are able to choose more effective strategies in problem solving while using minimal cognitive effort compared to novices. Put simply, experts are able to achieve better results because they bring together and use many seemingly intangible resources when they work, and they appear to do it effortlessly.

Just as with other fields, some clinicians are more effective than others with different clients (Lambert & Barley, 2002), and as a result, they get different results. Wampold and Brown (2005) found that for low-performing clinicians (in the bottom 25%), their clients had only a 20% chance of achieving reliable change in their level of functioning. Furthermore, they found that the "best" therapists (top 25%) did *better* than expected, and they did so consistently. The lingering question is "why?" Thus, it is not simply a matter that there are naturally gifted therapists and (conversely) naturally dreadful therapists. If it were so, then the therapists with poor outcomes would do poorly *all the time*. But, they did not do poorly all of the time. In fact, they were able to have a positive impact with some clients. According to Wampold (2005), "[t]he variance of outcomes due to therapists (8%–9%) is larger than the variability among therapists (0%–1%), the alliance (5%), and the superiority of an empirically supported treatment to a placebo (0%–4%)" (p. 204). So while it might be difficult to objectively quantify expertise in psychotherapy (Chi, 2006; Hubble et al., 2010), expertise *does* matter. So, if age, degree, or years of experience do not necessarily translate into expertise, how does one attain mastery?

According to Ericsson: "[t]he acquisition of expert performance can thus be described as a series of relatively stable states where each state has a set of mechanisms that mediate the execution of associated performance" (2006, p. 694). In other words, each level of a practitioner's development (Level 1, Level 2, Level 3) can be thought of as one of these "stable states," and each of the domains within are mechanisms that mediate the "execution of performance." According to Davidson and Sternberg (1998), "teaching meta-cognition skills in conjunction with the domain-specific skills seems to be more effective than teaching each type of skill separately" (p. 63). In other words, a domain encompasses all aspects (the breadth and depth) of a particular topic. Regardless of the field of knowledge, mastery of essential domains is what accounts for the differences between the *abilities and results* of novices *and* experts. Novices can learn the basics of the domain (the breadth) and, over time, develop a richer understanding of the subtleties of it (the depth). Thus, we have incorporated the discussion of linear and nonlinear thinking (metacognition) within each of the domains.

Generally speaking, during the first phase of learning (Level 1), beginners try to understand the requirements of the activity or discipline and focus on performing the tasks (basic listening and understanding, assessment, developing a therapeutic relationship) while avoiding gross mistakes. For example, a beginning therapist must deliberately practice Domains 1, 2, and 3, while the Level 2 practitioner is likely to deliberately focus on both the Level 1 domains (1, 2, and 3) as well as the Level 2 domains (4, 5, and 6). In the second phase, when people have had more experience, noticeable mistakes become increasingly rare, performance appears smoother, and learners no longer need to focus as intensely on their performance to maintain an acceptable level. After a limited period of training and experience—frequently less than 50 hours (say, after their first practicum experience), they develop an acceptable level of performance, and can automatically, and with minimal effort, perform these skills. But as their actions become automatic, practitioners cannot actively control and modify these behaviors. Some experts will at some point in their career give up their commitment to improvement and stop their deliberate practice to further improve performance. This leads to a plateauing, which results in premature automation of their performance. By contrast, however, expert performers who seek mastery consciously counteract this automaticity.

The "secret" to the process of mastery, as Ericsson et al. (2006) and others have identified, is *deliberate practice*. It has been identified as the active ingredient in mastery of any professional endeavor. As Horn and Masunaga (2006) have put it, deliberate practice is "... focused, programmatic, carried out over extended periods of time, guided by *conscious performance monitoring, evaluated by analysis of level of expertise reached, identification of errors, and procedure directed at eliminating errors*" (p. 601, emphasis added). In therapy and counseling, deliberate practice, among other things would entail such things as case review, self-reflection, and an understanding that the process of learning about therapy involves fitting its various parts into an organic whole. As such, the process of learning requires *the integration of what appears to be disconnected parts* (as Davidson & Sternberg, 1998, suggested).

It is our contention that if a person masters the linear and nonlinear thinking aspects of each of the domains (which we will describe in the next chapter) for a particular level of development, the end result will be a more effective and personally satisfied clinician compared with trainees who do *not* undertake this. Furthermore, as a therapist progresses from level to level and masters the domains of each successive level, he or she will be able to be more effective with a greater versatility in the same way that "master therapists" are.

There are two limiting factors to the model of deliberate practice and attainment of mastery. First, the work is mentally demanding and requires concentration at a level that cannot be sustained for long periods of time (approximately 5 hours a day). Interestingly, that amount of time is true regardless of the field of expertise that is being pursued (sports, math, chess, or therapy!). The second limiting factor is that there is a "scarcity of optimal training environments and to the years required to develop the complex mediating mechanisms that support expertise." Even for individuals who are naturally "gifted," without the proper training environments, their full potential is not achieved. In addition, most other individuals, who *could* learn mastery, instead choose to focus on a supposed "lack" of natural talent, rather than a lack of proper training environments (that support deliberate practice). Sadly, this is true in counseling and psychotherapy. It is one of the reasons for the creation of this system of training.

How Will We Do This?

There are several key features that we have incorporated into this text in order to help "break down" many of the esoteric and theoretical concepts that we are addressing (paradoxical interventions, mastery, *advanced* nonlinear thinking) and make it more concrete for the reader. These include reviewing clinician attitudes and dispositions, and incorporating elements of deliberate practice such as case examples, nonlinear thinking exercises, transcribed examples of masters at work, and video examples of these concepts in action. We will describe them briefly, below.

Clinician Attitudes and Dispositions

In our introductory text (Mozdzierz et al., 2014), we added to each of the seven domains an accompanying clinician attitude or disposition that corresponded to that domain. And, just as we believe that there are universal domains that all master practitioners use—to some degree or another—we think that there are corresponding attitudes or dispositions that all practitioners seem to incorporate into their unique styles (see Table I.1).

Mozdzierz et al. (2014) described the first six attitudes/dispositions, and in this text, we will describe the seventh and final one, irony (see Chapter 2). Just as with domains, each of these dispositions are *additive*. For example, while connecting and engaging requires curiosity as the main nonlinear strategy for clinicians, assessment requires both curiosity *and* collaboration (just like it requires connecting and engaging). Focusing on the therapeutic relationship involves optimism and hope, as well as the capacity to be curious and collaborative. Effectively utilizing paradoxical interventions requires irony *as well as* mindfulness, self-soothing, pattern recognition, optimism and hope, collaboration and curiosity. Ultimately, we feel that each of these seven attitudes adds together to make a good "picture" of what a nonlinear thinking therapist considers when approaching a client, and we present them as a guide for what an aspiring *nonlinear* thinker considers.

Deliberate Practice Elements

The process of mastery is not a smooth "one-size-fits-all" process. *No two people are alike, nor do they learn in the same way, in the same style at the same pace.* This is an important awareness and one to genuinely assimilate and embrace. The reason for mentioning this is to predict that some people will have a difficult time in understanding the essence of certain material that we discuss and *that is natural and normal.* As much as possible in the present text, we want to circumvent some of those difficulties by providing *real* clinical case examples, discussion of those examples as well as exercises to further enhance the learning process.

Table I.1 Corresponding Clinician Attitudes or Dispositions for Mastery

Domain	Corresponding Clinician Attitudes or Dispositions
1. Connecting and Engaging	1. Curiosity
2. Assessment	2. Collaboration
3. Therapeutic Relationship	3. Optimism and Hope
4. Schema Dynamics	4. Pattern Recognition
5. Emotional System	5. Self-Soothing
6. Ambivalence	6. Mindfulness
7. Paradoxical Intervention	7. Irony

Case Examples

In this text, we have included a number of real-world case examples from our clinical experience. Each of these have been selected to illustrate the particular element of nonlinear thinking or paradoxical interactions. Many of these cases have reflection questions for the reader to practice some of the aspects of nonlinear thinking that is being presented (i.e., deliberate practice), as well as in-depth analysis of the case material and the implications of the intervention for treatment. Lastly, we have included some transcript material from two full-length cases (The Case of Ashley and The Case of Mike), the videos of which will be available online at: www.academicvideostore.com/video/principles-counseling-and-psychotherapy-essential-domains-and-non-linear-thinking-master or by going to www.academicvideostore.com and searching on the book title.

Nonlinear Thinking Exercises

Periodically in this book (and the advanced text), we will be presenting exercises, called "Exercising Your Nonlinear Thinking" that are designed to get the reader to think in nonlinear ways. Interestingly, many of these puzzles are ancient, and some are more modern. In addition, there are some riddles that require some nonlinear thinking that applies to the particular material or section of the text.

Examples of Masters at Work

According to Ericsson et al. (2006), "more-accomplished individuals in the domain, such as professional coaches and teachers, will always play an essential role in guiding the sequencing of practice activities for future experts in a safe and effective manner" (pp. 698–699). So another element of deliberate practice is watching experts performing the tasks that are being illustrated. In this text, there are transcripts with "master practitioners" demonstrating paradoxical interventions. These sections, we have titled "Don't take OUR word for it!" This allows readers to see how a particular master works with a client in the domain. These master clinicians' sessions will be embedded in the text for the reader to further illustrate the specific element of the domain, as well as the universal nature of the domain (i.e., used regardless of their theoretical orientation).

In addition, we have created an accompanying video component that shows master clinicians working with real clients and displaying the domain-specific skills. (This can be accessed by going to www.academicvideostore.com/video/principles-counseling-and-psychotherapy-essential-domains-and-non-linear-thinking-master or by going to www.academicvideostore.com and searching on the book title). This site will allow the reader to be able to watch various elements of each domain to be demonstrated. Lastly, there is produced "introductory" material for each domain that can be accessed by going to www.routledge.com/cw/Mozdzierz. This may be subject to university subscriptions, check with your local librarian for full access.

Summary

Although this process of mastery does take time, we don't believe that it must necessarily be a painful or mysterious journey. Coexistent with the educational purpose of this text, we also hope to demystify the seemingly unfathomable. We do not believe that the lengthy process of mastery should be an excuse for providing substandard therapy to clients. According to Ericsson et al. (2006) and others, mastery does not come from mindless practice (i.e., putting in x-hundreds or thousands of hours), without any structure or guidance. Mastery is achieved by *deliberate practice*. This type of practice is "focused, programmatic, carried out over extended periods of time, guided by conscious performance monitoring, evaluated by analyses of level of expertise reached, identification of errors, and procedure directed at eliminating errors" (Horn & Masunaga, 2006, p. 601). Specific goals are set at each successive stage of development and involve objective feedback about performance that help the learner to internalize how to identify and correct errors, to set new goals, to focus on overcoming weaknesses, and to monitor progress (i.e., *thinking like a master*). Level 3 practitioners are aware of how differently they think, feel, and professionally function from when they began their clinical practice. It is critical that they have learned to think in nonlinear ways. Nonlinear listening and becoming sensitive to the information it provides set the stage for nonlinear responding and interventions—those universal, transtheoretical, paradoxical responses to clients that have the capacity to stimulate and transform clients' perception and thinking while helping to resolve their ambivalences. It is to a further consideration of how master practitioners think and intervene in nonlinear paradoxical ways that this volume next devotes its attention.

1   Advanced Nonlinear Thinking

In the 2010 film *Inception,* Leonardo DiCaprio leads a team of corporate spies who infiltrate the dreams of wealthy executives to extract company secrets (about emerging products, trading strategies, business data, etc.) for their competitors and give them a strategic advantage. They use "shared dreaming" to be able to enter a dreamer's world and interact with the "reality" of the dream. Of course, the dreamer's world is often bizarre, unpredictable, and nonlinear in nature! The rules of the "real world" don't always apply, and often gravity, time, other properties of physics and rationality are warped and distorted. In order to be able to navigate this world, DiCaprio and his "crew" must be able to deal with the lack of predictability. In addition, there can be multiple layers of dreams ("dreams within a dream") where time progresses more slowly in the "deeper" dreams than they do in the "upper" levels of dreaming. So, an hour in one dream would seem like minutes in another, etc.

Of course, the field of psychotherapy has been fascinated with dreams from the beginning. Sigmund Freud, Carl Jung, and their followers have used the interpretation of dreams as a major technique in understanding the client's "inner world" and their motivations. However, dreams have also been a source of wonder for humans throughout history. In Plato's dialogue *Theaetetus,* Socrates states: "It is not difficult to find matter for dispute when it is disputed even whether this is real-life or a dream" (cited in Hayden & Picard, 2009, p. 16). And Socrates was not alone! The Chinese philosopher Chuan Tzu put forth a similar thought experiment about what was "real," being awake or dreaming. The French philosopher Rene Descartes went so far as to say "I can never distinguish, by reliable signs, being awake from being asleep" (as cited in Hayden & Picard, 2009, p. 17). It leads to the question: How can one be sure that *this* is reality, and not a dream? What if what we think are dreams actually is reality, and what if what we think is reality is just a dream? In which case, maybe you are just dreaming that you are reading this book!

But back to the film! At one point, DiCaprio and his team are contracted to enter the dream world of an heir to a multinational conglomerate. However, their mission is not to *steal* an idea, it is to *implant* an idea—a process called "inception." This requires the team to go "deep" into the target's psyche and change his perception of how he sees his world (viz. the conglomerate, his father, and his life's purpose) while at the same time making *him* think that the idea is his (not implanted). The inception process isn't easy, as the team has to go through multiple realities within the dreams and have to battle the "target's" natural defenses before getting to the "core" of his personality where the new idea—which will change his life—will be suggested and potentially accepted.

In many ways, this is analogous to what therapists strive to do. We enter the client's world, like entering a dream. We observe *their* perception of life, their relationships, and their problems that may or may not conform with the reality of these things. Often the rules of "reality"—time, space, etc.—are warped and distorted. And, just like in the movie, a therapist's "mission" is to help the client see things differently so that they will act or behave differently. In essence, we implant or suggest new ideas in clients' minds—in other words, inception! And if we are *really* good at it—just like DiCaprio and his crew—the client feels that he or she is the one who comes up with the answer by himself or herself (albeit with the therapist's help!). And while a MAJOR difference between *Inception* and psychotherapy is that it is ethically done with the client's consent, *how* to do this at the most sophisticated levels is the subject of this text.

Advanced Nonlinear Thinking

This chapter introduces the reader to the next level of nonlinear thinking, or what we call *advanced* nonlinear thinking. Advanced nonlinear thinking is an extension of what we described in our introductory text (Mozdzierz, Peluso, & Lisiecki, 2014). We will describe additional nonlinear thinking elements used by master practitioners to help clients. These include deductive and inductive reasoning, understanding double-binds, using Socratic questioning, first- and second-order change, and the role of creativity and expertise. First, we will begin at an "elementary" level!

Inductive vs. Deductive Reasoning

There are few characters in the world that have had the impact and staying power of the great fictional detective, Sherlock Holmes. First created in the 1880s by Sir Arthur Conan Doyle, as of the writing of this book, there are presently two successful television series based on Holmes and one successful film franchise currently in production. That is in addition to the countless books, previous movie and TV adaptations, and fan societies that have all been devoted to him. So what is it about Holmes, and his faithful companion Dr. Watson, that fascinates us so much almost 130 years after his creation? A couple of the key features of Holmes' character are his impressive powers of observation, and his powers of "deduction" (more on that below). Using just his mind (and his eyes), he seems to see things that virtually *everyone* misses. According to Holmes, he does not only "see," but he "observes":

> [To Watson]: "You see, but you do not observe. The distinction is clear. For example, you have frequently seen the steps which lead up from the hall to this room."
> "Frequently."
> "How often?"
> "Well, some hundreds of times."
> "Then how many are there?"
> "How many? I don't know."
> "Quite so! You have not observed. And yet you have seen. That is just my point. Now, I know that there are seventeen steps, because I have both seen and observed."
> (from *A Scandal in Bohemia,* Arthur Conan Doyle, 1892/1986, pp. 241–242)

Now think about something that you routinely do or see. Do you observe the most basic elements? For example, do you know how many times you chew something before you swallow it? Do you know the distance between your bed and the bathroom, or approximately how many steps it takes for you to get there? Can you name all of the apps on your smartphone's home screen? Why not? You do or see these things almost *every day!* Holmes would say, it is because you do not observe them. Instead, they become automatic and slide into the background, outside of our awareness. Deliberate observation (like deliberate practice, mentioned in the previous chapter, and later in this chapter) requires the individual to make these automated processes conscious. It means being mindful of small details, and not dismissing them. So what do you do with these observations once you have them? This is where Holmes' *other* "gift" —deductive reasoning, and its twin, inductive reasoning, comes in.

Deductive Reasoning

Deductive reasoning is a form of argument that uses the truth of the premises (or assumptions of a logical argument) to prove the truth of the conclusion. Usually, there are two (or more) premises from which a conclusion is drawn. If the premises are true, then the conclusion is believed to be true. For example,

1. This book is written in English.
2. You are reading this book.
3. Therefore, you can read English.

The truth of the conclusion "You can read English" is based on the truths of the first two arguments. In deductive reasoning, the "contrapositive" is also employed. In this case, if the book is not written in English, then you cannot be reading it. Since the conclusion is built on the arguments that begin with general principles, it is often said that deductive reasoning is "top-down" reasoning, though some philosophers believe that this is too simplistic (Johnson-Laird & Byrne, 1991).

In cases of deductive reasoning, the conclusion may be true, but it is true only for conditions (premises) set down by the argument. This is one of the limits of deductive reasoning. It is not generalizable (which is why many writers say that deductive reasoning goes "from the general to the specific"). This has implications for clients; they may take deductions and make broad generalizations when they should not, or believe the conclusions when they should not. Conclusions drawn from deductive reasoning should not only be evaluated for the truth of the premises, but for their overall validity and their overall soundness. The classic example of deduction that is sound (logically), but not valid would be:

1. All cats die.
2. Socrates died.
3. Therefore, Socrates was a cat!

Now, assuming that the deduction was pertaining to the ancient Greek philosopher and *not* to a pet feline named for him, then the argument is not valid. In order for an argument to be valid and sound, the conclusion and the premises must be true. For example, a client may say:

1. "Promotions only go to workers the company wants to keep."
2. "I didn't get the promotion at work."
3. "Therefore, I'm going to lose my job."

In this case, while the logic is consistent, the conclusion is not necessarily valid or sound, since the conclusion is not *necessarily* true. In reality, many clients come in absolutely believing that the conclusions that they have "deduced" are true. Usually "trapped" by this logic and rigidly applying the conclusions to their life will often trigger unpleasant emotions and/or ambivalence. These clients believe that they cannot get out of it. It is the therapist's job to use *inductive* reasoning to show them where their reasoning might be faulty.

Nonlinear Thinking Exercise: Deductive Reasoning

Create a likely scenario that a client may come into session with that is true based on deductive reasoning. Then create a likely scenario that is not necessarily true, but that the client believes is true, based on sound (though not valid) deductive reasoning. How would you handle it?

Inductive Reasoning

Inductive reasoning, by contrast, is reasoning in which premises are used to supply strong evidence in support of (but not necessarily absolute proof of) the truth of the conclusion. Inductive reasoning is used to draw general inferences from personal experience with specific events, thus it is considered to be a "bottom-up" process (Overholser, 1993b). So while the conclusions of sound and valid deductive reasoning, by definition, are supposed to be true, the truth of an inductive argument is considered *probable,* based upon the evidence given (Copi, Cohen, & Flage, 2007). Conclusions reached by inductive reasoning can be revised based on new information (vs. faulty reasoning in deductive reasoning). An example of a conclusion based on inductive reasoning is the following:

1. You like Coldplay's music.
2. Coldplay is releasing a new album soon.
3. Therefore, you will probably like Coldplay's new album.

In this example, the two premises are two observable facts, and the third is *likely* to be true, but not *certain* to be true (after all, maybe your musical tastes have changed, or Coldplay will release an album that is a "dud," either of which would change the veracity of the conclusion).

Clinically, one of the uses of inductive reasoning is to help clients differentiate between facts, their beliefs, and their opinions. According to Overholser (1993b),

> [t]he basic process in inductive reasoning involves analyzing similarities and differences among specific experiences in order to extract a general principle . . . and therefore can be used to help clients transcend their personal experiences and construct a broad view of reality.
>
> (p. 75)

By keeping a focus on logical reasoning, and critically reviewing the evidence, inductive reasoning is helpful in therapy. The therapist uses inductive reasoning to help the client to process his or her own experiences and draw reasonable conclusions, or to revise conclusions that he or she may have drawn based on previous experiences that may not be valid. For example, clients with a history of child abuse may conclude that they are flawed, damaged, or were the cause of their abuse. They may believe that they somehow deserve bad things that happen to them in life and expect them to happen. Many types of irrational thinking are based on inaccurate overgeneralizations that are based on schematized views of self, others, and the world. Clients will often seek information that supports these preestablished, schematized beliefs, which makes them self-perpetuating in nature. Inductive reasoning in therapy can help to correct and replace these idiosyncratic and dysfunctional cognitions by patiently encouraging clients to consider additional "evidence" (premises) and draw a new generalization (Overholser, 2010). Using inductive reasoning, clients might be asked about the events in their present life and whether they are "all bad" or if bad things happened, and then what might have been the logical cause of the events (i.e., "Is there anything going *right* in your life right now?" Or "When was the problem, not a problem?"). This collection of evidence allows for new patterns to emerge, new conclusions to be drawn, and new (and hopefully better) explanations for the individual's life to be suggested.

Nonlinear Thinking Exercise: The Missing Dollar Paradox

Here is a classic paradox that seems to make money disappear into thin air (Hayden & Picard, 2009)! Suppose three diners are at a restaurant. They are told that the total bill for dinner is $30. Each contributes $10 and hands them to the waiter. However, the waiter is then told by the manager that the diners have been overcharged and that their dinner should have only cost $25. She hands the waiter five $1 bills and tells him to refund the customers' money. Realizing that the 5 bills cannot be divided evenly by 3, he gives each diner $1 back and pockets the remaining $2. But there is a problem! If you consider that each diner has now contributed $9 each to the bill (for a total of $27), and the waiter pocketed the remaining $2, that only adds up to $29 ($27 + $2), NOT $30. *So what happened to the extra dollar?* Try to reason this out, the answer will be at the end of the chapter! (*Hint:* Use deductive and inductive reasoning).

Inductive Reasoning and the Use of Analogies

One common method of inductive reasoning that therapists can use to help is the use of analogies. Reasoning by analogy involves comparing two objects, events, or people based on relevant but not obvious similarities. According to Overholser (1993b), analogies can either be "intradomain" or "interdomain." Intradomain analogies involve exploring with the client similar problems from the past, or similar problems in different situations that they may have had and successfully dealt with, and then applying them to the present situation. This is related to looking for untapped resources or unused power outlined in Domain 2 (see Mozdzierz et al., 2014 for details). Interdomain analogies, on the other hand, require abstracting similarities across blatantly different events that may be outside the client's direct experience. Again, according to Overholser (1993b), these can be based on at least five different content areas: *natural, medical, mechanical, strategical,* and *relational* comparisons. Analogies based on *natural processes* use some well-known aspect of nature (i.e., a caterpillar withdrawing into a chrysalis but emerging as a butterfly as an analogy of growth) and draw a conclusion by applying it to a parallel problem situation. Analogies that are based on *medical practices* use descriptions of medical procedures as related to the problem area (i.e., cleaning dirt in a wound, which may hurt but will prevent infection to describe the pain of re-living the past). Analogies based on *mechanical processes* extrapolate from the actions seen in mechanical operations (i.e., a car "running on all cylinders" to explain healthy balance in life). *Strategical analogies* are analogies that are based on the tactical strategies involved in various activities, such as the planning required in chess to capture your opponent's queen, or the positioning of a tennis ball in your opponent's court, can help clients to see larger patterns from their random behavior. Finally, *relational analogies* are based on parallel relationships between two or more people, such as a parent-child relationship, teacher-student relationship, or supervisor-employee relationship (Overholser, 1993b, 1999, 2010).

Master Example 1.1: But Don't Take Our Word for It!

In this example of a transcript with a master practitioner, *Susan Johnson* (cocreator of EFT) works with a couple who is working through issues of being emotionally hostile to one another using an analogy to help the husband connect with his emotional experiences (Alexander Street Press, 2012).

Susan Johnson: "... Take that elevator down, and then you go into that softer feeling that you might not ever let yourself even feel if you were being strong and silent, the image that comes up for you is a baby crying, yeah?"

Husband: "Um, that was just the analogy that I used. I think that looking at the literature and listening to the tapes, it was probably a fear of failure, you know?"

Susan Johnson: "Is that right? Fear of failure?"

Husband: "Not being good enough for this particular relationship."

In Domain 4 (Mozdzierz et al., 2014), we discussed how the use of metaphor can help the process of assimilation or accommodation of clients' schema dynamics. The use of analogies in inductive reasoning can act in the same way by increasing the client's cognitive flexibility and helping them understand their problems from a different perspective. In the example above, Susan Johnson uses the mechanical analogy of "taking an elevator down" to invite the client to explore deeper meanings, while the client chooses the metaphor of a baby crying to explain his behavior as the result of a fear of failure. Inductive reasoning using analogies allows clients to look beyond their established views of their problem and take a new perspective by looking at the deeper structural similarities of two different events or processes. If done properly, analogies can help distill new and complex problems into a simpler and more familiar image (Overholser, 1993b, 2010). For example, a client with anger issues lashes out at people who are trying to help him, and then later regrets it. This behavior can be redefined with an analogy to reflect a wounded animal who strikes out when other people try to help. A sense of relief occurs when people realize that new problems can be dealt with by transferring familiar information to the new problem.

Finally, back to Sherlock Holmes. While he was famous for talking about his "deduction," as you were reading this, did you notice something about the contrast of deductive and inductive reasoning viz. the great detective? Holmes uses his observations of a "link" in a "chain of facts" that leads him to his inevitable conclusion (i.e., "I see you forgot your umbrella when you left your house this morning." The other person might answer "How did you know that?" "Simple, I noticed that although your jacket was dry, the inside of the collar was still damp, suggesting that you had recently been out in the rain, but did not have an umbrella to shelter you, so you turned up your collar. I also noticed that you had newsprint on your wrist that tells me that you used a newspaper to cover your head in the rain as you ran indoors and the ink ran down your arm."). Therefore, he reasons from the specific (observed "links") to the general (conclusion about the "mystery") and thus employs *inductive* reasoning. Again, for our purposes as clinicians, deductive reasoning fosters definitions where inductive reasoning fosters deeper understanding. Deductive reasoning sets the "rule" (i.e., schema dynamics) by which things are classified. Inductive reasoning is used to make the rules more flexible or universal (i.e., assimilation and accommodation of schemas). Just like deductive arguments, these "rules" or biases can distort the validity of inductive arguments and prevent one from forming the most logical conclusion based on the clues. Examples of these biases include the "availability heuristic," "confirmation bias," and the "predictable-world bias" (see Copi et al., 2007; Kahneman, 2011). We will have more to say about this later in the chapter. But if you were able to figure out the mystery of Holmes' "deduction/induction" and how it applies to clients, then grab your pipe and deerstalker hat, "the game is afoot!"

Double-Binds

In the 2010 Disney movie *Tangled*, the classic tale of Rapunzel is retold. In the story, Rapunzel is stolen as a baby from her parents by "Mother Goethel," an old woman who wants Rapunzel for her magical youth-restoring hair. She takes Rapunzel deep into the woods and hides her high up in a tower where no one will find her, and where she can enjoy eternal youth (courtesy of Rapunzel's magic hair). She raises Rapunzel as her daughter, caring for her every need, and telling her how scary and full of danger the outside world is. She tells her that she is "keeping her safe" and absolutely *forbids* her from *ever* leaving the tower. Rapunzel grows to be a smart young woman who dreams of seeing the outside world and, on her 18th birthday, asks Mother Goethel if she can leave. Mother Goethel gives her an answer in the form of a song (hey, it's a Disney movie!), called "Mother Knows Best." In it, she sings to Rapunzel that they stay in the tower to "protect" her from the scary world:

> Something will go wrong, I swear/
> Ruffians, thugs/
> Poison ivy, quicksand/
> Cannibals and snakes, the plague!

Then she suggests to Rapunzel that she is the safest bet for her:

> Mother's right here/
> Mother will protect you/
> Darling, here's what I suggest/
> Skip the drama, Stay with mama/
> Mother knows best!

It sounds like good advice, given all of the dangers in the world outside the tower! Then Mother Goethel "ups the ante" by subtly criticizing Rapunzel:

> Take it from your mumsy/
> On your own, you won't survive!/
> Sloppy, underdressed/
> Immature, clumsy—please!/
> They'll eat you up alive!/
> Gullible, naïve/
> Positively grubby/
> Ditzy and a bit, well, hmm . . . vague/
> Plus, I believe/
> Gettin' kinda chubby/
> I'm just saying cause I wuv you . . .

Ultimately, we see Rapunzel's resolve melt away into fear, confusion, and self-doubt. In other words, Mother Goethel *manipulates* Rapunzel into doing what *she* wants by creating conflicting emotional reactions from her, even though it is not what Rapunzel wants. Furthermore, she doesn't even know *why* Mother Goethel wants her to do it (she has no idea that Mother Goethel wants her just for her magic hair), but Rapunzel complies and withdraws her request. In other words, she is in a classic double-bind!

Double-binds were first described by Gregory Bateson and his colleagues in the 1950s. All double-binds have the following common elements (Gibney, 2006). First, the double-bind requires two or more people, with one person being the "victim" or recipient of the double-bind. The other person (or persons) are somehow the recipient's "superiors" (meaning that they have some power, influence or are respected), such as parents or supervisors. Second, the relationship with the "superior" must have some emotional intensity or importance to the "victim," to the point where they are afraid of damaging the relationship by not complying with the "superior's" wishes. Many times the "victim" will feel that their happiness or comfort lies in appropriately "pleasing" the other person, so they devote considerable time and resources to deciphering and understanding the other person's messages or dictates. Often, the other person will change their responses in a seemingly random way, which makes it hard for the "victim" to appropriately respond to the confusing messages. Finally, the experience of the double-bind is a repeated or reoccurring theme in the client's life. In other words, individuals who find themselves in double-binds have likely been in double-binds in the past (i.e., in their families of origin). Additionally, the two individuals are involved in an intense personal relationship in which one of them feels under pressure that it is vitally important to discriminate what sort of message is being communicated so she or he can respond appropriately. These types of relationships are typically complementary, where one person is in a position of power—for example, parent/child, teacher/student, boss/subordinate, where the "dependent" individual cannot survive without the other's cooperation. They need to "please" the other in order to survive.

Next, a series of "injunctions" or directives are placed on the recipient by the "superiors" (Gibney, 2006). They are the following:

1. A "primary injunction" (essentially a command) from the "superior" to the "victim" that usually restricts someone's behavior. It can take the form of one of two formats:

    i.   "Do *(some behavior)*, or I will punish you."
    ii. "Do not do *(some behavior)*, or I will punish you."
    iii. (Both i. and ii.)

    The punishment may include the withdrawing of love, the expression of hate and anger, or abandonment. This induces the "fear" element. For example, a spouse or partner may say: "I don't care what anyone else wants to do, I want to go to the movies tonight!"

2. A "secondary injunction" is imposed on the recipient, which conflicts with the first at a higher or more abstract level, with threats or punishments that imply that the relationship will be damaged or lost if not complied with. For example: "Do not notice the contradiction between my claim to be a loving parent and my willingness to withdraw my love from you." And: "Do not notice nor comment on the unfairness of this situation." "Do not question my love (even though I threatened to take it away in the first injunction)." "You must do *X*, but only do it because you want to" (with the implication that they had *better* do *X*). It is unnecessary for this injunction to be expressed verbally (looks of disgust, or sighs of contempt are frequent mechanisms that convey this). This induces the "confusion" element. Continuing with the example above, the spouse may say "But

I guess we can stay at home to watch the game you want to see on TV!" A sigh or a look of contempt or disgust would also accompany this.

3. If necessary, a "tertiary injunction" is imposed on "victims" to prevent them from escaping the dilemma. These can include "reversals" such as promises to be better, threats of harm to the recipient, the superior, or someone else the "victim" cares about (including children or pets). With this injunction, the "superior" implies that the "victim" is somehow in the "wrong," or that he or she is the cause of the problem situation (i.e., "What is wrong with this relationship resides in you," "You don't care about me," "You are messing with me"). Finally, with the example, the spouse or partner might continue by saying, "I never get to do what *I* want to do!" (making themselves seem like a perpetual martyr), or "You don't ever want to do anything together that's fun anymore" (implying that the "victim" is the cause), or more directly "You know there are plenty of other people out there who would be happy just to be with me!" (a direct threat to the relationship).

Thus, the essence of a double-bind is two conflicting demands, *each on a different logical level,* neither of which can be ignored or escaped. In other words, the logic for the first injunction must be clear, and the logic for the second injunction must also be clear or true. For a double-bind to be effective, the victim must be unable to confront or resolve the conflict between the demand placed by the primary injunction because it would violate the logic of the secondary injunction. So in the tale of Rapunzel, Mother Goethel says "If you leave the tower, you will get hurt in the scary world" (primary injunction), "I will love you, keep you safe, and take care of your every need as long as you stay right here" (secondary injunction), and "You don't have what it takes to make it out there, you are hopelessly incompetent!" (tertiary injunction). This is where the fear and confusion induces ambivalence, and it just becomes easier to comply or go along, like Rapunzel (Gibney, 2006).

Another element that makes double-binds so powerful are secondary gains. Secondary gains represent interpersonal or social advantages or, for example, actual financial compensations that are derived indirectly from symptomatic behavior. This is one reason why it is essential for nonlinear-thinking therapists to pay attention to the issue of ambivalence (see Mozdzierz et al., 2014) and the way it might be expressed in therapy: client behaviors have potential hidden benefits (i.e., secondary gains) associated with behaviors that are difficult to relinquish (Rogers & Reinhardt, 1998). In the double-bind, the "victim" cannot comment on the contradictory messages being expressed, either because they are not in a position to understand what is going on (i.e., Rapunzel doesn't know the full story about her abduction), or because they are confused, or are not allowed to directly question the "superior." This is usually due to the fact that the superior has some secondary gain or benefit from the "victim's" cooperation. The recipient feels that "Even if I want to get out, I can't do it without something truly bad happening." This leaves the victim torn both ways, so that whichever demand they try to meet, the other demand cannot be met. As a result, attempts to solve the dilemma in one instance (first-order change, see below) are not going to successfully resolve the double-bind. This was the case with Rapunzel not being able to resolve her impossible dilemma, so she chooses to comply with Mother Goethel and give up her dream. Consider the following example reprinted from the Domain 6 chapters of our introductory text:

Clinical Case Example 1.1: Trying to Have It All

A young, highly successful, accomplished, and attractive couple sought marital counseling due to emotional distance that had grown between them for a variety of reasons. Both earned six-figure salaries, both had graduate degrees, and both had exceptionally bright future career prospects. They had made progress in understanding the basis for their emotional distance from one another and sufficiently working through certain crises.

During their fifth session of therapy, which had been spread over the course of approximately 2 months, the discussion turned to how their work schedules, career paths, and future choices concerning careers affect their marriage. The woman bemoaned the fact that she was tired of seeing others taking credit for projects she had designed and seen to completion and being promoted as a result of her efforts. Very tearfully, she lamented the fact that she was very nearly within grasp of being given a promotion that would clearly mean recognition, success, and her future career path. As the oldest child in her family of origin, she felt she had been achievement , career-, and success-oriented since early childhood, thus reflecting strong family values of what constitutes self-worth.

At the same time, she began to sob that she knew that her children desperately needed her at home at this critical preschool time in their lives. Although she could change her employment status with her current company to part-time, she knew that it would be the death knell for a strong upward career move and the promotion, recognition, and status she covets. She also recognized that if she devoted more time and attention to her children—who need her at home—she could return to full-time employment in the future and resume her achievement orientation. But she also believes that by then, she would be an "also-ran" in the company thick with high achievers.

In the case example above, the woman is in a double-bind that is created by the *circumstances* of her life and not necessarily by another person. In this case, the important thing to remember is that the client's schema dynamics may also play a role in double-binds. Often schema-dynamics form the secondary injunction. The primary injunction in this case was that she was "becoming distant" from her family and she needed to spend time with them. The secondary injunction was that she wanted to be a "success" in her career (and her self-worth was tied to it). Finally, the tertiary injunction was that she neither wanted to be an "also ran" at the company or a "bad mother" to her children (identity level). As a result, she was caught in a seemingly impossible dilemma (we will discuss this case some more below).

Previously, we (Mozdzierz et al., 2014) noted that clients are ambivalent about issues that are troubling them, *and ironically,* they are ambivalent about getting the help that they need to resolve the problem for which they have sought treatment! In fact, Olson (1972) made three observations about clients entangled in double-binds that shed light on this finding:

1. The more dependent the relationship is where there is a double-bind, the greater the resistance the client may have to clarifying the confusing communication from the "superior" (since it might jeopardize the relationship).
2. As a result, before anyone can truly improve a relationship, they must be willing to risk losing it.
3. Relationships that are in the greatest need for change are the ones that will resist the change the most, even if that change would dramatically improve the relationship.

This can be seen in reluctant or resigned precontemplators (see Domain 2, Mozdzierz et al., 2014) or in cases of domestic violence in which power and control (through the use of double-binds) are used to keep the abused partner in the relationship. Consider this example with a master practitioner:

Master Example 1.2: But Don't Take Our Word for It!

In this example, master clinician *Leigh McCullough* works with a woman who is in an abusive relationship. In this brief segment, the client expresses her ambivalence about getting a divorce (Alexander Street Press, 2012).

Leigh McCullough: "Right, right. I guess what I was thinking is, um, again you keep saying: 'If I could just not provoke him.'"

Marcy: "Just until I get enough saved up to leave him. You know, and just for us to have an understanding that we're not, we don't belong together. And I just wish he would understand that we don't belong together 'cuz we really don't."

Leigh McCullough: "Why is it that you, you need him to understand? Why do you think he will understand?"

Marcy: (crosstalk) "'Cuz it, 'cuz I want it to be a mutual divorce. I don't want to fight over nothing. I just . . ."

Leigh McCullough: "I see."

Marcy: "I'm tired of fighting."

> *Leigh McCullough:* "It's not some magical thinking. You've got a man who is
>   punching you in the face . . ."
> *Marcy:* "Yeah, I know. Wishful thinking, yeah."
> *Leigh McCullough:* "It's magical thinking that there's gonna be some 'reasonable'
>   divorce here. You're, you're wishing for something that's clearly not going to
>   happen."

In the example above, the client is trapped in an abusive relationship and is hesitating
to leave because she feels that somehow *she* is responsible for her husband "understanding" the reasons why the relationship is ending. McCullough must help the client to disengage from this pattern of thinking. As a result, clients express their hesitancy to therapy
itself in the form of noncompliance with the therapist, *because sometimes therapy itself
is a process that naturally produces a double-bind* (as evidenced in the vignette above)!
At times, therapy produces the feeling of being *pulled in two directions* (i.e., "I want to
change, but I don't want to be forced to change") while *wanting to have one's cake and eat
it too* (i.e., "I know that I need outside help to change, but I don't want to give up control"), and ultimately finding oneself stuck *between a rock and a hard place* (i.e., "I can't
stay the same, but I'm not sure I want to change"), which is our definition of ambivalence
(see Domain 6 in Mozdzierz et al., 2014).

At the same time, therapists are placed in a double-bind of their own! In order to be
successful in creating an effective therapeutic alliance, a therapist must align with, or
"join" the client. This involves seeing things from the client's perspective (even though
you may not necessarily *agree* with them). This builds rapport with the client as they
begin to feel that the therapist "gets" them. However, the very next thing that the therapist tries to do (vis-à-vis a type of "inception" process) is to encourage them to alter and
change their way of seeing or doing things. In other words, they take the very perspective
that they have just adopted in order to join with the client and then try to convince them to
change it in some way (called reframing—we will cover this in greater detail in Chapter 2).
Asking a client to do this risks the very alliance that the therapist has tried to build. This
brings up a paradoxical situation called an "auto-double-bind" (Panichelli, 2013), which
can be formulated as follows:

To be a good therapist, you must *at the same time* obey *statement 1 and statement 2:*

1. *Achieve joining:* see the problem through the eyes of your clients (and let them
   know about it).
2. *Do not do # 1.* Achieve reframing instead.

Of course, you cannot obey the first injunction *and* obey the second. "Every therapist
who attempts to actively reframe the clients' problem is confronted with a paradoxical
situation: If the therapist thinks that another interpretation would be more appropriate,
how can he or she still acknowledge the clients' own interpretation and inherent suffering?" (Panichelli, 2013, p. 441). In the case example with McCullough, *she* is in an "auto

double-bind" as she tries to align herself with the client, and at the same time "disturb" the client enough to get out of her domestically violent relationship. Understanding such ironies is part of the challenge and excitement of becoming a therapist. In fact, master practitioners use this to create "positive double-binds" that take the injunctions in the original double-bind, deconstruct them, and move the client from the "lose-lose" proposition of the double-bind to a "win-win" in the therapeutic "positive double-bind" (Gibney, 2006), which we will demonstrate in the form of paradoxical interventions in the following chapters of this book. Because of its clinical ubiquity, and because of the intense nature of double-binds, we feel that it takes real, *advanced* nonlinear thinking to understand and help clients deal with them. One of the more powerful methods for helping clients to understand and resolve double-binds is the Socratic method, or Socratic questioning.

The Socratic Method

Originated by the philosopher Socrates (BCE 469–399), the Socratic form of inquiry (called "the elenchus") used questions to systematically alter the students' perceptions or beliefs about a subject and arrive at a conclusion that the teacher wants them to arrive at without actually "giving" the student the answer (Overholser, 1993a). Socrates would accomplish this by asking a series of questions designed to elicit responses that would lead the student to see the faults of his own way of thinking or admit their ignorance, and then begin to use logic rather than their own beliefs to decide what was true or valid. Often, Socrates would use a student's belief as a starting point and then ask questions that would show the weakness of that belief in the form of a forced choice of either (1) the student's position, or (2) a slightly more morally/ethically superior one. In its original form, publicly revealing the fallacy of the student's ideas was humiliating and meant to humble him from arrogance or stupidity (Overholser, 1993a, 2010).

For example, a student might say: "Stealing is never justified, it is breaking the law." Socrates (or the questioner) would clarify with a question, "So one should never break the law?" Socrates would then begin the questioning with a follow up like "The law is important. Would you say that the purpose of the law is to preserve life?" The student would affirm that as an absolute, from which the questions would continue: "Isn't the preservation of a human life more important than upholding the law?" The student would be forced to abandon his belief for the slightly better one, "Yes it is, since the law is there to preserve human life," which Socrates would use as the basis for the next question or choice. "So, if a person's life was in jeopardy, he would be justified breaking the law?" Each student response would be the building block for the next question that would invariably lead the student away from their starting position, and to the position that Socrates ultimately was advocating: "If a person is starving to the point of death, he would be justified breaking the law to steal bread in order to preserve his life?" The student, having answered the preceding questions in a way that leads him to this point, would answer yes, at which point Socrates would proclaim that the original premise ("Stealing is never justified, it is breaking the law") was wrong and needed to be modified.

Socratic Questioning in Therapy

Systematic questioning (i.e., Socratic questioning) is not merely a rhetorical technique, but also represents an advanced nonlinear therapeutic strategy for helping clients make changes. It involves an interaction of question format (kind of questions), specific content (what the question asks), and relational process issues (the relationship between counselor and client). According to Overholser (1993a):

> Systematic questioning involves the use of a graded series of questions designed to facilitate independent thinking in clients. The questions involve the active and collaborative involvement of both therapist and client. Also, a progressive series of questions can be used to shape the client's thought processes.
>
> (p. 67)

Socratic questioning focuses clients' attention on their thought patterns, and allows them to see, through a systematic process of directive questions, how their long-held beliefs are untested and probably untrue. As with Socrates' original method, Socratic questioning begins with a good understanding of the client's beliefs, or stance. In order to accomplish this, the clinician must have a thorough grasp of the client's presenting problem and desired goals, as well as have an understanding of the client's faulty logic or cognitive distortions (i.e., skewed premises leading to flawed deductive reasoning and/ or double-binds). Then the therapist must have an idea about how to lead the client to discover their maladaptive cognitions and subsequently change those faulty beliefs that prevent the client from getting what he or she wants. The purpose of Socratic questioning in cognitive therapy, according to Beck, Wright, Newman, and Liese is to lead the client "to examine areas that the patient has closed off from scrutiny" (1993, p. 29).

Socratic questioning is central to cognitive and cognitive-behavioral therapies, as well as rational-emotive behavior therapy (Carey & Mullan, 2004; Ellis & Dryden, 2007; Overholser, 1993a). Indeed, this was a major technique used by Aaron T. Beck when he originally developed cognitive theory (Beck, Rush, Shaw, & Emery, 1979) to help clients see how their cognitions contribute to their problems. Yet, despite the centrality of Socratic questioning, there is considerable disagreement over a precise definition of Socratic questioning (Carey & Mullan, 2004; Overholser, 1993a, 2010).

Overholser, in a series of articles (1993a, 1993b, 1994, 1995, 1996, 1999), attempted to define the Socratic method for clinicians. He outlined seven types of questions that are commonly used in Socratic questioning. They range from simple to complex.

1. *Memory questions.* Memory questions require clients to remember specific facts and details. Examples of memory questions include: "When did the problem first begin?"; "When was the last time it happened?"; "How old were you when it happened?"; etc. Memory questions establish the facts from which a Socratic dialogue can proceed, but they do not *advance* the argument at all. According to Overholser (1993a), they are "a means to an end instead of an end in itself" (p. 68), and the answers do not represent a high level of understanding because they do not elicit reasons, just facts.
2. *Translation questions.* Translation questions require clients to "change the information or ideas into a different but parallel form" (p. 68) in order to help identify gaps in the

client's understanding. It takes the client outside of the immediate context and puts them in a similar one. Some examples of translation questions include: "What does it mean to you?"; "How can we make sense out of this?"; "What would your mother say about this?" Translation questions can be useful with therapeutic analogies, pattern detection, and inductive reasoning, each important aspects of the Socratic method and advanced nonlinear thinking.

3. *Interpretation questions.* Interpretation questions help clients uncover relationships among facts, definitions, skills, or generalizations. A guiding premise of Socratic questioning is that clients learn more when they discover relationships on their own, rather than simply having it explained to them. An interpretation question may follow insight gained in one area of a client's life and invite them to apply the knowledge, insight, or pattern to another area (Overholser, 1993a). Examples of interpretation questions might include: "What does it mean to you?"; "What can we learn from it?"; "How does that information change the way that you see other areas of your life?" Also, interpretation questions can help clients interpret symbolism from inductive analogies (i.e., "So if it is important to keep a car tuned up so it runs properly, shouldn't the same apply to your relationships with other people?").

4. *Application questions.* Application questions "ask clients to apply information or skills to a specific problem situation . . . encouraging clients to focus on areas that have been discussed previously and now need to be applied" (Overholser, 1993a, p. 68). Application questions are used to bring knowledge, skills, or insights that the client already has into his or her conscious awareness. These questions are analogous to ones used in solution-focused approaches and can include, "What have you tried to correct this problem in the past?" or "Has there ever been a time when this problem was not a problem?"

5. *Analysis questions.* Analysis questions ask clients to solve a problem by taking larger issues and breaking it down into its constituent parts. Analysis questions help clients to develop a more conscious awareness of their thought processes that are used for reaching logical conclusions. These are processes used in many mindfulness-based approaches (e.g., ACT, DBT, etc.). Examples include: "What do you think is causing this problem?"; "What evidence do you have for that?"; "How would you know if you are right or wrong?" Analysis questions stress the fact that conclusions must be based on adequate evidence and encourages the client to use inductive and deductive reasoning (Overholser, 1993a).

6. *Synthesis questions.* Synthesis questions "encourage clients to solve problems through the use of creative/divergent thinking. The therapist should not have a preplanned answer in mind and expect the client to generate the same answer. Instead, questions should suggest many different possible solutions" (Overholser, 1993a, p. 68). These questions represent a more abstract and sophisticated thought process, often relying on the use of inductive reasoning to connect diverse elements into a meaningful pattern. Examples of synthesis questions include: "What are some other ways of looking at the situation?" or "How do you see X and Y relating to one another?"

7. *Evaluation questions.* Evaluation questions ask clients to make a value judgment according to specified standards. First, the appropriate standard is identified and then a determination is made regarding how closely the particular idea or behavior meets

these standards. In many ways, this is one of the quintessential types of Socratic questioning since evaluation questions compare the client's actual performance to the standards. Examples of evaluation questions include: "How close do you think you came to that ideal?"; "How would you rate your marriage?"; "How do you feel about yourself as a person?"; and "What would it mean for you to achieve your goal?" Evaluation questions can also help clients clarify and integrate their thoughts and feelings, which is an important goal of the Socratic method (Overholser, 1993a, p. 69).

A general principle of Socratic questioning is to start with a broad topic or belief and ask progressively more specific questions that get the client to address precise behaviors. These are often called "leading questions," and their format is designed to emphasize higher-level cognitive processes: "The leading question contains an implied assumption, often serving as a spotlight to focus the client's attention onto a specific area. However, the phrasing of the question should not push clients toward one response over another" (Overholser, 1993a, p. 71). Leading questions get clients to critically reflect on their views of certain topics or issues. While the questions should not bias the client's response, at the same time, the use of two alternatives require the client to advance his or her thinking in a way that will provide insight or make progress. Likewise, there is balance that must be struck between too much and too little structure in the questions themselves. Clients who feel that the conversation is too much like an interrogation are not likely to participate (and may even bolt from therapy). Instead, the Socratic questioning process should (a) require the client to think rather than just answer, (b) should shape the client's responses to refine their understanding of complex issues, and (c) alternate between Socratic and non-Socratic dialogue. According to Overholser (1993a),

> Instead of asking clients to remember facts and details, Socratic questions are more likely to encourage the analysis, synthesis, and evaluation of different sources of information. The content of Socratic questions focuses on developing independent problem-solving skills in the client.
>
> (p. 72)

Finally, there are some caveats to using Socratic questioning. Specifically, younger clients, or cognitively impaired clients who cannot process verbal interaction or are more concrete thinkers, may find the process confusing or demeaning (Overholser, 1993b). In addition, clinicians are cautioned not to let the Socratic questioning become disrespectful, or a "cross-examination," thereby damaging the therapeutic alliance (Carey & Mullan, 2004). We will discuss some of the other elements to the Socratic method, including the use of inductive reasoning, universal definitions, and clarification of virtues/values.

Elements of the Socratic Method: Inductive Reasoning, Universal Definitions, Self-Improvement, and Clarification of Virtues/Values

Many people believe that the Socratic method begins and ends with Socratic questioning. However, this is a very limited (and incorrect) definition (Overholser, 2010). Earlier in this chapter, we described the difference between deductive and inductive reasoning.

In fact, the Socratic method relies heavily on *inductive reasoning* to help clients understand underlying patterns, identify general principles, or use analogies to move away from the "specific" to the "general" (Overholser, 1993b; 1994). In fact, uniting disparate items of data, and creating patterns, is the heart of both inductive reasoning and the Socratic method. Taking the client's observations of the events of her life and generating *universal definitions* (i.e., "So, 'being successful' to you would mean . . . ?") can be used to refute problematic definitions or beliefs that the client may have. Creating universal definitions by abstracting commonalities from the client's experiences teaches the client to objectively evaluate their perspectives and changes the way that they see things. According to Overholser (1994), "[t]he goal is not to invalidate the client's perception but to increase the client's awareness of alternate views" (pp. 290–291). Once they are aware of these alternative views, they become more flexible and realistic in their schematized view of self, others, and the world; they are able to question their beliefs without being threatened by the questioning (Overholser, 1995; 2010).

Implicit in the Socratic method is the idea that while the therapist is a guide, it is the clients who ultimately must come to the realizations and insights that the therapist is steering them toward. The process of *self-discovery* is a central component of the Socratic method and is fostered by the questioning. Universal definitions only have real impact and meaning for the client if they are rooted in the client's experience, and if they can be applied to the client's problem. As a result,

> the client is not an opponent to be changed but a colleague in a mutual quest. . . . The Socratic therapist stops short of doing the work for the client. Instead of explaining why the therapist believes a particular problem seems to occur, it is better to explore the client's understanding of the problem.
>
> (Overholser, 1995, p. 290)

Self-improvement in the Socratic method, according to Overholser (1996), involves an understanding of the interaction between self-knowledge, self-acceptance, and self-regulation. When these are understood, then the client's long-term life goals can be clarified and utilized to help the client. Socrates understood the importance of self-awareness by saying: "the unexamined life is not worth living." Yet, this seems to be the sad state of affairs for most people today (becoming so busy with school, job, Internet, television, Facebook, Twitter, and other distractions) that they never stop to think about larger questions like their life goals, or moral and ethical values. Self-acceptance, a key feature of many mindfulness-based approaches (like ACT, DBT, etc.), can be hindered by a lack of self-knowledge. As a result, clients have unrealistic goals or standards for themselves that can become easily upset when their lives do not go the way they believed it should (i.e., fail to get the job they wanted, or are disappointed with a romantic partner, etc.). Finally, self-regulation "refers to the ability to control short-term impulses and desires in favor of long-term goals" (Overholser, 1996, p. 556). So when individuals do not get what they want in life because of poor choices that they may have made, and then they overreact emotionally and don't understand why their anger or depression is so "out of control," the Socratic method in conjunction with empathic understanding can be used to soothe and help the client become more flexible in their approach (viz. inductive reasoning and universal definitions). Thus the client and therapist can work toward the client becoming more self-aware, self-accepting, and self-regulating (and thus, self-improving). These are the hallmarks of a master practitioner using advanced nonlinear thinking.

While self-discovery is an important part of the Socratic method and therapy in general, Socrates felt that there was an ultimate and crucial end-point for people to lead a "good" life: virtue.

> Virtue focuses on long-term issues, such as the good of one's moral character, whereas vice involves an emphasis on immediate, tangible satisfactions. . . . According to Socrates, misbehavior is due to ignorance about what is in our best interests in the long run.
>
> (Overholser, 1999, p. 137)

Socrates centered his discussions on the five "cardinal" virtues: wisdom, courage, moderation, justice, and piety. However, the virtues are closely intertwined, so when clients are addressing issues related to one, they are also touching on the others as well (Overholser, 2010).

Master Example 1.3: But Don't Take Our Word for It!

Consider this example from master practitioner, *Steve Andreas* (creator of Neurolinguistic Programming) and how he responds to Melissa's inference (Alexander Street Press, 2012).

Melissa: "It's that revenge thing."
Steven Andreas: "Okay!"
Melissa: "But then there's part of me that wants to let it go."
Steven Andreas: "Okay! Now what would revenge do for you?"
Melissa: "Make me feel better."
Steven Andreas: "That'd make you feel better. I'd like you to feel better. I don't think revenge is the best way to do it, it's a way. Now, tell me . . . tell me this. Close your eyes and go into wild revenge fantasies, what would you do if you have . . . if you were totally omnipotent and you had all the power in the world and you could take revenge on this guy and beat him into a bloody pulp or whatever. How would that make you feel?"
Melissa: "Like I won."
Steven Andreas: "Okay! So, would you feel stronger?"
Melissa: "No, I'd still feel equal."
Steven Andreas: "Equal! So you feel unequal now?"
Melissa: "I want him to feel the hurt that I felt."
Steven Andreas: "Yeah! And that would make you feel equal?"
Melissa: "Hmm . . . hmm . . ."

Problematic behavior is the result of clients' lack of self-awareness and not fully understanding the impact of their behavior. However, lasting change (second-order change, see below), or effectively removing oneself from a double-bind, can be accomplished by clarifying values or virtues, through the process of the Socratic method. In the example above, Steven Andreas uses Socratic questioning (in particular, interpretation, analysis, and evaluation questions) to help Melissa see not how she values equality, but how her actions to hurt her ex-boyfriend would not really make her feel equal. It requires a mindful effort on the part of the client, as well as on the part of the therapist, to effectively guide the client toward this understanding and action. Make no mistake about it, as Kahneman (2011, p. 413) notes, such work requires real effort and cognitive strain. Next, we will discuss the therapist's qualities necessary for utilizing the Socratic method.

Therapist Qualities and the Socratic Method

Attempting to accomplish these through Socratic questioning, inductive reasoning, and clarification of virtues can come across as paternalistic, if the therapist is not careful. However, in order to counteract this, it is helpful for a therapist to keep two concepts in mind: "Socratic ignorance" and intellectual modesty. Socratic ignorance "requires that the therapist maintain a general attitude involving a disavowal of knowledge" (Overholser, 1995, p. 283). In the family therapy literature, this is often referred to as a "not-knowing" stance (Mozdzierz et al., 2014). Socratic ignorance means that the therapist admits that he or she is not certain of any "knowledge" objectively and that most statements are the result of some faulty process including individual beliefs and personal opinions (Overholser, 1995). True "knowledge" is based on factual information that has been reasoned and tested. Beliefs are claims by an individual that have not been empirically reasoned but may be accurate, while opinions are personal preferences that are unquestioningly accepted and cannot be proven to be true (Overholser, 1995). Socratic ignorance and other elements of the Socratic method frequently reveal that many examples of purported knowledge by clients are merely beliefs or opinions.

In addition to Socratic ignorance, therapists must also approach clients with intellectual modesty. Intellectual modesty is a genuine desire to learn from clients, their life experiences, and ways to help them overcome their problems and live life better (Overholser, 1999). This genuine curiosity about the client *enhances the therapeutic relationship because the therapist avoids the role of expert*. As a result, therapists do not overestimate their skills or abilities and remain skeptical of their own knowledge (Socratic ignorance) while pressing the client on their own beliefs and opinions. Intellectually modest therapists are unafraid to ask questions to which they do not know the answer, because they accept that they are not the source of all knowledge about the client, nor are they the repository of all answers and wisdom. In fact, Socrates viewed his students as associates, just as an effective master practitioner maintains a collaborative stance (see Mozdzierz et al., 2014, Domain 4). In fact, by demonstrating one's own ignorance and curiosity, it invites the client to do so as well, thus deepening the relationship and increasing the probability that clients will be willing to share their personal experiences and derive deeper meanings from them (i.e., self-exploration, clarification of values, etc.).

For a concrete example of Socratic questioning, and the therapist use of these, consider this excerpt from the Case of Ashley:

Therapist:	You know, I am going to go out on a limb here and say that you probably don't take a lot of these days off? In fact, I *bet* you have the most days stored up?
Ashley:	[SMILES SLIGHTLY] Yeah, its funny you say that. I've maxed out my accrued vacation days and they say that if I don't take some this year, I will start to lose them.
Therapist:	And how many do you have?
Ashley:	[SHEEPISHLY] Almost 6 weeks worth.
Therapist:	And I'll bet that you feel guilty when you *do* take vacation days . . .
Ashley:	I try to make long weekends, or stretch a holiday by a day. Those are my vacations. I can't take more than that.
Therapist:	So why is it that other people can take time off but you can't?
Ashley:	I can—
Therapist:	But you just said you can't?
Ashley:	[sighs] It's complicated . . .
Therapist:	I know it seems that way, but it really isn't if you wanted it to be.
Ashley:	[A LITTLE HURT] What do you mean?
Therapist:	I can see that disturbed you [Ashley NODS HEAD YES SLIGHTLY] but you see, while you think that you have organized things well, you really haven't?
Ashley:	What do you mean?
Therapist:	Because YOU have to do all the work and everybody else gets the reward. Let me ask, when something breaks or "goes down" at the hospital, what happens?
Ashley:	Well, there are backup systems.
Therapist:	Right, I assume backup power, backup data storage, etc., right?
Ashley:	Sure.
Therapist:	But in your office, do you have backup systems?
Ashley:	Sure, for the computers and data . . .
Therapist:	But there is one thing that doesn't have a backup . . .
Ashley:	Me.
Therapist:	Yep. And what happens when you "go down?" There is no backup. Who replaces you?
Ashley:	No one right now, but they *could* replace me.
Therapist:	Is that what you are afraid of? That they'll replace you?
Ashley:	Yeah, that's part of it.
Therapist:	And that is why you have to work harder than everybody else? Because you don't want to be cast aside, cast away?
Ashley:	[SLOWLY] Yeah . . .

In this example, several elements of the Socratic method are present. First, the therapist utilizes evaluation, analysis, and synthesis questions to get Ashley to reflect on her beliefs about her place at work. He uses inductive reasoning and creates a mechanical analogy ("backup systems at the hospital") to bring to light how her flawed reasoning has gotten her into a difficult position at work. Finally, the therapist helps her to explore some beliefs she has about herself and her place in the world so that she can begin to clarify her values (viz. her self-goals and virtues) thus developing alternative views as Overholser (1994) advocated. Using the Socratic method, Ashley begins to move from a more rigid (long-held fictional assumptions) to a more flexible (alternative) view of her situation. For another example of a master practitioner at work, consider the following example with William Glasser:

Master Example 1.4: But Don't Take Our Word for It!

In this example of a transcript with a master practitioner, *William Glasser* (creator of Reality Therapy) works with a woman who is deciding about whether to commit to a relationship or not (Alexander Street Press, 2012).

William Glasser: "Human beings have a variety of needs, that's one of the things that I teach, and one of the needs is freedom. Do you think that your need for freedom is kind of something that's important to you?"

Ann Mary: "Absolutely."

William Glasser: "Hmm . . . hmm. It sounds that way to me that everything you've talked about is it, I mean, that song, 'Don't fence me in,' and you remember . . ."

Ann Mary: "Yeah!"

William Glasser: "You look like the kind of person that doesn't want to be fenced in and . . . and Chicago doesn't fence, and this is kind of a big place and you go here and there."

Ann Mary: "But I don't you know I don't know, he's . . . he's a wonderful guy, and he is great to me, and I just don't understand why I'm so hesitant."

William Glasser: "Well I think, you've explained I guess about this as clear as you can on why you're so hesitant. It's one thing to see him every other weekend or every weekend and so another thing, when you're with him a lot of the time, I said, in this summer you were with him for about a month or something, how long were you with him down there?"

Ann Mary: "About 3 weeks."

William Glasser: "Three weeks and . . . and that was in the beginning of the relationship too."

Ann Mary: "Right."

William Glasser: "And that's when things were sexually hot and all that kind of stuff?"

Ann Mary: "Yeah, everything was 'love and sunshine.' So, I don't know. And then I feel bad if it doesn't work out, and it's like I'm kind of in a lose-lose

> situation here, you know? If I do end it, I will lose it; if I do marry him and I hate it, I lose, you know? So I don't know."
>
> *William Glasser:* "Had you ever had a win-win situation in your relationship?"
>
> *Ann Mary:* "No. I've never had one of those either, so . . . No, I really wouldn't know, you know?"
>
> *William Glasser:* "This is as far as the personal treatment of this man by you; this is about as good as you've had? Is this what you'd say?"
>
> *Ann Mary:* "Oh, yeah, absolutely."

In this example, Ann Mary is clearly in a double-bind. Her long-distance partner wants to marry her, and while she cares for him and doesn't want to hurt him, she is afraid to lose her freedom. Glasser uses elements of inductive reasoning (going from her specific situation to more general ideas of relationships) and the Socratic method (evaluation and synthesis questions) to help her clarify her values and her goals for herself. According to Overholser (2010), using the Socratic method in therapy can be a vehicle to help clients "find their natural skills, talents, and penchants in order to help them grow into useful qualities and productive habits. The Socratic method adheres to the metaphor that 'you can only help an acorn grow into an oak tree.'" (p. 359). Using the Socratic method is part of advanced nonlinear thinking because it goes beyond approaches that just meander and "float" by aimlessly, but rather seeks to understand the client on a more substantial level in order to help resolve double-binds, and guarantee long-term, second-order change. We will discuss that issue and its connection to the other elements of advanced nonlinear thinking.

Nonlinear Thinking Exercise: Two Paths, Two Guards, One Question!

While we have been discussing Socratic questioning, and double-binds, here is a nonlinear exercise with a little bit of *both*. It is an ancient riddle that goes back over 2,000 years (Hayden & Picard, 2009). Here is a version of it: You stand at a fork in the road with two paths that have a door at its entrance. Next to each of the two doors, there stands a guard. You know the following things: (1) One path leads to Paradise, the other to Death. From where you stand, you cannot distinguish between the two doors. Worse, once you start down a path, you cannot turn back. (2) The guards are identical twins in every way. The only thing that is distinguishing about them is that one of the two guards always tells the truth. The other guard always lies. Unfortunately, it is impossible for you to distinguish between the two guards.

You have permission to ask one guard one question to ascertain which path leads to Paradise. Remember that you do not know which guard you're asking— the truth-teller or the liar—and that this single question determines whether you live or die. The question is: What one question asked of one guard guarantees that you are led onto the path to Paradise, regardless of which guard you happen to ask? Before you read on, think of what question you would ask.

The question to ask, which would guarantee that you would get the information you need to make the best choice, is: "If I asked the 'other' guard, 'which door should I pick to lead to Paradise?' which door would he indicate?" Whatever the answer is, take the door "opposite" to what's indicated! Why? With a dichotomy (a question with only two answers), lying about the correct answer is the same as telling the truth about the wrong answer. Regardless of whom you ask, they'll have to say the same thing and point to the wrong door. Confused? Let's think it through, together. Suppose you ask the question to the guard who always tells the truth and he is standing at the door for Death. He will tell you that the other guard would say, "Pick the other guard's door." If you ask the guard who always lies who is standing at the door to Paradise, he will say to pick his brother's door (the path to Death). Then the answer is simple: Pick the opposite door of whatever the guard tells you to choose! Even if you change who is standing in front of which door, the answer is still the same.

So what does this have to do with advanced nonlinear thinking? First, it is a type of double-bind (unless you get the right information, you risk death, but you can't necessarily *trust* you are getting told the truth!). Second, in order to arrive at a solution that would be successful, you have to employ some inductive reasoning, and then you have to ask the question in a way that will get you the answer you want (Socratically, of course!).

Please note that with this (and subsequent) exercises, getting the answer right or wrong is not as important as understanding the thinking behind the right answer. Once you understand that, then you will have a better appreciation of advanced nonlinear thinking!

First- and Second-Order Change

The purpose of any therapy is to produce change. Whether it is stopping a problem behavior (e.g., smoking, alcohol use), a disturbing impulse (anger, eating disorders, etc.), or correcting long-held beliefs and patterns of interaction (e.g., personality disorders, destructive relationship patterns, etc.), the overall goal is *change*. However, while most change is *good*, not all change is equal in value, or duration. In fact, according to noted family therapists Watzlawick, Weakland, and Fisch (1974), change can be described as either first-order or second-order. For clinicians, this is an important distinction that impacts the long-term success of any therapeutic endeavor.

Based on Whitehead and Russell's (1910–1913) "Theory of Logical Types," Watzlawick et al. (1974) described first-order change as representing direct attempts to coerce change *on the same level of reality* (i.e., within the same "logical type," or class). Examples would be: arguing with a spouse and demanding that he change his behavior; insisting that a loved one stop drinking; managing anxiety by avoiding potentially threatening situations; etc. Such change efforts are "first order" because *they represent the same level of reality and the same logical type or same class of behaviors* (i.e., "I don't like what you are doing, I want you to stop it." First-order changes can also be those things that clients have been *trying* as "solutions" to their problems (i.e., using nicotine patches, or avoiding a threatening coworker). They represent *linear thinking* and are mostly ineffective in bringing about the sort of long-term changes that people desire. They represent attempts to bring about change by applying the same "common sense reasoning" as is applied in the physical world of change (e.g., "The room is too dark, so I'll turn on the light switch").

First-order change refers to alterations or variations in a system that leaves the fundamental organization of that system unchanged. It is superficial in nature, and the change may reduce a symptom or resolve surface issues. Examples of this include time management strategies or behavioral changes (i.e., diet, smoking, etc.). In terms of accommodation and assimilation of schema, first-order change can be seen as the equivalent of assimilation (see Mozdzierz et al., 2014 for details). It works within the existing structures of the schema to create change but doesn't require the individual to change their outlook on the world. If the person is stable and healthy, then a simple problem-solving approach will be sufficient to put an end to the problem. Let's be clear about this: *Successful first-order change should not be trivialized!* For example, many psychosocial approaches use skills training. The value of skills training, like all approaches, lies in being able to apply the skills appropriately to clients in an appropriate context. Skills training generally does not address (or alter) the larger schema dynamics. It does help clients to cope, however, with life situations, and it helps them assimilate new information (skills) into existing schemas. As a result, it can be *very* effective in alleviating suffering in some situations. But many times, clients interested in linear solutions report that they have "tried that" and have found such methods unsuccessful. *Nonlinear listening* reveals comments such as "I tried that, and it didn't work" as clinical clues that something more dynamic is operational. For example, if a client is in a double-bind, then first-order change will not do much to address the double-bind, and it may even strengthen it (since it will only address one level/injunction that will trigger the secondary injunction, and be *very* unpleasant for the client trying to make changes). So, if the individual has deeper, underlying issues, then merely addressing the first-order change will not make a major impact on the individual that will last once therapy ends. At this point, change at the second-order level is necessary, and interventions that address larger schema dynamics are appropriate.

Second-Order Change

In the 1999 film, *The Matrix,* Keanu Reeves plays the role of Thomas Anderson, a computer programmer by day, and a computer hacker named "Neo" by night. He is convinced that something is not right with the world around him, and he seeks out the answer to the question: "What is the matrix?" He encounters a band of resistance fighters who tell him that the world around him is the matrix, and that it is a virtual reality that every human being is plugged into as slaves. As the control agents for the matrix are closing in on them, Neo must make a choice: swallow the blue pill and remain in the matrix, or swallow the red pill, unplug himself from the matrix, and join them in their fight to save humanity. He must choose one or the other, he cannot save humanity and remained plugged into the matrix. Of course, he swallows the red pill and learns the true nature of the matrix and fights to change it. The difference between staying in the matrix and leaving it is a good metaphor for describing the difference between first- and second-order change. While Neo is in the matrix and doing his computer hacking, he may be making small disruptions, but he is not affecting the control that the matrix has. Once he decided to leave the matrix, he is able to make massively sweeping changes that permanently change the matrix (and ultimately free humanity).

Just like *The Matrix*, second-order change takes place on a different level (e.g., schema accommodation, or reappraisal, see Mozdzierz et al., 2014). It is defined as "change in which the fundamental structure of the system is overhauled so that, in addition to problem solving and symptom reduction, the system is permanently redesigned" (Murray, 2002, p. 168). With second-order change, the rules that govern the structure of the system change, which can include changes in communication or how a person relates to the problem or another person (Davey, Duncan, Kissil, & Fish, 2011). Watzlawick et al. (1974) summarized the essence of what is involved in second-order change thusly:

a. Second-order change is applied to what in the first-order change perspective appears to be a solution, because in the second-order change perspective this "solution" reveals itself as the keystone of the problem whose solution is attempted.
b. While first-order change always appears to be based on common sense (for instance, the "more of the same" recipe), second-order change usually appears weird, unexpected, and nonsensical; there is a puzzling, paradoxical element in the process of change. Applying second-order change techniques to the "solution" means that the situation is dealt with in the here and now. These techniques deal with effects and not with their presumed causes, the crucial question is *what* and not *why*.
c. The use of second-order change techniques lifts the situation out of the paradox-engendering trap created by the self-reflexiveness of the attempted solution and places it in a different frame (as is literally done in the solution of the "nine-dot" problem) (pp. 82–83).

How is second-order distinct from first-order change? According to Davey et al. (2011), "it is distinct because it refers to changes in the interrelationships within the system and that the underlying rules shift in second-order change" (p. 105). So for example, if a couple frequently has arguments over money, where one partner asserts the right to spend more because he or she makes a higher salary, and the other person feels inferior because he or she does not, then a therapeutic goal of reducing the number of arguments would be an example of first-order change. However, working with the couple to redefine their relationship to money, or discuss the symbolic and emotional elements about money and their definition of each other relative to it, or reframe the arguments about money as attempts to get closer to one another and meet their emotional needs, that would be a definition of second-order change. It would create a new balance point or equilibrium in the relationship away from the issue of "who makes more" and toward a point of care and satisfaction with each other as equal partners working together. To be effective at the second-order level of change, therapists must

- understand that *linear* solutions are most often just the first step in understanding a client's problem;
- intervene in a fundamentally paradoxical manner (one that is seemingly absurd to the client);
- realize that it is necessary for an individual to face and resolve the ambivalence that he or she is feeling *now*, rather than focus on past hurts, distant causes, or future fears; and
- help create accommodations to an individual's schema by *altering his or her perspective* (i.e., changing the context and prompting a reappraisal of circumstances) regarding the problem.

In fact, second-order change is SO powerful that when Fraser and Solovey (2007) analyzed the relevant literature on therapy and its effectiveness, they asserted that second-order change is a common element in all effective psychotherapies—a "golden thread" that unifies all effective treatments. Table 1.1 summarizes examples of the nonlinear nature of Fraser and Solovey's (2007) conclusions. For example, if a client's tendency is to move away from the problem (a first-order change that temporarily stops the problem), then the paradoxical intervention (and second-order change) suggests that a client be directed to move toward the problem (but with a prosocial rationale for doing so). For example, if a person is conflict-avoidant, his or her tendency would be to please and placate in order to avoid a confrontation. Second-order change would require the individual to *provoke* the confrontation and be prepared to resolve it. Obviously this would require understanding any underlying double-bind that might be in place. Such double-binds make the conflict avoidance attractive. Therapists can then employ elements of the Socratic method to help the client discover any faults in their beliefs related

Table 1.1 Differences in First-Order vs. Second-Order Change

If the client's tendency in attempting to solve a dilemma (i.e., "first-order" change) is to . . .	Then the paradoxical intervention (i.e., "second-order" change) is to . . .
. . . go away from the problem.	. . . go toward the problem.
. . . overpursue the problem.	. . . stop and reverse the pursuit.
. . . not attend to the problem.	. . . acknowledge the problem and take necessary problem-solving action.
. . . be overly complex.	. . . simplify the problem and narrow problem-solving efforts.
. . . overintervene in everyday ups and downs.	. . . tolerate and accept the natural unpleasantries of everyday living.
. . . simplify difficulties to the point of trivializing things.	. . . honor the complexities of the problem or situation.

Note: Adapted from Fraser and Solovey (2007).

to conflicts, as well as clarify their values (which would help them make a more effective argument in the confrontation). Understanding first- versus second-order change also includes if a client is oversimplifying the problem. In such instances, a first-order level of change would work to help the client to manage the constituent parts, while a second-order change would honor the complexity of the situation. This is *nonlinear/paradoxical* because it does not "logically" flow and is seemingly absurd to the client—though it contains an element of truth. For this reason, second-order change is a part of advanced nonlinear thinking.

Clinical Case Study 1.2: More Than Just a Paycheck

A 45-year-old man, who immigrated from Honduras 22 years before, came in to consult with a therapist for feelings of depression following a mild heart attack. He has been married for 20 years and has 4 children aged 18, 15, 11, and 8. He begins by talking about his problems with his business. He is the owner of a clothing distribution warehouse that he built from the ground up. He acknowledges that he has difficulty turning over much of the day-to-day control of it to his younger brother, despite the fact that business has not appreciably suffered during his recuperation while his brother has been in charge. The client reports that his wife has often joked that his work is "the other woman" in his life, but he quickly states "I want my company to be successful because everything I do, I do for my family. There is no one else in my life. And if I don't work, they won't eat!"

The situation became very serious when the client went back to work before being released to do so by his doctor, and began to experience some chest pains. The client was asked: "What would be different in your life if this heart condition improved or went away?" The client was puzzled for a moment, then answered: "Well, I wouldn't be stuck at home doing nothing. I'd be able to go back to work!" Gaining a clue about the purpose of the client's behavior, the therapist, inquired about the client's home life. He stated that he felt like a stranger at home, and that his wife "ruled the roost." He felt like he did not have a place there and that (aside from his financial contribution to the family), they are able to get along without him. He saw himself as a success building a company from "nothing" and providing for his family here and in Honduras. He was especially proud that he'd achieved his dream of giving his children many of the things that he did not have. He valued his role as a provider but was unsure *how* to provide anything other than money at home. Now he felt he had nothing to offer them.

The therapist was able to summarize the client's situation by saying: "Up to now, work is somewhere that you can escape from your family. Except now that is killing you! What good are you, or all of your hard work, to your family if you are dead? Do you believe that is what they really want?" The client silently nodded his head in agreement. As a result of Socratic questioning, the client was able to express that he felt lost regarding his family, and unsure about how to rebuild his relationship with them. He was asked how he was able to "build something from nothing" before. If he was "starting from nothing," he knows how to be successful, because he had done it before. The client recalled that he worked hard and watched people who were more successful than he was. He learned from that and even had a "kind-of-mentor." When the therapist asked who he saw as being successful "providing" at home, he said that his wife was. The therapist suggested that he apply his earlier successful strategy to his wife and ask for her help. Initially, this was a challenge, as his wife held "traditional" male/female gender roles, but the client was able to ask for and take direction from his wife. Pretty soon, he was rebuilding his relationship with his wife and his children. At termination, his wife was beginning to take college courses to pursue her dreams of fashion design, while her husband assumed a greater role domestically.

Recently, two studies have looked into the experience and understanding of second-order change. First, Murray (2002) surveyed clients who had participated in therapy and felt that they had experienced second-order change. She found that second-order change "takes place within certain contexts, and is associated with factors such as insight, being able to confront a problem, and developing a new perspective of the problem, of the world, or of self" (p. 168). Clients described their experience of second-order change as "transcendent" or "moving beyond or stepping outside of a set of perceived restrictions, confines, or limitations—largely in terms of systems of meaning" (pp. 168–169). Indeed, this is very similar to the goals of the Socratic method described above. Further, she found that clients felt that second-order change gave them a greater sense of self-acceptance, personal power, and inner peace (or self-regulation), again reminiscent of the aims of the Socratic method. Murray also found that clients who experienced second-order change were able to "uncover the self" or clarify their values, and were able to better organize their lives, above and beyond the problem area that they came to address. This is clearly demonstrated with the husband in Case 1.2, above. Finally, there were changes that allowed clients to be able to view themselves and their relationships with others in a different way, which is consistent with removing one's self from double-binds (appropriately managing boundaries, clarifying values, and taking responsibility for one's actions, to name a few).

Even more recently, Davey et al. (2011) performed a Delphi study (a research method that surveys "experts" in a given field) to look at the definition and meaning of "second-order change" within the field of marriage and family therapy (the field that created the notion of first- and second-order change). Conceptually, the experts coalesced their answers around the ideas that second-order change alters the interactional patterns between family members, which shifts the context of the problem so that the problem behavior is not reinforced or triggered. As the people within the system change, the system itself changes, and it is as if there is no "room" for the problem behavior anymore. For participants engaged in second-order change, they endorsed the ideas that the relationship between family members goes from unilateral and competitive to a dynamic and collaborative process. Also, in relationships where there is second-order change, individuals will move away from trying to manipulate the other person to connect with them out of a personal feeling of anxiety, but instead out of a genuine empathy with their partner's experience. Again, this sounds like the outcomes described above from the Socratic method, as well as a shift away from double-binds. It also seems to be congruent with the results that master practitioners are able to achieve through the use of nonlinear thinking.

Davey et al. (2011) also found that there were some unique challenges in teaching new therapists about second-order change. Specifically, they recommend teaching an understanding of multiple perspectives that encourages students to shift from a purely individual perspective toward truly understanding the systemic nature of human relationships. In particular, they felt that training should help students "who live and work in a linearly focused world to epistemologically move toward a systemic understanding" (p. 108), or what we would call *nonlinear* thinking. In addition they recommend creating learning environments that help students begin to create their "philosophy of change" and how their role as a therapist facilitates the change process. Additionally, panelists agreed on challenging therapists to see interactions rather than individual pathology, using case studies, the observation of live sessions, providing live supervision, and reviewing videos from master practitioners. We feel that this is an important part of mastery, particularly as it relates to deliberate practice and expertise. In the next section on advanced nonlinear thinking, we will discuss these elements, as well as an important emergent property of this that is important for master practitioners: creativity.

Deliberate Practice, Expertise, and Creativity

In the introductory chapter of this text, as well as in our previous text (Mozdzierz et al., 2014), we described the phenomenon of "deliberate practice" and its impact on mastery, owing to the work of K. Anders Ericsson and his colleagues (Ericsson, Chamness, Feltovich, & Hoffman, 2006). Deliberate practice on the way to mastery is not a casual or automatic process where a person "puts in their time" and obtains mastery of a particular field. Instead, skills and knowledge must be acquired, practiced, and then refined through feedback and repetition. While the acquisition and basic levels may be able to be attained relatively quickly (within 50–100 hours), further improvement requires more concentrated efforts. According to Ericsson et al. (2006):

> [t]he principal challenge to attaining expert level performance is to induce stable specific changes that allow the performance to be incrementally changed.... Deliberate practice is therefore designed to improve specific aspects of performance in a manner that assures that attained changes can be successfully measured and integrated into representative performance. Research on deliberate practice in music and sports show that continued attempts for mastery require that the performer always try, by stretching performance beyond its current capabilities, to correct

some specific weakness, while preserving other successful aspects of function. This type of deliberate practice requires full attention and concentration.

(p. 698)

In this text, and in our previous text (Mozdzierz et al., 2014), we have added elements that help to exercise a person's nonlinear thinking, as well as provide opportunities to interact with clinical material in a creative and sophisticated way, in the same way that Davey et al. (2011) suggest. However, there is a further benefit to developing advanced nonlinear thinking in order to achieve mastery as a clinician!

Creativity and Expertise

If it hasn't been clear by this point, the therapeutic process is one that requires a great deal of thought and skill. As we have shown, improvements in performance, and the attainment of mastery is caused by changes in cognitive mechanisms (i.e., advanced nonlinear thinking). However, achieving mastery results in an interesting cognitive by-product, namely, *creativity*. "Expertise facilitates creative thinking because deliberate practice enables the would-be creator to develop new techniques or skills, that allow him or her to go beyond what had previously been accomplished in the domain" (Weisberg, 2006, p. 768). In other words, mastery of a given field provides the launch pad for creativity and redefinition of the way that things had been done before. Experts push the boundaries that had been previously set.

Weisberg (2006) examined the connection between creativity and expertise. Using case studies of masters from music (Mozart, the Beatles), visual arts (Pablo Picasso, Jackson Pollack), and the sciences (Craik and Watson's discovery of the shape of the DNA molecule, Thomas Edison's invention of a functional light bulb), he followed on Ericsson's notion that "creative advances are the highest expression of expertise" (p. 781). From this he produced evidence that suggests three assertions that link expertise and creativity:

1.   Expertise is necessary for creativity.
2.   Innovations come about as the result of extension of techniques resulting from practice.
3.   Creative advances based on expertise redefine their domains.

He defined two separate, but important types of expertise: domain-specific and general expertise. Domain-specific expertise is expertise where creative advancements are built on knowledge that is based on the past history of innovation in that field. This may be a transfer of knowledge into a new situation. General expertise is *not* dependent on knowledge from a given domain or field, but based on general knowledge in other fields that inspire a creative and novel application into the expert's field. For example, the Beatles' use of orchestral instruments in some of their works represented domain-specific expertise (still within the musical field), whereas the Wright brothers' use of a control system for wings was based on their observations of what birds do to change their wing shape in order to maintain flight (general expertise). In short, experts use their knowledge and expertise to pick up important cues in the situation or problem and anticipate (based on pattern recognition) where different solutions will take them.

Conclusion

In this chapter, we have attempted to broaden the definition of nonlinear thinking, begun in Mozdzierz et al. (2014), into *advanced nonlinear thinking*. We feel that these sophisticated elements are important to understand as part of the work of master practitioners in order to move into the heart of the seventh domain, using paradoxical interventions and understanding the nonlinear thinking behind it. This requires mastering all six previous domains and applying general expertise to generate a new and different approaches or solution, which can change the ways that clients see themselves, or their problems. In this way, an expert clinician, who applies creative innovations is able to act as a change agent and be effective in clients' lives (very much like in the movie *Inception*). Next, we will move into a general definition of paradoxical intervention, and understanding the first class of paradoxical interventions: the Neutralizers.

Answer to the Missing Dollar: The truth is that there *is* no disappearing dollar. It is a matter of nonlinear accounting! First, while the logic of the math in the problem is solid, its conclusion is flawed and invalid (deductive reasoning). The reality is that the meal was $25, the waiter pocketed $2, and refunded $3. That adds up to the $30 (inductive reasoning). The flaw was that the $2 "tip" to the waiter was counted *twice* ($27 + $2), while the $3 refund was not counted at all!

2 The Basics of Paradoxical Interventions and the Neutralizers

In the 2012 blockbuster film, *The Avengers,* a group of superheroes must join together to combat a global threat. Most of the main characters are flawed heroes (Iron Man, Captain America, Thor), but one is especially flawed: Dr. Bruce Banner, aka The Incredible Hulk. Of course, the Hulk is a super strong, and mostly mindless, green monster that is triggered when Dr. Banner gets angry. Throughout the film, the other characters try to figure out how Dr. Banner maintains control of his anger. At one point, Tony Stark (Iron Man) says: "Man, you really have got a lid on it! What's your secret? Mellow Jazz? Bongo Drums? A big bag of weed?" But Dr. Banner never tells them. Ultimately, the heroes get ready for a battle with an alien army bent on destroying the Earth. Needing all the help that they can get (as a giant alien monster is about to crush them), Captain America says to Bruce: "Uh, Doctor Banner, I think now might be a good time for you to get angry." At which point, Banner looks at him and says: *"That's* my secret, Cap: *I'm always angry"* and immediately transforms into the Hulk (who proceeds to smash the alien into the ground). In other words, in order to control his transformation into the Hulk (by getting angry), Dr. Banner does the *opposite* of what everyone thinks he ought to do (try to remain calm, not get angry, etc.), which is counterintuitive! This is the essence of a paradox, and it is the focus of this chapter (and the rest of this book).

Paradoxical interventions represent perhaps the most sophisticated and elegant of the *advanced nonlinear thought processes* demonstrated by master practitioners (*regardless of their theoretical orientation*). As such, explicit use of paradoxical interventions is a hallmark characteristic of Level 3 practitioner development and is the last of the seven domains that master practitioners employ to help clients. We begin this chapter by defining paradox and how it can be viewed from both the client's perspective and from the clinician's perspective as they relate to advanced nonlinear thinking. We will examine some of the *basic elements* and concepts regarding the "how to" of implementing nonlinear thinking and using paradoxical interventions. In this regard, we provide examples of reframing that help define it and its central place in therapy. We will also demonstrate how *nonlinear* listening provides the input that a therapist needs in order to respond to clients in a variety of circumstances. Then we will introduce the first and most basic type of paradoxical interventions: the Neutralizers.

What Is a Paradox?

> A great truth is a statement whose opposite is also a great truth.
>
> —Niels Bohr

There are actually several different ways of defining or looking at what a paradox is. The *Random House American College Dictionary* (2006) defines paradox as follows: "A statement or proposition seemingly self-contradictory or absurd, and yet explicable as expressing a truth" (p. 878). For example, Supreme Court Justice Oliver Wendell Holmes, Jr. once opined that "No general proposition is worth a damn!" Well, his statement *is actually a general proposition (or statement)* and itself should be considered worthless (according to Judge Holmes). There is an element of "truth" in his proposition, but it is contradicted by itself, hence a paradox.

Another understanding is that paradox can also be viewed as a statement or situation that contains two true elements that cannot simultaneously coexist, although most often they do coexist, which defies logic, or is counterintuitive. That is, although each statement is true, when put together, they don't seem to make logical (i.e., linear) sense. In fact, the word paradox actually comes from Greek and means "beyond belief." As a brief example of this view of a paradox, we cite a classical paradox in Figure 2.1.

If "Everything in this box is a lie," then the statement must be the truth; but if the statement is the truth, it says that everything in the box is a lie! Both statements can't exist simultaneously, although each statement can be considered "true." Hughes and Brecht (1979) have similar illustrations of paradoxical statements referring to a rectangle with the statement, "It is false that there is a true statement within the rectangle [of Figure 2.1]" (p. 8). Another similar paradox to Justice Holmes' statement and Figure 2.1 is the "liar paradox." In it, Epimenides of Crete (BC 600) was reported to have said: "All Cretans are liars." Himself being Cretan, he should be lying, but if he lies, his statement isn't true, however, then he is not lying, and so on and so on! "The statement has an irreconcilable contradiction and is said to be 'undecidable,' being true and false at the same time" (Watzlawick, Beavin, & Jackson, 1967, p. 193). Hence, it is a paradox. So how can something absurd and incomprehensible also be *helpful* in therapy?

From the Practitioner's Perspective

In order to understand how to use paradoxical interventions in treatment and thus encourage second-order change, each of the two nonclinical definitions of a paradox described earlier is relevant. The first definition of a paradox presented above is pertinent to a practitioner's perspective. That is, an explicit paradoxical intervention consists of seemingly self-contradictory and sometimes even absurd therapeutic perspectives about a client's circumstances. Although they are seemingly self-contradictory, or even absurd,

---

Everything in the Box is a lie.

Figure 2.1

effective paradoxical comments contain an element of truth. As Watzlawick, Weakland, and Fisch (1974) suggest, such comments change the conceptual and emotional meaning and fit the "facts" of a client's situation even better (i.e., more positively) than the troublesome perspective that they have been maintaining (Panichelli, 2013).

In many of the chapters in our introductory text, when a *nonlinear* response to a client's concerns was illustrated, a paradoxical intervention was utilized. For example, in Chapter 11 of our introductory text, the therapist suggested to his client (Clinical Case Example 11.1: Schemas, Emotions, and Symptoms) that she was "stuck" in an emotionally abusive marriage because she wanted to be a "winner." Being a "winner" was represented in her frame of reference by continuing to be "the wife" of a continually philandering husband—she was the "winner" compared to the women with whom he philandered because *she was still the wife.* Staying in the marriage can be viewed from two perspectives: (1) From the wife's perspective, getting a divorce would have made her a "loser" because she would have "lost" her husband to another woman—she would have finished second, just like in the early memory that she reported in treatment; and (2) from the therapist's perspective, why would anyone want to stay in such an apparently demeaning and denigrating marital arrangement and, in addition, subject her children to neglectful treatment from their father? The therapist was able to see that her staying in a bad marriage made her a "winner" *from her point of view.* Therefore, to be effective, the therapist *must understand* the client's point of view while still holding a different opinion of it (recall from the previous chapter that this is the essence of the therapeutic "auto double-bind"). That point of view thus contains an element of truth, from her perspective; hence, *a paradoxical interpretation of her behavior* helped the client find new meaning. That new meaning was something positive, namely she felt like a "winner" as long as she was the wife in her otherwise inexplicable self-denigrating behavior of staying in an overtly abusive marriage, without financial support for their children, while her husband continuously indulged himself with other women and expensive habits. However, the therapist's comment was not just another perspective; it was *specifically relevant to the client's belief system and a core schema,* namely, wanting to be a "winner."

From the Client's Perspective

Bohart and Tallman (2010) and Miller, Hubble, Duncan, and Wampold (2010) have focused attention on a semi-neglected important variable in psychotherapy research: the client's perspective. The client's perception of the quality of therapeutic relationship is more highly correlated with outcome than is the *therapist's* perception (Bohart & Tallman, 2010). Such information and many more findings regarding clients' perceptions are important and powerful (Miller et al., 2010). As a result, no paradoxical intervention can be deemed effective without discussing the client's perceptions of paradoxical interventions and how they must fit the client's perceptual model in order to have positive therapeutic impact.

Paradoxical interventions are therapeutically effective because they mirror the tension of a client's ambivalence or dilemma. This pertains to the *client's perspective* on her circumstances and how she experiences paradoxical interventions. In fact, the second general definition of paradox given above (i.e., a statement that contains two true elements that cannot coexist simultaneously, yet do coexist) is the same as the one for a double-bind described in Chapter 1. The resolution of the ambivalences can't be found in a client's struggle with her problematic symptom such as vacillating endlessly, becoming immobilized, trying to escape, or letting fate decide. As Watzlawick et al. (1974) indicated, such efforts are all members of the same "class" or "logical type" of effort. Instead, resolution comes from a different "class" or "logical type" of effort—the practitioner's new *reinterpretation* (e.g., absurd or perhaps illogical) of the client's dilemma and circumstances (not unlike in the movie *The Matrix*). Using advanced nonlinear thinking, the practitioner's reinterpretation of the client's dilemma results from a nonlinear understanding (i.e., a different "logical type") of the client's schematized world-view, their feelings about it, and understanding how the present circumstances create ambivalence and bind them up in problematic behavior. Such understanding unbalances the "tension" and presents new possibilities that accommodate client schemas, reappraises the current problematic circumstances, and resolves ambivalence (by using inductive reasoning). The client sees things from a different point of view that allows both seemingly inconsistent possibilities to be true, which allows for the possibility of second-order change.

As an example, a young man says, "I want to be with Jane, the love of my life, but she wants to get married. I would marry her; but I am afraid to lose my freedom. Jane expects a commitment, and I don't want to lose her. As a result, I've become very anxious and depressed and I'm barely functional. But, getting married would compromise my freedom!" This young lover cannot have it both ways and may seek a counselor or therapist to help him regarding what he should do. He truly loves Jane, and he truly loves his freedom (i.e., to come, go, and do as he pleases), but from his vantage point, he can't have both conditions be true at the same time—one has to go. Jane is telling him that it is time for him to make up his mind about what he wants! She either wants to "take things to the next level" or move on with her life without him. This set of circumstances (i.e., the demands of the situation and the client wanting both Jane and his freedom) creates ambivalence for the client, and he becomes stuck between a rock and a hard place. Anxiety, nervousness, and depression develop, and ultimately provide an "excuse" of sorts from the prospect of having to choose between Jane and his freedom. Continued preoccupation with nervousness, anxiety, and so on prompts him to seek treatment for his symptoms as a compromise to his dilemma. Thus, he has found a way to have his cake and eat it too, but at the price of experiencing and suffering with his symptoms. In the process, his self-esteem is preserved because he has a "reason" for not addressing the life circumstances that demand attention (i.e., the choice of whether or nor to get married). Therefore, from the client's perspective, it is not *him* but the involuntary symptomatic behavior that "prevents" him from making a choice.

There are several important considerations involved in a therapist actually conveying paradoxical interventions in a way that maintains the therapeutic alliance. The first is the *therapist's conviction* that, indeed, there is a positive element of truth to what she is conveying to her client (see Luborsky et al., 1999). The therapist must be able to see, feel, hear, and understand the element of truth in the paradoxical intervention, which represents nonlinear thinking. It is also important to understand that the "truthfulness" of the intervention is relative and not absolute. It is also essential that a clinician understands and believes that *this is* the best way to facilitate client movement.

Nonlinear Thinking Exercise: Moore's Paradox

English philosopher G. E. Moore put forth the following famously absurd statement: "It is raining outside, but I don't believe that it is." Now think about this for a minute. In the first half, a fact is asserted ("it's raining outside"). This is easily verifiable (just look outside). Then there is the personal *assertion* ("but I don't believe that it is"), which flies in the face of the logic or reality of whether it is raining or not. The really *absurd* part is that the person says definitively that it is raining, but then seems to dismiss it because they don't believe that it is. The *final* absurdity is that actually both parts of the statement can be true at the same time (which is the definition of paradox)! It is true that it could be raining, and it can also be true that a person doesn't believe that it is (Hayven & Picard, 2009).

Now, think about this in terms of clients in therapy. Often they will be presented with facts, or they themselves may present the facts, but then their beliefs will (seemingly) dismiss those facts. Consider the parent who says "My son was suspended from school, but I don't think he did anything wrong!" Or "I saw my wife out with another man in a restaurant, but she would never cheat on me!" And finally, "I got a DUI, but I don't have a problem with drinking!" Each is a version of Moore's paradox. There is a fact, and then there is an assertion of belief that could be equally valid. Taken together, however, they are absurd and seemingly contradictory. However, they are the realities that clients often come into therapy with. Clinicians can try to address them in a straightforward (or linear) way but will find themselves trapped by the paradox. OR, they can use a nonlinear approach and apply a paradoxical intervention. In any case, it is understanding the client's inherently nonlinear (and even paradoxical) thinking that creates or contributes to their problem that will help the clinician to effectively address their problem.

Linear approaches to helping a client resolve her ambivalence and dilemma (i.e., first-order change) usually fall far short of desired outcomes, but nonlinear paradoxical interventions can be very helpful. A client perceives a paradoxical intervention as two statements of fact (or truths) that seemingly cannot coexist, but do. That prompts a client to constructively react (emotionally) against her therapist's interpretation or directive and her own symptom, behavior, or complaint. A paradoxical intervention prompts an emotional response that either broadens a client's perspective in order to see her problem in a different way; or advocates for the status quo (or maintaining the problem), which shows the client that the problem is within her control (in the same way the Socratic method can help a person get out of a double-bind). To make sense of such interventions, clients are required to shift their perspective or reappraise the problem or symptom, often using inductive reasoning, in a way that allows therapy to move constructively forward.

Returning to the example above, if the young man's therapist gave him a benign but firm directive *not* to make a decision with his current symptoms of anxiety, depression, and nervousness (i.e., "strong emotional conditions") because it might be the wrong decision made under emotional duress, he would essentially be intervening in a paradoxical way. The therapist is advising that the client do what he is already doing—"do not make a decision"—*but for benign reasons.* Such a directive contains absurdities because the client is already not making a decision, and the therapist is agreeing with the client (after the client has defined his not making a decision as a problem). The therapist may add that it is generally not a good idea and not in anyone's interests to make a decision under such strong emotional conditions (an element of truth). This promotes an affective expression that highlights the client's flawed thinking and behaving. We begin the "how to" process with Clinical Case Example 2.1.

Clinical Case Example 2.1: Depression and Mourning

An 82-year-old man was referred for treatment because of depression combined with his mourning following the death of his wife. She had died of a heart attack 2 weeks shy of their 50th anniversary. Quite tearfully, the client explained that he blamed himself for the circumstances surrounding her death. She had gone out into the yard to perform a small garden task, when she collapsed and died. He thus blamed himself for not finding her on the sidewalk sooner so that he might have been able to revive her or call paramedics. By the time he did find her and called the paramedics, she was beyond resuscitation.

While in group therapy, he talked about how he no longer does any chores around the house, with the possible exception of preparing some very meager meals for himself. He especially talked about how many "projects" his wife had left for him to do, from fixing a curtain rod to washing and waxing floors. He then expressed the wish that, "If I could only talk to her and give her a message or get a message from her, I could feel much better." The therapist suggested to the elderly gentleman that perhaps a different way of looking at the situation was that the "projects" that his wife had left for him were, in a way, messages to keep him busy at a time when he would be very lonely. In effect, the client was told that the unfinished projects would be as messages from his wife that she loved him because she did leave so many things for him to be busy with. The client's response to this redefinition was a smile and the simple statement that, "I never looked at it that way."

Consider how the therapist's comment to his elderly client in Clinical Case Example 2.1 fits both of the two definitions of the general term paradox. To explain: The paradoxical intervention was seemingly absurd because tasks to do around the house are just that: tasks to do around the house. The emotion(s) created by those tasks are primarily *negative/avoidant* in nature. He was given an opportunity to *reappraise* at his wife's demise and the tasks she left from another vantage point previously unavailable to him: Those tasks could represent "messages from her" to keep him busy and persevere. *That meaning* was unavailable to him because of the very strong emotions constraining his ability to see another meaning in his wife's death. Thus, from the client's point of view, the idea that his wife was communicating with him met *his* schematized view as to what it was that he needed to help him contend with her being gone and his being alone—the tasks became messages. Her demise was no longer of the same "logical type."

The specific goal and intended effects of this redefinition were to help the man cope with his wife's death as a result of a new understanding. The different and more benign definition of his wife's demise provided a measure of comfort. He was cognitively "stuck" in a repetitive negative mind set filled with self-reproach, creating a double-bind. Although not all redefining results in such new understanding, very often perceiving new meanings to problematic life circumstances can provide significant emotional relief (e.g., tranquilizing or calming) to clients.

We present Clinical Case Example 2.2 to illustrate.

Clinical Case Example 2.2: Redefining a Complaining Wife

A man whose wife discovered him in an adulterous affair came to therapy struggling to maintain his marriage. He wanted to learn how to deal with his wife, his guilt, and his fall from grace in the eyes of his children. At the same time, he had great difficulty in reconciling certain patterns he had observed in his marriage even *before* his brief affair. Although "mortified" by his own behavior, he maintained that his marriage was far from perfect prior to his affair. Communications with his wife were characterized by seemingly incessant questioning that always ended up with her "never being wrong." Their children had made the same observation of their mother: that she "always had to be right." Everyone likes to be right, but an extreme need to be "right" (or never "wrong") can be aggravating to others. This pattern of relating left the husband feeling like he was "groveling" and constantly apologizing without ever feeling as though he was being forgiven for anything, let alone for having had his affair.

Obviously, he was interpreting what his wife's behavior was all about, and he didn't like what he was feeling. Seeing that the man had made some very keen observations about his marriage both pre- and post-affair, the therapist first gave the dispirited man a note of encouragement by complimenting him on his recognition of the pattern in his marriage. Knowing that this man was a highly paid executive in a very responsible position, the therapist asked the man if he was a "data-driven" manager. He enthusiastically responded, "Yes!" The therapist then offered the following "prosocial" paradoxical explanations by stating that his wife was not very much different from many women who, by questioning their husbands, were looking for information. For someone who has a privately vested interest in being "right" (i.e., "perfect"), however, there can never be enough information. Being "right" and having the information to be "right" are what make her "tick."

The man responded by enthusiastically noting, "That puts it so differently! I take it (i.e., privately logical) as questions—like how I was brought up with my mother and father constantly demeaning me. I was verbally abused by my mother and father for my first 20 years. When I hear those questions from my wife, it's like I'm being verbally abused. It might be me overreacting to circumstances of verbal abuse in my childhood. That's intriguing if that's the case. I never think to answer the questions because I'm too pissed off!"

Consider how Clinical Case Example 2.2 fits the definitions of a paradoxical intervention. First, the paradoxical intervention was seemingly absurd because it didn't fit the picture that the client had painted about his wife (complete with "independent corroboration" from his children) as a nagging and controlling woman who alienated everyone. Such a picture of his wife is stimulated by his long-held schema dynamics (i.e., verbal abuse in childhood that predisposed him to getting entangled into a double-bind). However, when he looks at his wife's behavior from another vantage point previously unavailable to him, a more benign (i.e., positive, prosocial) interpretation of his wife's behavior (seeking information) becomes more acceptable to him as the underlying need or value is clarified. Thus, from the client's point of view, the idea that she may have a more benign purpose for her questioning behavior mollifies and accommodates his predefined (schematized) idea about her. This helps him to reappraise his beliefs and emotional reactions toward her, as well as embrace a different nontroubling perspective. It is "nontroubling" (i.e., belongs to a different logical category) because he does not associate it with the abusive interactions he had with his parents. Thus, her questioning is not of the same "logical type" of verbally abusive behavior as that of his parents; it is of a different "type" of behavior. The new interpretation of his wife's behavior allows him an avenue of opportunity to continue to stay in the marriage, which is something that he wants to do. He has a "new relationship" to his wife's behavior (thus, second-order change is achieved). Otherwise, he is stuck with his double-bind: "To leave the marriage is to fail miserably, but to stay in the marriage is to continue to take abuse (which my schemas won't allow me to do)!" Make no mistake about it, the wife's behavior paradoxically contains two truths: Her behavior is annoying and stimulates negative associations of the husband's badgering by his parents, and simultaneously, it is simply a call for information.

As with other elements in this text, *nonlinear listening* is important in determining what a client needs. In general, *linear listening* reveals that clients who need tranquilizing complain that they are "upset." They use a wide variety of linear descriptors to convey their upset such as *anxious, nervous, stressed, confused, down, overwhelmed, pressured, depressed,* and so forth. Those words are accompanied by phrases such as "I can't take it anymore," "I'm coming apart at the seams," "I've got to *do* something," "I can't stand the pressure any longer," "I don't know what to do," "I want to end it all," and "I'm doing all this stuff (i.e., 'spinning my wheels') but not getting anywhere" (endlessly vacillating)." Such clients may come for treatment in a "crisis" (e.g., "in emotional turmoil," or "emotionally upset") because they are literally exhausting themselves (and others) and unable to calm themselves. Their particular situation may reflect a long protracted period of being unable to resolve a situation that seems to get worse with everything they do. Or it may be a more recent and immediate traumatic crisis with which they can't cope. In couples and family therapy, a client may complain that a spouse or family member is not as concerned as he is, not putting in the same effort as he is, or not (re)acting the same way that he is.

In most such instances, as suggested by Mozdzierz, Peluso, and Lisiecki (2014), clinicians must listen not only in a linear manner but also for

- *Congruence* (does the client really want the help she is seeking for herself as the identified client?)
- *Absence* (is what the client *verbalizes* as the problem really the problem?)
- *Presence* (what is her agitated behavior saying that she is not telling verbally?)
- *Inference* (what is the client telling me that she *doesn't* want?)
- *Resistance* (how does a client respond to a concrete linear suggestion—does she "Yes, but . . ."?)

Assessing for themes, determining a client's schema dynamics, understanding the client's emotional system, and determining the source of her ambivalence also are important for the therapist to know. Each of these elements provides the *nonlinear-thinking* clinician with information about what a client needs from therapy, as well as provides the building blocks for paradoxical interventions.

Reframing: The Essential Precursor to Paradoxical Intervention

In the *Star Wars* movies, Jedi master Obi-Wan Kenobi initially tells a young Luke Skywalker that his father, Anakin Skywalker, was "betrayed and murdered" by the evil villain Darth Vader. Thus in Luke's eyes, Vader is a purely evil character. When Luke rushes off to duel Vader and free his friends, Darth Vader reveals the truth to Luke (and the film audience) that he *is actually* Anakin Skywalker—or that is, he is Luke's father! When Luke confronts Obi-Wan about this fact, Obi-Wan tells him, "Your father was seduced by the dark side of the Force . . . he ceased to be Anakin Skywalker and became Darth Vader. When that happened, the good man who was your father was destroyed. So what I have told you was true . . . from a certain point of view." Luke, incredulous at this explanation (because it was the basis for all that he thought was good and bad in the universe), questions him further, to which Obi-Wan simply explains, "Luke, you are going to find that many of the truths that we cling to depend on a certain point of view." The new explanation "forces" Luke to reappraise his assumptions from a new point of view, at which point Vader no longer is an evil villain, but a pitiable person who is in need of redemption. He now has a "new relationship" with his disdain for Darth Vader.

One of the most powerful ways that paradoxical interventions accomplish this transformation of meaning is by broadening the client's perspective and altering their context (*through the appraisal processes in the emotional (limbic) system;* see Chapter 10 of our introductory text). Numerous authors (e.g., Fraser & Solovey, 2007; Mozdzierz, Lisiecki, & Macchitelli, 1989; Mozdzierz, Macchitelli, & Lisiecki, 1976; Omer, 1981, 1991, 1994) have emphasized contextual considerations as important in the development and use of paradoxical interventions. As we have sought to demonstrate, context includes the objective facts, the subjective appraisals of those facts and emotions driven by the client's schema dynamics (view of self, view of others, etc.). It is from within a given context that ambivalence is created, problematic behaviors emerge, and solutions are discovered. Paradoxical interventions help clients to broaden their perspectives using contradictory (or absurd) statements (often condensed in metaphors) that contain elements of truth. When clients experience two messages that seemingly cannot coexist, but do, they typically react by saying, "I never thought of it that way before!" This relieves tension, facilitates the resolution of dilemmas (i.e., underlying ambivalence), and makes a more lasting (i.e., "second-order") change. Hence, enlarging the perspective and context from what schema dynamics have typically permitted provides a client with an opportunity to disengage (i.e., stop struggling) and allow a new focus/engagement to emerge ("from a certain point of view").

Reframing, or *redefining,* is a *nonlinear* paradoxical intervention that provides new meaning for a problematic concern. "Reframing" was initially defined by Watzlawick et al. (1974) as:

> To reframe . . . means to change the *conceptual and/or emotional setting or viewpoint* in relation to which a situation is experienced and to place it in another frame which fits the "facts" of the same concrete situation equally well or even better, and thereby changes its entire meaning.
>
> (p. 95, emphasis added)

A simple example of reframing would be telling the husband presented earlier in this chapter in Clinical Case 2.1 that his wife's nagging perhaps represents a distressed attempt on her part to gain his attention and engagement with her. Obviously, a complaint about a wife constantly nagging expresses a view by the husband as a "negative" attribute. When the same nagging is viewed as an attempt to facilitate the husband's engagement, the identical wife behavior takes on a positive connotation. The same "facts" (i.e., the wife's alleged "nagging") are conceptually changed so that they can be seen as compatible with an entirely different and more positive meaning.

Generally, reframing offers a *positive* implication or significance to what a client has been appraising as negative or problematic. Thus, it is most typically *unexpected* and requires a client to *reappraise* her concern (e.g., symptom, complaint, circumstances, behavior, or beliefs), most often in a different and more positive way. Upon understanding what the therapist has paradoxically reframed, the process of *reappraising* something that has had negative meaning can produce emotions and their concomitant feelings that are calming, liberating, relieving, and change stimulating. Ekman (2007) calls this *reflective appraisal*. All of the paradoxical interventions that we describe in some way involve the process of reappraisal[1] or reframing. As discussed in the previous chapter, the use of such reframing is universal in the therapy literature (e.g., see Mozdzierz et al., 1989).

Mindfully Being Alert for Opposites

A major orienting principle in understanding "how to formulate and apply paradoxical interventions" concerns making use of *dialectics*. Dialectics is the process of contrasting a thing with its *opposite* in order to create a new meaning. Goldberg (1980) offers particularly helpful philosophical insight into the "true" meaning of things and how paradoxical is the truth of what clients believe and what practitioners tell them:

> I assume that truth is paradoxical, that each article of wisdom contains within it its own contradictions that truths stand side by side. In Western thought logical sequences rule our reason and . . . dominate our psychology . . . our attitudes, feelings, and behaviors rest upon assumptions which we rarely question. The core assumption in many instances is of a logical, sequential universe in which if *A* is true and *B* is logically the converse, the *B* cannot be valid. In the paradoxical mode each may be simultaneously *meaningful*. Contradictory truths do not necessarily cancel each other out or dominate each other, but stand side by side, inviting participation and experimentation.
>
> (pp. 295–296)

In terms of reframing or redefining, the dialectic process involves looking for an opposite meaning contained in what it is that a client is describing as problematic.

Looking for Positive Meanings in the Negative

In advocating for a symptom in order to effectively use paradoxical interventions, a practitioner can ask herself, "What is something *positive* that a client's symptom, complaint, etc., accomplishes? Does it help a client to avoid, excuse, postpone, achieve a private sense of triumph (albeit at a price), etc.? Does it provide a possible 'solution' to the client's struggle with ambivalence? What positive *new meaning* can be derived from the symptom?"

The training of clinicians is to learn about psychopathology, defense mechanisms, DSM diagnoses, personality disorder syndromes, etc., all of which are necessary but all of which can interfere with understanding a client in a more encouraging way. That is, classical understandings of psychopathology, defense mechanisms, diagnoses, etc. can interfere with practitioners' seeing something other than the pathological maladaptive aspect of a client's behavior. When something positive can be gleaned from what it is that the symptom, behavior, complaint, or the like accomplishes, positive effects are conveyed to the client in an encouraging and thoughtful manner. For example, if a client is avoiding something, new meaning is found in reframing it as preventing something bad from happening. If he is postponing something, new meaning can be found in reframing such postponement as an indication that the client is not yet prepared for something and it is better to be prepared before committing himself. Can anything good happen from being unprepared for something?

Advocating (Benignly) for the Status Quo

When a therapist *advocates (benignly) for the status quo,* she suggests or instructs a client *to continue* with certain symptoms or behaviors but for benevolent purposes. Remember that a client's symptoms represent the end product of their attempts to resolve dilemmas. Those dilemmas are created due to ambivalences experienced when a client's schema dynamics are found incompatible with life's demands or the circumstances that clients are facing. Advocating for the status quo must be done in a *benign* manner to provide an opportunity for a client to maintain schemas until such time as he feels safe enough to modify them and address life's demands more constructively or the circumstances change. Thus, *he can have his cake and eat it too;* at the same time, continuing the behavior produces feelings of discomfort at the lack of change. This is paradoxically absurd because it sends a message to clients to keep engaging in a problematic behavior that they want to change. It is paradoxical because the intervention is working to change the behaviors by telling the client *not* to change the behavior.

When advocating (benignly) for the status quo, it is important to remember that a client has typically been "fighting" (i.e., with herself, her symptom, despairing, etc., or with other people, e.g., being resistant, rejecting, or forming impasses). As a result, when using a paradoxical intervention that advocates (benignly) for the status quo, a therapist "unites" with the symptom or complaint in a way that is accepting, embracing, and endorsing, while empathically acknowledging a client's right to feel the way she does and be the way she is. Acceptance and joining are important considerations, for they encompass the contextual and prosocial aspects of paradoxical interventions. Such interventions authenticate a client's experience. That allows a therapist to assume a position of symptom advocate while reinforcing the therapeutic alliance. Such behavior gives a client nothing, or at least less, to be resistant to or "against." The therapeutic "leverage" and energy a client has invested in her symptom are advantageously and ironically utilized to help her.

Searching for Previous Solutions

Another nonlinear principle useful in planning and implementing paradoxical interventions is to identify not only what the complaint is but also what the client has tried to do about it (as well as tracking what typically has happened as a result). What a client has done represents her "solution"—even if it is unsuccessful—to her symptom or complaint. Ironically, often when a client discovers her solution to be ineffective, she typically engages in doing more of the same. For example, a typical complaint is "I can't sleep!" A client will then report all the ways she has tried to make herself sleep. This is a contradiction. No one can "make" himself or herself fall asleep; we have to *allow* ourselves to fall asleep. Or, for example, when a client's spouse or partner is unresponsive to subtle messages, the same messages are repeated but louder, and often times with increasing amounts of emotional acrimony, but to no avail.

Therapists understand that behaviors, symptoms, and complaints do not have just one meaning, and that a different view of their situation is necessary for lasting (i.e., "second-order") change. Then it becomes possible to understand that *reframing* provides that other meaning—more constructive and benign—that the client hasn't come upon. Thus, if a client continues with a symptom or complaint, he is cooperating with the therapist and moving in a more constructive direction; if the symptom is abandoned, the client is also served. As Luborsky et al. (1999) noted, the therapist's belief in what she is paradoxically suggesting is important in helping a client believe in it.

It is important to remember that such *interpretations are not forced upon a client.* They are simply offered for client consideration. *A therapist must never fight with a client.* Despite what is demonstrated in movies and TV dramas in which a "therapist" *definitively* tells a client what he has done right or wrong, fighting/confronting a client, is not very productive (Beutler, Moleiro, & Talebi, 2002; Fraser & Solovey, 2007; Norcross, 2010). Instead, a therapist must always approach the client in a spirit of being a friend seeking a deeper understanding of the client as well as more detailed information from him. One approach to this, outlined in Chapter 3 of our introductory text, can be seen in a clinician adopting a stance of "not knowing" (often thought of as the "Columbo"[2] approach). This presents a therapist as less threatening and potentially allows a client to disclose more information (e.g., "I know what I mean when I say that I'm anxious, but I'm not sure what you mean when you say you were anxious"). The nonlinear-thinking therapist utilizes *impressions* to deliver a paradoxical intervention in the form of vague statements such as, "I noticed that. . . . It occurred to me. . . . Could it be that . . .?" This allows clients to absorb paradoxical directives without becoming defensive.

Advanced Nonlinear Thinking and Paradoxical Interventions

Remember that clients are *invested* in their symptoms, which *may not make common sense* to a practitioner. They are invested so because those symptoms most often represent "solutions," albeit painful and inappropriate ones, to clients' problems. Recall the discussion of double-binds in Chapter 1 when clients are stuck between the primary and secondary injunctions. They have to find a solution even if it is "problematic." Dealing with the problem logically/linearly leads a person to conclude that they cannot control or influence it, feel helpless to change their circumstances and thus seek help. Such solutions, whether clients recognize it or not, have helped to excuse them from accepting responsibility for personally troubling circumstances that they cannot solve more directly without some sort of psychological "price" to pay. Such individuals will "fight" to keep the advantages that their symptomatic or strange behaviors afford them. The "fight" takes the form of resistance to make changes in therapy. *That's the client's perspective,* and the client may or may not be aware of maintaining that perspective.

Research by Wright (1960, 1962) points out how tenaciously human beings will hold onto "solutions" (i.e., "perspective" or schemas) that they have developed to nonclinical problems solving. Wright placed subjects in an experiment to score points with a "multiarmed-bandit" but didn't know that the scoring of points was in reality "noncontigent." That is, there actually was no connection whatsoever between a given subject's particular responses (i.e., his performance) and scoring points. Then, on the last block of trials, all of a subject's responses are given points. After initial blocks of trial-and-error attempts to score points, no matter what they were actually doing, in the last block of trials the subjects believed that they have found a "magic formula." However, it is based on faulty reasoning—usually *deductive* reasoning—that is flawed and leads to *invalid* conclusions. Subjects became incredulous and unable to accept being told that there is no magic formula and the experimenter has been giving them points no matter what they do. Some of the subjects became incensed in learning this from the experimenter. Some of the subjects claimed it was the experimenter who is deluded. Paul Watzlawick (1976b), in commenting on this most enlightening research, is very incisive:

> This . . . [is] the essence of a universal human problem: once we have arrived at a solution—and in the process of getting there, have paid a fairly high price in terms of anxiety and expectation—our investment in this solution becomes so great that we may prefer to distort reality to fit our solution rather than sacrifice the solution.
>
> (p. 54)

Watzlawick is not specifically referring to behavioral and emotional problems; his depiction of how invested we human beings are in our "solutions" is apropos of what happens in clinical circumstances. Patients can be and often are resistant and will "fight" in many different ways, some more obvious and some less so, to maintain the advantages that their symptoms give them rather than face prospects of failure if their problems were to be addressed more directly. Paradoxical thinking and the interventions that follow from such thinking represent constructive ways of approaching human beings' substantial resistance to making changes. Change is difficult for human beings whether it is change regarding the normal things of everyday living or change regarding the way we think and behave in dire emotional conflicts. If the reader should challenge this, we ask the following: "How difficult or easy was it for you to change something important in your life?"

When clients experience dilemmas (i.e., approach–approach, avoidance–avoidance, approach–avoidance, and double approach–avoidance; see Domain 6, Mozdzierz et al., 2014), they typically feel highly ambivalent, which places them in a double-bind. The double-bind (or dilemma) contains two true elements or injunctions that cannot exist simultaneously: "If I choose to address this issue in a direct way, it will go against my schematized world-view" (e.g., "I am afraid that I might fail, or lose something that I value"). At the same time, if a person unconsciously reasons, "If I don't face this issue, and it won't go away, I am failing to meet what I perceive that 'life' (i.e., responsibilities, obligations, natural expectations for self-reliance, other people, my own preferences, etc.) is demanding of me." The person is thus stuck in their ambivalence. The symptom (e.g., vacillating endlessly, becoming immobilized, trying to escape, or letting fate decide), however, allows for these to coexist, though at a price (e.g., a person's health, anxiety, depression, insomnia, general functioning, etc.). This price creates a "tension" that requires some sort of "resolution." When clients try to "resolve" the dilemma on their own, however, without understanding the underlying ambivalence and the paradoxical nature of their wanting their cake and eating it too (i.e., a double-bind), the typical results are highly dissatisfying and only add to their apprehension and confusion. As a result, using advanced nonlinear thinking to create paradoxical interventions is what master practitioners use to help clients out of their dilemmas. We begin to discuss exactly how, next.

Nonlinear Exercise: The Barber's Paradox

"I'd never join a club that would have me as a member!"

—Groucho Marx

Suppose there is a town with just one barber, who is male. In this town, every man keeps himself clean-shaven, and he does so by doing *exactly* one of two things:

1. Shaving himself; or
2. Going to the barber.

The question is: Who shaves the barber? Think about it. All men are clean-shaven, and we know that the barber is a male (though some versions omit that, and the solution is that "the barber is a female" but that is not the case here!). The rule that forces the paradox is that he must be clean-shaven by doing *exactly* one of the two things: shave himself or go to the barber. But if he shaves himself, he is going to the barber (himself) and thus doing *both* at the same time. If he goes to the barber (himself), he is shaving himself (and likewise doing both at the same time). So how can he follow the rules: Be clean-shaven, and only do one of the two options?

This is very similar to the paradox that states: "Every rule has an exception." By its very definition, this presents a paradox. The statement "Every rule has an exception" is a rule, which should have an exception, except if the rule that "every rule has an exception" *does* have an exception, then the rule would no longer be valid because it would be proven wrong. So what is correct? That every rule has an exception or that there is a rule that doesn't have an exception (which makes the original statement wrong)?

Both of these (and Groucho's statement) are a phenomenon of philosophy called self-reference. Self-reference means that the person or idea that is being referred to is the speaker. Most times, this is not a problem (we make "I-statements" that refer to ourselves all the time), but there are times when it creates a logical paradox, as in the cases above. This is particularly true when a person uses "circular" logic, which continues to refer back to itself. The barber cannot shave himself, but there is no one else to do it, and he must be clean-shaven, but cannot shave himself. Or "I would not belong to a club that would have me as a member. So if I am not a member of a club, I would want to belong to it, but if I belonged to that club, I would not want to belong to it, etc." Clients may find themselves in this kind of pattern by saying: "I would never become addicted to anything, but I can't seem to stop smoking. But I would never become addicted to anything so I won't stop smoking, because by stopping smoking, I would be admitting that I was addicted to nicotine." Circular reasoning, or systems thinking, is the cornerstone of Family Systems Theory (and is a major part of nonlinear thinking). Master clinicians use these to both understand client behavior, AND use it to get clients *out* of their problematic thinking. This can often be used with the Socratic method and inductive reasoning to encourage clients to reject or break out of double-binds. Understanding the self-referencing paradox, and how clients get themselves into problematic behaviors, why they cannot seem to break out of them, and how to use the same advanced nonlinear thinking to get out of them is a core element embraced by master practitioners.

Categories of Paradoxical Intervention

Paradoxical interventions can be categorized according to what it is that a practitioner is attempting to accomplish in responding to a client in a nonlinear manner. While some paradoxical interventions help a client to find *new meaning* (i.e., something positive) in their symptom, circumstances, complaint, etc., other paradoxical interventions "prescribe" the symptom (i.e., advocate that a client postpone what they are already postponing, reproduce or engage in a symptom or complaint for constructive purposes, etc.). To clarify, practitioners use paradoxical interventions to

1. *Neutralize* the negative impact of aggrandizing and critical, negativistic, inflammatory, or disparaging remarks directed at the therapy or the therapist
2. *Tranquilize* and help to calm clients upset and overwhelmed with emotion
3. *Energize* and (positively) mobilize client resources in more useful rather than useless directions
4. *Challenge* client behaviors that are disruptive to client functioning and/or well-being

Although paradoxical statements and perspectives—by nature of their contradictory or absurd elements—challenge clients' views of their circumstances, they do so by supporting, and endorsing a client and *joining* rather than opposing symptoms, complaints, problem behaviors, resistance, and reactance. Thus, they utilize the therapeutic auto double-bind (see Chapter 1) to create second-order change.

We begin our discussion of the various categories of paradox with what we have called "Neutralizers": how such interventions can *neutralize* client behaviors that can be disruptive to treatment. The following chapters provide definitions, descriptive case examples, and rationales for other types of paradoxical interventions.

Clinical Attitude and Disposition: Irony

"Irony is a disciplinarian feared only by those who do not know it, but cherished by those who do."

—Soren Kierkegaard

"Irony is the form of paradox. Paradox is what is good and great at the same time."

—Friedrich Schlegel

"At a time like this, scorching irony, not convincing argument, is needed."

—Frederick Douglass

In the O. Henry short story *The Gift of the Magi,* a poor husband and wife struggle to buy their spouse a special gift for Christmas. The wife knows that her husband would like a platinum chain to go with a precious pocket watch that he has, while the husband knows that his wife, who has gorgeous hair, would love fancy hair accessories and combs to adorn her hair. However, since they are poor, neither has the money to get the other what they want. So the wife sells her hair to the wigmaker to get the money to buy the chain, while the husband sells his watch to get his wife her combs. When they go to give each other their gifts, they realize that each has sold the very thing that the other person's gift was meant for. *This* is an example of irony, commonly defined as a sequence of events that are incongruous or provide a contrast between "what might be expected, and what actually occurs" (*American Heritage Dictionary,* 2011).

According to the *Oxford English Dictionary* (2007), irony is defined as "A condition of affairs or events of a character opposite to what was, or might naturally be, expected; a contradictory outcome of events as if in mockery of the promise and fitness of things." As a result, we feel that the appreciation of irony is a key clinician disposition for being able to appropriately understand and use paradoxical interventions. Clearly, to understand the irony of a situation requires many of the same nonlinear thinking components that we have advocated. For example, many of the same methods for understanding the nonlinear nature of communication (listening for congruence, absence, presence, inference, and resistance) are the same for appreciating irony. It is the incongruence of a situation that makes one appreciate the historical irony of President Ronald Reagan's assassination attempt in 1981. When John Hinkley fired his weapon, none of the bullets directly hit the president. It was only as he was being rushed into his bullet-proof limousine (which was designed to protect the president from gunshots) that he was struck in the chest by a bullet ricocheting off of the car. Likewise, the tragic irony of Mrs. John Connally (wife of the Governor of Texas) saying to President John F. Kennedy, "You can't say that Dallas doesn't love you today, Mr. President" as he was riding in the motorcade on November 22, 1963. Moments later he was shot and killed. Finally, there is the historical irony of the iconic photograph of President Harry S. Truman holding up a copy of the *Chicago Tribune* on the morning after the 1948 election that had the bold banner headline "DEWEY DEFEATS TRUMAN" when actually, Truman had won.

Truly to understand irony is to understand that life can be unfair, and sometimes cruel. This is the reality that clients face when they come to therapy. In fact Casadei and Giordani (2008) state that irony, humor, and the "clinical point of view" share common cognitive denominators (or what we would call nonlinear thinking). They argue that each is a creative process that require an embracing of the "darker" side of the self, and to be able to empathically communicate to another person. In fact, they even link therapeutic irony with the Socratic method (*advanced* nonlinear thinking!). Understanding irony allows for joining to occur and provides clients and therapists a way to be able to introduce contradictory or conflicting emotional information for the client to reflect upon and change their perspective or behavior.

Clearly, it is the master practitioner who has developed a general nondefensive and paradoxical mind-set—not as a "technique" but as a nonlinear way of thinking about such corrosive client comments, the treatment process, and even life itself. A therapist's neutralizing responses evolve from a nonlinear mind-set. Indeed Schlegel's quote above ties the ideas of paradox and irony together. Of course, an appreciation of irony is crucial in advanced nonlinear thinking, and useful in employing the Socratic method, and understanding double-binds. This means sometimes using irony to respond to a client's negativistic comment about the therapy or therapist, and perhaps agreeing with it wholeheartedly; hyperextending a client's point further than the client intended; using humor; "looking at the flip side"; or adopting a neutral stance. Natural differences in clinicians' personalities have much to do with what sort of response (i.e., humorous, ironic, "straight," etc.) they can comfortably deliver in replying to caustic client comments (see Mozdzierz et al., 1989).

Neutralizers: The Primary Paradox

Neutralizers represent a class of interventions that are closest to having a generalized nonlinear paradoxical mind-set. In most instances, the neutralizing influence and effects of a "primary paradox" consist of a simple, unexpected, ironic therapist response to certain disagreeable types of client verbalizations or behaviors. There are several nonlinear assumptions underlying the need for the use of *neutralizers*. The first assumption concerns clients' potential use of negativistic, disparaging, etc. comments. *Neutralizers are therapeutic responses that are meant to defuse the potential of disparaging client comments to undermine the work of the therapist and/or therapy.*

How Neutralizers Work

A metaphor that may be helpful in describing the meaning and impact of neutralizers on clients' behaviors is that of an antacid—a relatively simple compound whose purpose is to neutralize the destructive, corrosive activity of acid in the digestive tract. For example, imagine someone consuming a large meal of spicy food. The stomach secretes hydrochloric acid in significant quantities in order to digest the spicy food into nutritious energy for the body—an obviously useful and beneficial function. In some instances, however, as a result of a particular menu choice, the once-helpful acid continues to pour out, eating away at the lining of the stomach. In addition, the acid can back up into the esophagus, a part of the digestive tract that has little protection against stomach acid, and causes a painful, burning sensation (commonly referred to as heartburn!).[3] All of this results in a disruption of pleasurable activities and causes significant discomfort. Within a few minutes after chewing two antacid pills, however, the antacid neutralizes the stomach acids and stops the pain of heartburn, providing significant relief.

In the same way, for any number of reasons, some client behaviors are disruptive to the therapy, acting very much like an acid. Such attitudes or behaviors can have corrosive effects that can prevent the development of or eat away at a therapeutic relationship or alliance. By paradoxically counteracting clients' negativistic or disruptive comments (e.g., by making an absurd statement that contains two true elements that seemingly cannot coexist) and rendering them harmless (or at least noncorrosive), neutralizers act like an antacid that soothes a client's acidic comments.

The following list of particular client behaviors that can be disagreeable and disruptive to treatment is suggestive but not exhaustive:

- Negativistic, inflammatory, or disparaging remarks directed at the therapy or the therapist (possibly due to being mandated for treatment or in the precontemplation stage)
- Aggrandizing, elevating comments that put a therapist on a pedestal (from which he or she can be toppled and the treatment sabotaged)

By responding with neutralizing paradoxical interventions, the therapist does not confirm, deny, dispute, or otherwise react or overreact to a client's accusations or statements (as outlandish as they might be), but rather attempts to "neutralize" them (see Table 2.1). Such neutralizing interventions are an especially important consideration in addressing the need to nurture, preserve, and maintain the therapeutic relationship.

We add a cautionary note to the use of the "*P*'s of the paradox," as we have called them: Paradoxical interventions do not replace the necessity of "working through" issues that a client brings to therapy. Although at times such interventions represent major aspects of therapeutic success, at other times they facilitate overcoming the corrosive impact of resistance, reactance, and pessimism by changing the client's relationship to the problem from one of fear or avoidance, to encouragement and hope. At all times, it is the client who defines what a successful outcome is and what is useful to her. That is why it is so important to solicit feedback from clients about the impact and success of treatment—or lack of it (see Miller, Duncan, Brown, Sparks, & Claud, 2003; Miller, Duncan, Hubble, & Wampold, 2010).

Neutralizing Disparaging Comments

For some clients, disparaging comments may be intended to provoke what the client believes to be an inappropriate counselor response, thereby providing the client with an

Table 2.1 Possible Aggrandizing, Disparaging, Inflammatory, and Negativistic Client Comments, and Possible Practitioner Responses

Client Comment	Type of Client Comment	Possible Neutralizing Therapist Response
"You don't seem interested in me!"	Disparaging of the therapist	"That's interesting. Let's explore that."
"Last session, you gave me several examples of clients to illustrate valid points. I didn't like that. I've listened to other people all my life, and this is my time for someone to listen to me!"	Expression of negativism by the client	"Thank you so very much for showing me the sort of trust that allowed you to express that to me."
"You don't seem to like me!"	Inflammatory	"Hmmm. Tell me more about that."
"WOW! Your fee is really high!"	Negativistic and inflammatory	"I disagree—it's outrageous. At the same time, I don't know anything that isn't expensive."
"I don't want to be here!"	Negativistic	"I don't blame you. You didn't ask for this."
"You're confusing me!"	Disparaging and possibly inflammatory	"I sometimes say things, and they don't come out right."
"You're my last hope."	Aggrandizing and perhaps setting up the therapist or therapy for failure	"I like to believe that there are numerous practitioners who are able to help you. Let's put our heads together and see what we can accomplish."
"You come very, very highly recommended."	Aggrandizing and perhaps setting up the therapist or therapy for failure	(With humor) "I deny everything unless I have a chance to talk to my lawyer."
"Dr. Smith says you are absolutely the best and will solve my problem."	Aggrandizing and perhaps setting up the therapist or therapy for failure	(Said with humor and mild exaggeration) "I don't know about that Dr. Smith and how he tends to exaggerate everything."
"This discussion is very difficult."	Possibly negativistic	"I'd like to caution you that most likely tonight, you are going to be thoroughly exhausted. Many clients have reported such exhaustion following the sort of session that we're having."

excuse for leaving treatment prematurely or being uncooperative in other ways. Typically, these individuals are in the precontemplation stage and thus try to leave therapy (or otherwise be uncooperative) without feeling responsible for doing so. For example, in the film *Good Will Hunting* (see Van Sant, 1997), as part of his probationary plea bargain to work with a math professor at MIT, Matt Damon's character, Will Hunting, must go to therapy (against his will). Arrangements are made for him to see a therapist, whom he mocks, followed by another therapist, with whom he repeats his mockery before being seen by Robin Williams' character, Sean. In each scene with the other therapists, the mocking behavior that Will displays is designed to disrupt the therapeutic process. In each case, he is successful. When he finally starts to see Sean, he attempts to sabotage the therapy, just as he had done before. Will begins to jokingly critique a painting that Sean had done and begins to probe his personal life. When Will hits upon the subject of Sean's deceased wife, Sean became enraged and grabs Will by the throat (which, we would emphasize, is *neither* paradoxical nor *ethical!*).[4] When they meet again, Sean takes him for a walk to the Charles River. He explains his behavior, and then he describes why Will does what he does. He explains that he uses his intellect to push people away, but in doing so, he never really experiences life. He says, "I could ask you about love, and you would probably quote me a sonnet." Will is at a loss for words, reacts with silence and stonewalling in therapy, but eventually begins to engage in treatment and opens up to Sean. In other words, Sean effectively *neutralizes* Will's negative behavior. From that point on, Will begins to open up to Sean and address his issues. Therapists who do not respond appropriately to disparaging client comments may be reflective of a failure to engage clients, which contributes to the high "dropout" rate in therapy (see Mozdzierz et al., 2014).

Master Example 2.1: But Don't Take Our Word for It!

This excerpt is taken from a family therapy session with *Monica McGoldrick* (author of *Genograms* and *Ethnicity and Family Therapy*) as she works with a teenage daughter, her father, and her step-mother (Psychotherapy.net, 2006).

David: Ah, Monica, I've been thinking a lot about last week and, uhm, I still feel that it's important that we focus on the present and not so much on the past.
Monica McGoldrick: Hmm.
David: Uhm, I mean, we spent a good deal of the session last week, as an example, talking about Michelle's grandmother, who Michelle saw for all of about 4 months total in her entire life, and I really think we need to focus on the present and Michelle's behavior, which is continuing to be very difficult.
Monica McGoldrick: I have to tell you that, from my perspective, the past really influenced the present in such important ways that we cannot not deal with that. But I'll tell you what. Let's start with what's happening now, that, you know, obviously there's something that you wanted me to understand that you think I don't yet understand. So why don't you tell me what, what that is.

In the case example, McGoldrick knows that the client is being disparaging, but she hasn't been able to forge a connection with David yet, so she doesn't have a strong enough footing to confront his resistance. In addition, she is aware of the auto double-bind inherent in her position (i.e., she has to "join" with David, but not "go along" with what he wants because it will take them away from what needs to be dealt with therapeutically). Instead, she used a neutralizing comment to work *with* David's hesitation, go with his concerns, and look for ways to connect them with the family history that seems to be the cause of their current distress.

Neutralizing Aggrandizing Comments

Another nonlinear assumption involving neutralizers concerns clients' potential use of aggrandizing, idealistic comments that flatter a therapist but may subsequently be used to hold the therapist responsible for the potential future failure of therapy. A client is ultimately responsible for making progress from treatment. The client gets the credit for gains made, and he or she is responsible for making changes. The therapist is a facilitator of change and bears responsibility for making certain that all possible salient domains of therapy are appropriately brought to bear. Therapists create the conditions that are necessary for a client to move through the stages of change and cope more effectively and constructively.

Master practitioners are skilled in recognizing and benignly responding to overt and subtly disparaging comments to nurture the therapeutic relationship and heal ruptures to well-established alliances. A therapist must never deliver neutralizing comments with contempt, sarcasm, or any other form of defensiveness or hostility—the purpose of a "primary paradox" is to simply *neutralize* clients' depreciating, aggrandizing, and so on comments in order to allow therapy to continue. Maintaining such a *nonlinear* mind-set is what master practitioners do to understand the purpose of a client's comments and then effectively neutralize any acidity or aggrandizement of the therapist. This is in keeping with the initial goals of early treatment, namely, to always keep sight of establishing and maintaining rapport, nurturing and preserving the healing potential of the therapeutic relationship or alliance, and *not provoking* further client negativism or premature termination.

Power Struggles, Ambivalence, and Precontemplators

As discussed in Chapters 12 and 13 of our introductory text, clients who come to therapy are often in a state of ambivalence about giving up their problem behaviors. Even if they verbally express a desire to rid themselves of a bad habit or immobilizing behavior, they may struggle when a therapist attempts to intervene. Clients often misrepresent themselves to their therapists, pleading that they need help in making a change (i.e., the theme of despair in introductory text, Chapter 5). If the therapist succumbs to such pleading (i.e., the side of making changes), it allows clients to argue strongly for staying the same (i.e., something they appraise as and feel "safer" with because its effects are a known quantity). Linear-thinking therapists who fall into this trap are vulnerable to finding themselves in "power struggles" with clients. The reality is that entering into verbal harangues with a client, mobilizing defensive responses, and arguing are quite counterproductive, only accentuate feelings of ambivalence within a client, and all too frequently lead to premature termination (Beutler et al., 2002; Horvath & Bedi, 2002). *Neutralizing* power struggles is the most effective way to handle such traps. Consistent with Miller and Rollnick's (2002, 2012) work with motivational interviewing, we have found that offering no direct obstacles to a client's resistance, uncooperativeness, or symptomatic behavior is the most "antacid-like" and productive approach. According to Beutler et al. (2002), a therapy setting that is devoid of an overt struggle for power and has a spirit of mutual respect is more effective. This is the effect of a neutralizing paradoxical intervention. It allows for the therapist to avoid power struggles with clients, while at the same time fostering a therapeutic alliance. Consider the challenge in Clinical Case Example 2.3.

Clinical Case Example 2.3: Neutralizing the Rebellious Behavior of a Reluctant Nun

A nun was referred—actually, "ordered"—by her Mother Superior to go for treatment. She was overtly unhappy about being forced into treatment with reduced professional responsibilities, but because she had taken a vow of "obedience," she reluctantly and unhappily complied with the referral. She made it abundantly clear that she felt betrayed at being sent for therapy. Assessing her grave reluctance to be in therapy, the therapist gingerly broached the subject, and she agreed that she did not want to be in treatment.

Although she was very devoted to religious life, she felt unappreciated and that her colleagues perceived very negatively. This clearly colored her perceptions and interactions with others, which she made clear to the therapist from the beginning. Neutralizing the toxicity of her position, the therapist empathically said, "I really don't want to see people who don't want to be here. It's counterproductive. People benefit the most from counseling if they are willing participants." With that, she seemed to perk up. It seemed to the therapist as though she perhaps wasn't feeling quite so "forced" to be in treatment. He then asked if he might make a "suggestion," to which she agreed to listen. He then proceeded to ask, "How would it be with you if we were to agree to three more sessions spaced out every other week? Almost anyone can tolerate me for three sessions (said jokingly). (In recognition of the intended humor, the nun smiled appropriately.) During that time, you can tell me your story of what led to your being sent here and how you are feeling about it. At the end of that time, if you don't find anything of value in our discussions, I will be happy to write a letter to your Mother Superior informing her that we have concluded our business." She smiled and readily agreed to the proposition. As part of the agenda for the third session, the therapist brought up the three session trial, and the good nun indicated that she thought she would like to continue for a while longer. She ended up staying in treatment for 6 months, finding herself more and more committed to acknowledging, understanding, and changing some things about herself that she had long neglected.

Questions

1. What was the nun's dilemma?
2. What was the "neutralizer" paradoxical intervention used? How was it effective?
3. Discuss the paradoxical nature of the reframing for the client (i.e., two true elements that were mutually incompatible, yet true) and the counselor (an absurd or contradictory statement that contains truth).

By and large, neutralizers are used to insure that a therapist does not provide a client with an excuse for leaving treatment prematurely. That was the therapist's primary intention in Clinical Case Example 2.3. What *was* paradoxical about the intervention were the two true statements that the therapist made: (a) implying that staying in therapy was counterproductive unless it was voluntary; and (b) acknowledging that the client had been forced into therapy and was expected to stay since she had taken a vow of obedience. It acknowledges that the client is in a double-bind (go to therapy or else; but you have to *want* to change even though you don't want to; and you can't be a good nun if you don't obey), *and* it acknowledges the therapist's auto double-bind of needing to join with the client (i.e., empathize) and get her to accept that she needs to change some things about her.

It is necessary to deconstruct these events to understand the subtleties of this intervention. The client's ambivalence in Clinical Case 2.3 concerns having taken a vow of obedience (i.e., a religiously based, solemn promise to follow the orders of her Mother Superior) and being in a situation that she, as a person, did not want to be in. As a result, if the client was going to benefit from treatment, her perception of the therapy would need to change from something forced upon her to something that she chose to do. The therapist aligned himself with the client by providing her with what she wanted and felt she needed (i.e., early termination of treatment, which was in keeping with her feeling of being forced into treatment). But, he also suggested that they could perhaps renegotiate their arrangement after three sessions. Again, this allowed the client to make a *choice* about being in treatment, or to put it paradoxically: She could have a choice even though she felt that she had no choice! The intervention essentially addressed both aspects of her ambivalence: She was staying in treatment for three more sessions and 6 more weeks, which allowed her to feel good about keeping her vow of obedience. Being provided an option to terminate treatment early allowed her to keep faith with *herself and her desires* to not be in or need therapy. Her schema pertaining to self-identity dictated that she follow her vows. The therapist's option allowed her to leave treatment early with a good conscience and keep her vow of obedience—she could have her cake and eat it too.

The intervention neutralized the acidic effects of her negative reaction to being "ordered" to go to therapy, which she demonstrated toward the therapist. In addition, when the therapist communicated that he understood her predicament (of being "forced"), he communicated respect for the client, supported her position, and in fact agreed that therapy is most effective and beneficial with people who want to be there—similar to "agreeing with a twist." This allowed both client and therapist to work on creating a therapeutic alliance. Finally, the therapist augmented the impact of certain truths: Therapy *does* work best with people who want to participate in it; they could conclude their work, albeit very limited, early; and he was willing to write a letter in support of their work being concluded after 6 weeks of "brief" therapy. Using that frame of reference, however, if he could stimulate the client to agree to a course of three sessions, they would have a good chance of fostering a strong enough relationship to make a better determination about what the client needed regarding counseling. All of this could not have been accomplished without the neutralizing paradoxical intervention.

Dealing With Precontemplators/Mandated Clients

Clinical Case Example 2.3 (i.e., the reluctant nun) is reminiscent of the precontemplators discussed in Chapter 4 of our introductory text. In that particular case example, precontemplation is prevalent and the client is in the first stage of Prochaska and DiClemente's (1984) stages of change model. This determination is incorporated as part of the domain of assessing client readiness for change, needs, strengths, and goals. In Chapter 4 of the introductory text, we detailed how clients in the early stages of change model are often unwilling or not ready to commit to change. We also discussed the research of Prochaska and DiClemente (2005), which determined that failure to move a client from a stage of precontemplation to the preparing for action stage in the early phase of therapy typically resulted in premature termination (as seemed likely with the nun in Clinical Case Example 2.3). According to Norcross et al. (2011), clients in the precontemplation stage require a clinician to take on a "nurturing parent" role to get them to engage in therapy, whereas clients in other stages required different tailoring of the therapeutic encounter (i.e., clients in the contemplation phase needed a practitioner who acted as more of a Socratic guide). As a result, a neutralizer paradoxical intervention is going to be the most effective way to manage the client, while maintaining the therapeutic relationship; especially as each type of precontemplator (rebellious, reluctant, resigned, and rationalizing) can embroil the therapist in a power struggle.

Consider this example from the case of Mike:

Therapist: We weren't able to talk much on the phone when we set up the appointment. How can I be of help to you?

Mike: I'm a computer software engineer. I work for a small company that creates a web-based presence for companies to do business, etc. So I got into a heated discussion with a co-worker—who was an idiot, by the way—and she complained to my boss . . . who's really not my boss because I operate independently, and I was forced to. . . . I got written up at work for cussing out a coworker, she was—Look. Let's get one thing straight from the "get-go," I don't want to be here. I am told that I have a "temper" and that it gets me in trouble with people from time to time. I don't think that I am any different than anyone else. I don't go looking for a fight, but I don't back down from one either. I think that is part of what's wrong in the world, people don't stand up for themselves. Well, everyone gets in the way of me doing my job. They don't do what I want, they go behind my back, or they are incompetent and change their minds and I have to rewrite a program all over again.

Therapist: So you like what you do? [MIKE NODS HEAD YES]. And you don't like it when people don't do their job and get in the way of you doing your job, right?

Mike: Yeah, right.

Therapist: Well, I'm kind of the same way. I like to do my job too. I help people do their jobs and their lives better, *if* they let me. If they don't let me, it gets in the way of me doing my job. You know what that's like, right? Look. I don't know you well enough to know if your problem is a big one or just a small one. It is big enough that you're here today. Let me learn a little bit more about you and we'll see what we can do about things to make them better. What do you say? Let me do my job . . . ?

Mike: [WEARILY LOOKS OVER THE TOP OF MIRRORED SUNGLASSES] Alright . . . But look, when I was a teenager, I was forced to go to counseling, and it didn't do anything. The woman I went to see was all touchy-feely and had candles and incense . . . I thought she looked more like a gypsy or a fortune teller! Anyway, I said "enough of this" and bolted.

Therapist: Yeah, I've known a few folks like that in my time. Sometimes people just don't mesh. Their styles don't match. So, if that starts to happen with us, you'll let me know before you bolt? [SILENCE] If you do, I promise no incense and candles . . .
[BOTH LAUGH]

Mike: OK.

Neutralizing Client Compliments, Exaggerated or Otherwise

At first, it may seem "absurd" that you need to neutralize a compliment from a client. After all, it is quite exhilarating to hear someone say, "You saved my life . . . you changed my life . . . you come very highly recommended by someone that I really respect greatly . . . I could not have gone through this without you . . . if I had a father like you I wouldn't have . . . etc." The strongest recommendation that we can make is to resist the temptation to succumb to such praise and admiration. Therapists can also enjoy receiving compliments just like everyone else does. So why is this a problem? The logic is quite simple: If the therapist is the responsible agent for the changes that the client has made, then the therapist is also responsible for failure of the client to make changes, partial successes, or relapses. Each individual is responsible for his or her behavior and justifiably deserves credit for the hard work involved in making adjustments necessary for having a more satisfying life. Likewise, each individual must also be held accountable for their behavior despite poor genes, horrendous early family life, abuse, poor opportunities in life, etc. The therapist's responsibility is to facilitate the change process, to act like a catalyst for change, or act like a nonreactive "crucible" (see Mozdzierz et al., 2014), and to provide the encouragement, atmosphere, and circumstances in which a client can explore making changes.

Another consideration is that complimenting a therapist can also be a manipulative test by the client. By holding the therapist on a pedestal, the manipulative client can readily claim a failure of the treatment due to the failure of the therapist. It is a practitioner's clinical judgment that determines whether a complimentary comment is overdone, manipulative, etc. Clinical Case Example 2.4 provides an illustration of the therapist responding in a supportive and endorsing manner with a metaphor to a client who seemed too effusive in her gratitude.

Clinical Case Example 2.4: Perhaps a Bit Too Effusive

A married woman in her early forties entered treatment for help with a drinking problem. Her drinking seemed related to feeling overwhelmed by her accumulated responsibilities without much of a sense of being appreciated by others for her efforts. In treatment (initially weekly, then biweekly, then monthly until discharge), over a period of months, she made numerous connections between periodic overconsumption of alcohol and feeling unappreciated. Her drinking declined over the course of a year in treatment with no evidence of abuse, and she began demonstrating other healthy choices. She decided to terminate therapy and rightly so since she had obtained her treatment goals. In the last two scheduled treatment sessions, she made profuse declarations of how grateful she was to the therapist for his help, "wisdom," understanding, etc. The therapist, a "seasoned" practitioner, silently questioned the effusiveness of the client's feedback. In light of the fact that the woman had a history replete with her being pleasing, cooperative, conforming, exceeding expectations, etc., only to ultimately find fault with others who did not express sufficient gratitude for all of the pleasing behaviors that she felt she had been living.

As a result of the therapist's judgment, instead of basking in the glory of the client's praise, he related a therapeutic metaphor. The metaphor suggested that when moving a grand piano up to the fourth floor of a building without an elevator, there is always someone who is doing the "heavy lifting." He further suggested that there also was someone who was carrying the piano bench up the stairs and encouraging the heavy lifter(s), ". . . a little more to the left . . . careful not to hurt yourself . . . take a break . . . you're doing a lot of work . . . that piano is really heavy and you are doing a good job . . ." As a conclusion to the metaphor, the therapist suggested that he felt much like the person who was carrying the piano bench to the fourth floor, while she was the one doing the heavy lifting.

The metaphor allows for *some* credit to be given to the therapist for his contribution to the therapeutic endeavor, whatever the client may have perceived them to be. At the same time, the metaphor makes it clear that the major responsibility and credit for the outcome is clearly with the person doing the "heavy lifting." At other times, a grateful client may be expressing uncomplicated "true" feelings of appreciation for the help provided by the therapist and the therapy. Human beings can be and most often are truly grateful for help and kindnesses rendered to them. But, how does one accept the gratitude and yet return appropriate and well-deserved credit to the client? In such instances, what is a practitioner to do regarding compliments offered? Once again, as illustrated in Clinical Case Example 2.4, nonlinear thinking is useful. To accept the grateful and sincere compliment is to accept responsibility for the positive outcome in therapy. To reject the sincere compliment is to potentially offend the client. The answer is to express humble gratitude for the thoughtfulness of the compliment and to make certain that the client knows that "It is *you* that was doing the hard work outside of therapy to get where it is that you wanted to go!" Such an understanding is to acknowledge both sides of the ambivalence involved.

Before we finish this chapter, we have a follow-up exercise in neutralizers. Consider the common client statements in the left column. Then decide what type of statement it is (neutralizing a disparaging comment, neutralizing a compliment, etc.), and come up with an appropriate neutralizing statement.

Table 2.2 Exercise in Neutralizing Client Comments

EXERCISE PART 1	EXERCISE PART 2	EXERCISE PART 3
1. Describe what sort of comment (i.e., aggrandizing, disparaging, inflammatory, or negativistic) each of the following client statements might be. 2. Is the client's comment directed toward the problem or toward the therapy or therapist? What is the difference? 3. What might be a client's purpose in making such a comment?	1. Defend each of the interpretations made above.	1. What was *your* reaction to each of the possible counselor comments above? 2. Did you expect the sort of response that is indicated? 3. How does each comment address the possible purpose a client may have had in making the comment? 4. After this exercise, what other sort of *neutralizing* responses might you make to such client comments?
CLIENT COMMENT	TYPE OF CLIENT COMMENT	POSSIBLE NEUTRALIZING THERAPIST RESPONSE
"I don't know if I'm getting anything out of this."		(How would you respond?)

(*Continued*)

Table 2.2 (Continued)

CLIENT COMMENT	TYPE OF CLIENT COMMENT	POSSIBLE NEUTRALIZING THERAPIST RESPONSE
"Judging from what I've seen and heard from you, I don't seem to be getting any relief, and I don't know if you can help me."		(How would you respond?)
"I'm thinking of finding a new therapist."		(How would you respond?)
"You never talk to me."		(How would you respond?)
"You absolutely saved my life!"		(How would you respond?)
"I couldn't have done this without you."		(How would you respond?)
"Have any of your clients ever committed suicide?"		(How would you respond?)

Conclusion

In summary, neutralizing is an important way of defusing and detoxifying comments and situations that are potentially hazardous to the development of a positive and fruitful therapeutic relationship. We emphatically reiterate that neutralizing represents more of a nonlinear (i.e., paradoxical) mind-set than it does a "technique." The use of neutralizer paradoxical interventions helps to address essential therapeutic tasks such as helping to engage clients when they may be reluctant to do so, resolving potentially toxic situations, moving a client along the stages of change, and developing and preserving the therapeutic alliance. The use of neutralizing agents is but one aspect, however, of how to think and respond in a nonlinear manner utilizing paradoxical interventions. We venture forth into still other aspects of nonlinear thinking as we discuss the tranquilizers.

Notes

1. The term "reappraisal" is specifically used because of its brain-based implications. The amygdala is a part of the limbic system that plays a central role in identifying threats and/or positively valenced elements.
2. As reported in Chapter 4 of our Introductory Text, Columbo is a fictional detective from a TV series of the same name starring Peter Falk. Columbo typically presented himself as somewhat bumbling, confused, not understanding, quizzical, needing clarification, forgetful, and the like. All of which were devices to portray himself in a nonthreatening light. Doing so allowed him to gradually elicit a truer picture of what was going on.
3. The reader is advised that not all stomach conditions reflect eating spicy foods. Gastric esophageal reflux disease (GERD), stomach ulcers, and other serious conditions can also cause stomach upsets.
4. Clearly this is an instance of countertransference that is inappropriate. In real life, such therapist behavior could be subjected to charges of assault and a malpractice legal action.

3   The Use of Tranquilizer Paradoxical Interventions

Whenever you fly on a commercial airline, you have to listen to the inevitable "safety briefing" before take-off. And whether it is your first flight, or your ten-thousandth flight, they are all basically the same! Somewhere in the flight attendant's briefing is a seemingly absurd statement is made, which does not seem to make sense. "In the event of a decrease in cabin pressure, oxygen masks will descend from the ceiling. . . . If you are traveling with children, place the mask over your mouth first and tighten the straps before attempting to help a child." The phrase strikes a chill in the heart of any parent who would gladly give their life for their child! The idea that one would take care of himself before their child is seemingly absurd. However, the reality is that it does make sense. If, in an emergency, the adult passes out due to lack of oxygen while fumbling to put a mask on their child, then both the adult and child are in trouble! On the other hand, if the adult puts the mask on himself first and maintains consciousness, then he is able to help the child—increasing the possibility of both of their survival. Tranquilizers, the type of paradoxical interventions that we will present in this chapter, work in the same way. They get the client to stop behaving in a meaningless or destructive way (i.e., the equivalent of trying to put the child's mask on before your own and possibly passing out) and instead focus on what will be productive behavior (i.e., put the mask on your own face first, *then* put on the child's).

Definition

The "tranquilizers" represent a group of paradoxical interventions that help to calm people whose behavior is getting in the way of solving their problems. Individuals in need of "tranquilizers" usually feel that their lives are "out of control" and that they can't seem to calm themselves, nor can they see that what they are doing is generally causing more harm than good. Outside of precontemplators and mandated clients—who are generally hostile toward therapy, initially—many of the remaining clients who come for treatment present themselves with some sort of frenetic (i.e., frenzied, feverish activity) and unproductive behavior. For all of their "activity" (on the surface), the reality is that they feel immobilized. They cannot seem to "move forward" with their central issue or problem, but feel that they *need to do something*. Often what they do is either distracting (i.e., "busy work") or destructive (i.e., yelling, saying something inappropriately, doing something to make the problem worse). As a result, the client's frenetic behavior needs to be "tranquilized." Thus, the first order of treatment calls for these clients to be calmed, understood, soothed, and reassured (because they are presenting themselves as "upset"). Indeed, many clients respond that they feel much better after a therapy session because of the soothing influence of the therapist, the therapeutic relationship, and the therapy context, namely, it is a "safe place."

But calming a client in and of itself is not an end point. In fact, (and here is the paradoxical side of it) the client has to be "tranquilized" in order *not* to be immobilized! It is the master clinician who realizes that just because someone is *doing* something doesn't mean that they are *accomplishing* anything! They recognize that these clients are ambivalently stuck between their schema dynamics (views of self, others, or the world) and circumstances that they face (or don't *want* to face). When a therapist intervenes by using one of the tranquilizers, however, a symptom or complaint is transformed so that it no longer accomplishes what it was originally created to do. For example, if a client has used procrastination as a way to avoid failure but comes to therapy to "cure" her procrastination, a therapist might recommend that the client "postpone" tackling this issue until she is *really* ready. At this point, the client is confronted with the idea that her procrastination is out of control, which is a sign of failure (and contrary to her schematized view of herself). She might then decide to "prove" that she can accomplish tasks, and no longer procrastinate. Her procrastinating behaviors are successfully "tranquilized," and the therapist can begin to explore the more substantive issues of what the perceived failure or threat might be.

The therapeutic task is to determine a way (or ways) to "tranquilize" such clients' fears, anxiety levels, and so on without frightening them out of therapy! The therapist must remember that the energy that clients use to embroil family members, coworkers, and eventually the therapist into their issues is oftentimes a manifestation of ambivalence. The problem is that the client's "activity" is *not* helping but rather hurting her. If it continues, it will jeopardize the therapy. It is the same type of dysfunctional or immobilizing effort that keeps a client from more constructively dealing with her circumstances. Therefore, the behavior must be tranquilized to move forward. *Tranquilizing comments, interpretations, or suggestions are designed to calm, relieve pressure, deliver psychological reassurance, emotionally sedate clients with humanistic concern, and potentially restore a measure of emotional equilibrium to them.* Without such calming, they are otherwise prevented from fuller participation in therapy and the achievement of more specific therapeutic goals.

Tranquilizers and Advanced Nonlinear Thinking

As a client engages with his double-bind and ambivalence (e.g., procrastination behaviors), the therapist also engages in the client's dialectical struggle (e.g., advocating for change while also recommending caution regarding what change will mean). That is the *nonlinear thinking* at the heart of Miller and Rollnick's (2002, 2012) *Motivational Interviewing*: "Rolling with the Resistance," "Developing Discrepancies," "Agreeing with a Twist" (which we introduced in Domain 6, see Mozdzierz, Peluso, & Lisiecki, 2014), and (of course) paradoxical interventions. Paradoxical tranquilizer interventions have the added benefit of addressing the client's schema dynamics (Domain 4) and emotional system (Domain 5) as well as their ambivalence (Domain 6). When that happens, clients have an opportunity to feel relieved, calmed, or "tranquilized." At the same time, feeling calm and relieved, the client can begin to think more clearly and may be more receptive to therapist input and therapeutic movement. When calmer, clients have an opportunity to take stock of their ability to cope with issues, engage in planning, set attainable goals, and make more reasonable decisions. As a result, the tranquilizer works to create a shift away from the "trap" of the double-bind and the wasteful energy of the frenetic behavior using inductive reasoning and the Socratic method, the tranquilizer can create a shift that leads to second-order change. We next discuss applications of each of the types of tranquilizer paradoxical interventions.

Types of Tranquilizers

We have identified four types (or "*P's*") of "tranquilizer" paradoxical interventions: *permission, postponement, prohibition,* or *persuasion* (see Mozdzierz, Macchitelli, & Lisiecki, 1976). Each of them seeks to interrupt dysfunctional behaviors, symptoms, complaints, and so on by proposing the absurd idea that a client continues doing the (negative) thing he is doing or avoiding the more adaptive thing that he doesn't want to do. The Level 3 therapist understands that a client's symptoms and manifestations of ambivalence have been generated to serve a function and a purpose, namely, to excuse him from some possible threat or failure or to protect self-esteem (hence, ambivalence).

Permission

Permission is the verbal tranquilizer by which a therapist gives her client the authority to continue with present behavior or have his symptoms or complaint, albeit cast in a slightly different and more positive light. This directive is seemingly absurd because the client comes to therapy wanting to be rid of the burdens imposed by his or her symptoms or complaint. Our experience supports the idea that it is not only the symptom or complaint alone that discourages individuals. Rather, it is clients' *feeling of struggling* (unsuccessfully) with their problem that adds to their suffering along with the redundant, useless, circular, and no-win solutions they have attempted. Of course, such struggling only makes their situation worse by prompting feelings of frustration, helplessness, and loss of control. A therapist giving a client permission to have his symptom makes such an intervention paradoxical because it absurdly proposes a constructive purpose for continuing with the present problematic behavior for which the client is seeking help to change. Consider this example from master practitioner Robert Wubbolding.

Master Example 3.1: But Don't Take Our Word for It!

This excerpt is taken from a session with *Robert Wubbolding* (master clinician and author in Reality Therapy), as he works with a man who is facing a life-threatening illness. Notice how he uses permission to help the client to change his worry over his health (Alexander Street Press, 2012).

Robert Wubbolding: You know, see, I have a little motto, if something works, do more of it. And if something doesn't help, do less of it.

John: I like that.

Robert Wubbolding: It's the essence of the kinda counseling, the work that I do. (crosstalk)

John: Okay. I think what I've done is kinda like knocking my head against the wall and trying to make something work.

Robert Wubbolding: Yeah. And maybe stop worrying about dealing with this thing.

John: How do I do that?

Robert Wubbolding: By doing more of those things that work.

John: Okay.

Robert Wubbolding: That's why I said, if you were good at denial, we'd be trying to help you deal with that, but you're not good at denial. You're, you're good at taking it on board. So, maybe, maybe the opposite is better for you, is to, to, to do some things that would distract you, and taking that on board.

John: Yeah, you know, very much.

In this example, Wubbolding understands John's frenetic behavior ("like knocking my head against the wall . . .") is being counterproductive. His obsessing over his health status is actually having a negative toll on his health. However, he understands John's schema dynamics (reflected in not being "good at denial," and taking things "on board") and sets the stage for the paradoxical intervention of taking on distraction by suggesting that John consider doing more of "what works" for him (not denying, but "taking on" distractions). The reader will note how important it is for a therapist to not only have successfully engaged and established rapport with his client but also to have established a therapeutic alliance. If the therapeutic relationship isn't well developed, then the preceding comments could be misinterpreted by the client as cynical or mocking, which would only arouse client resistance while continuing with their problem behaviors. As a result, for basic *reframing* to work, the therapist has to see the positive in the negative behavior and using inductive reasoning to convince the client that it is so. Furthermore, as previously discussed, therapist conviction is also important regarding the "element of truth" contained within each example of giving permission. Clinical Case Example 3.1, which illustrates how paradoxically giving permission made an impact.

Clinical Case Example 3.1: One More Child to Raise

Another example that shows how nonlinear paradoxical permission can act like a tranquilizer for a client's symptomatic behavior comes from a female client who was in her late 40s. Referred to therapy for depression by her psychiatrist, the client complained of restlessness, lethargy, increased irritability, and feelings of hopelessness. To add to her woes, she had also recently been diagnosed with borderline hypertension (although not high enough to require medication).

Reluctant at first, she openly expressed her doubts about therapy. The client reported that she was happily married for over 25 years, and had three children, the youngest of whom was about to graduate from high school and move out. She was looking forward to being an "empty nester," having more time with her husband as well as for herself, and to start developing "adult relationships" with her children. Less than a year before, however, the client's younger sister was hospitalized for drug abuse—one of many such hospitalizations. In addition, the sister's 6-year-old daughter came to "temporarily" stay with her. At that time, she was the only person who could assume care for her niece because the child's father was, likewise, a substance abuser. Other family members, including the child's paternal grandmother, agreed to help during school breaks, summer vacations, as well as other times during the year whenever the client needed a break. When she actually asked for help, however, no one ventured forth. In fact, when she complained, she was chided by her brother, who asked her, "You think you're the only one with problems?"

At this point, she felt trapped: On the one hand, she really loved her niece and felt badly for her. By all accounts, the niece was a well-behaved little girl. On the other hand, she did not like the idea of sacrificing herself and the rest of her adult life to raising another child, telling her therapist, "I've raised my own, already."

When the counselor hypothetically mentioned to the client that she could turn her niece over to someone else in the family, or even to the child service worker who would place her in a group home, she adamantly refused to consider it, saying, "I couldn't do that!" Upon being given *permission* to do what she was complaining of, she raised objections. She was a firstborn child who took on the role of family caretaker after their mother died a few years prior, saying: "Her mantle had passed on to me." It is clear that her self-schema dynamics dictated loyalty to the role of caretaker and that this situation put her in a double-bind. It was equally clear that a common-sense linear suggestion would not be effective in bringing this woman relief from her torment. The therapist's nonlinear assessment determined that the woman needed relief and calming. As a result, he suggested, "It seems to me that you are very interested in being her (the child's) aunt, and doing all the things that an aunt would do; but you are not interested in being her mother." The client immediately seized on the idea and agreed. The therapist continued, "It doesn't seem fair that you are forced to be her mother because no one else will be." Again, the client agreed. In the same vein, the therapist continued, "The thought of you just 'giving her up' would relieve you of the problem; but, the idea of giving up on her is not very palatable to you." This nonlinear assessment clearly reflected the *ambivalence* that the client felt. She became quiet and nodded in agreement as the therapist added, "But what would happen to her if something happened to *you?*"

The client was stumped. The therapist persisted, "I mean, what would happen if you died suddenly in a car accident, or got sick and developed some life-threatening condition that made it impossible for you to take care of the child? Who would do it?" The client admitted that she didn't know but that "something" would have to happen. The therapist suggested that this might be worse than "giving her (niece) up"; it would be abandonment! The therapist further suggested that she already had a condition that was beginning to make it difficult for her to stay healthy—borderline hypertension. The client was told about the interplay between hypertension, heart disease, depression, and cancer, and that if she continued to ignore her health, her body would force a solution to her problem that she might not like!

So how was this intervention paradoxical? Let's look at it from both the counselor and the client's perspective. From the counselor's perspective, the absurd or contradictory statement that contained an element of truth was the idea that this woman, who was the only person in the family to take this child in, might actually *abandon* her.

From the client's perspective, the two concepts that were true but couldn't coexist were that she *did* want to be relieved of the responsibility of raising this child *and* that she felt that she was "ordained" to be the child's parent figure (a schematized view of self, revealed in the phrase that her mother's "mantle had passed on to me"). In other words, these are the two "injunctions" for the double-bind. At this point, the client agreed that if things continued the way they had been going, something would have to happen. Thus, the therapist used the Socratic method to create the "positive" double-bind using permission. The therapist invited the client to think about developing a "contingency plan" with other family members and the child's welfare worker about what might happen. It was further suggested that she might want to brainstorm with these interested parties to take steps now and give herself a break before it was too late.

Hence, permission (and tranquilizers in general) calms and frees a client from the pressure of being "backed into a corner" relative to her ambivalence. When individuals perceive that they are in a psychological corner (whether they put themselves there or not), they usually feel that they have only one choice (i.e., rigid defensiveness, or "black or white" thinking). Such thinking leads to constriction in their actions (i.e., doing what is "safe" by not acting at all), even if this continues to bring them trouble. This is one of the reasons why a "direct-assault," or linear, thinking by a therapist typically results in resistance from a client. If a client feels that her back is to the wall and that she lacks trust in her therapist, she is highly unlikely to hear (let alone heed) the interpretations or suggestions of the person giving her counsel. Permission gives a client the "psychological space" and authorization to step out of the corner that she is backed into (i.e., her dilemma) and begin to consider other alternatives. Using advanced nonlinear thinking, like Socratic questioning, the therapist is able to utilize the paradoxical intervention to clarify her values and see her situation differently. It is paradoxical in nature because clients *expect* a therapist to tell them to stop doing whatever it is that they are doing—possibly in an authoritarian or disapproving manner—just like others in their life have most likely done. When a therapist "rolls with the resistance" and gives a client "permission" to continue with her behavior while rendering a "plausible explanation" for doing so, the client is given room to question the "plausible explanation" underlying a behavior that she knows to be problematic.

In this example, the client was in a classic *double approach-avoidance* dilemma or a double-bind. When the client was given permission to actively think about giving up the child, as well as recasting her role from its present status of being mother and sole nurturer to her desired status of being aunt and a support to the child, she was able to feel less trapped by the double-bind. The therapist's comments provided an opportunity for her to reappraise her situation (again, using a Socratic approach), resulting in a more schema-friendly emotional response and corresponding positive feelings. Once she was given permission to be freed from the self-imposed tyranny of "I must take care of her (i.e., be her mother), because no one else will," "No one will help me," and "It's so unfair," she was able to reach out to other family members and ask for help.

As a result of the *permission* inherent in the therapist's paradoxical suggestion, the woman was able to write family members a letter explaining her situation, her concerns, and her disappointment. As a result of exploring her feelings in therapy, she decided that she really didn't want to give up the child, but rather wanted some relief. In addition, she reported feeling less depressed, more energized, and able to enjoy life more. As an added note, the child also benefited because she now *did* have a contingency plan for her care!

Postponement

Postponement refers to encouraging a client to delay or prolong a decision, required action, or felt need to act into the undefined future and make a mistake (or make things worse). A crisis situation usually requires the client to make a decision that can arouse considerable anxiety and uncertainty. *Uncertainty is toxic to human beings.* Fear of failure is often the underlying issue that inhibits clients from making a decision they need to make. Of course, making *no decision* can, and often does, lead to increased uncertainty. Although making no decision when one is called for in life can sometimes be a "successful"[1] strategy, the impending need for a decision due to life's circumstances can precipitate a crisis for the client. The pressure to make a decision increases feelings of ambivalence, uncertainty, and fear of failure, especially if it entails doing something that the client fears doing because the outcome is not guaranteed (or making a commitment to a particular course of action *at this point in time*). Oftentimes, such individuals will have exhausted their capacity to cope by vacillating, becoming immobilized, or trying to escape—but the circumstances have forced a crisis necessitating a decision (see Mozdzierz et al., 2014 for details). In fact, research into neuroscience has found that there are structures in the brain that seem to be triggered when faced with a dilemma that seems to paralyze action (Hsu, Bhatt, Adolphs, Tranel, & Camerer, 2005). The last option (besides making a decision) in resolving their dilemma is to let fate decide, which may result in a negative outcome for the client and produce the failure that the client fears. Encouraging a client to paradoxically postpone a decision provides significant relief to a client (i.e., tranquilizing), enabling a reestablishment of a sense of certainty (i.e., "The therapist is telling me it's ok to postpone this"), control, calming, and providing an enormous sense of relief that is desperately needed at times of significant apprehension. It is often much better to deal with the consequences of postponement than it is to deal with the consequences of a decision that one feels ill prepared to face. Under conditions of *relief,* a client increases his or her chances of making a more well-reasoned decision in the future. Clinical Case Example 3.2 is a good illustration of this.

Clinical Case Example 3.2: Malingering or Not?

A man came into therapy following a serious injury on the job. He worked in a prison system and had been severely beaten by a disturbed inmate approximately 2 months earlier. Even though he was due to return to work within the month, he did not feel ready to do so. Although he had recovered from most of his physical injuries, he still complained of "headaches." A neurologist had ruled out a physical cause for the headaches, but he continued to report that they still occurred several times a week. Malingering was ruled out, because this man strongly identified with his role as a corrections officer and had received several meritorious commendations from the state for his work. In addition, he had made some attempts to return to duty earlier but was nonetheless plagued by headaches. Later in treatment, he acknowledged being fearful of returning to work, a hypothesis that the therapist had formulated earlier in treatment. As a result, he began to restrict his activities outside his home for fear of triggering a headache that would leave him vulnerable. It was clear that he was on the way to developing a full-blown panic disorder or agoraphobia.

Questions

- How would you describe the client's dilemma?
- What behavior, symptom, or complaint might need to be tranquilized? How is it creating problems for the client and getting in the way of therapeutic progress?
- How might you intervene using paradoxical postponement with this man? Discuss the paradoxical nature of the tranquilizing approach you are suggesting for the client (i.e., two true elements that are mutually incompatible, yet true) and the counselor (an absurd or contradictory statement that contains truth).

The therapist made a reasonable assumption that the client's headaches might be an unconscious means of avoiding going back to work. In effect, the headaches were an expression of his inability to make up his mind about what he wanted to do with his life. So, the therapist suggested that the client specifically *not* think about going back to work for at least the next week. He was given *permission* to *postpone* going back to work—something that he was already postponing. The therapist told him that perhaps he could think about going back to work after that, but until then, his sole focus was to think about getting "well." The client was also instructed that if he felt that he wanted to go somewhere out of the house, that he should, but only in the company of someone else in the event that he might get a headache.

The next week, the client reported having only one or two headaches that were "mild" and that he had been able to go out to shop with a relative. He complained that it was limiting to have to ask for someone to come and wait for him, because he had never been accustomed to being "helpless." The therapist suggested that for the next week, he should still not think about going to work, but that if he wanted to go somewhere outside the house, he could go by himself as long as he felt it was "safe." Again, the following week, the client reported only mild headaches and that he had been successful in going out by himself. Gradually, the issue of returning to work began to be discussed, beginning with the client putting on his uniform at home but not leaving home while wearing it; then driving to work but not going in; and eventually returning to work. At the same time, the therapist began to discuss with the client the possibility that part of his symptoms might be "an invitation" (i.e., a positive redefinition of something that was very negative) to explore other career options. Prior to the accident at work, this man might have rejected such an idea. Now, he admitted that he was beginning to think of other things that he could do with his life. This opened up a new avenue of discussion that eventually led to the client enrolling in college courses to change careers. Still another example might illustrate the variety of circumstances in which clients are experiencing an urgency to make a major decision but are unprepared to do so.

Master Example 3.2: But Don't Take Our Word for It!

In this example of a transcript with a master practitioner, *William Glasser* (creator of Reality Therapy) works with a woman who is deciding about whether to commit to a relationship or not (Alexander Street Press, 2012).

William Glasser: Yeah, it's pretty good.
Ann Mary: Yeah, exactly, and you know, I don't know. I don't know.
William Glasser: Well it's good that you don't know. What is your hurry?
Ann Mary: Well it's, I feel like you know I also try and please people and I feel like I would be making everybody happy if I just did this, but I don't know.
William Glasser: Well, everybody has your life kind of plotted out for you a little bit. You are 35 years old, and people probably have known you had unsatisfied relationships, they'd like to see you what they call "settle down."
Ann Mary: Absolutely.
William Glasser: And all that stuff and . . . and I mean settle down doesn't sound that exciting to you.
Ann Mary: No it doesn't.
William Glasser: How about excitement? Is there any excitement in your life I mean?

So in this example, Glasser uses postponement to expose the client's double-bind and then open up some of her real concerns. First, the elements of the double-bind: (1) "Marry this guy or else!" (*demands of life*); (2) "You don't want to disappoint people" (*schema dynamic*); and (3) "You're not getting any younger, so hurry up!" At each level, the logic is clear, and they each provoke an emotion based on values that the client has. For her part, Ann Mary's doubt about the relationship (her ambivalence) has allowed her to vacillate endlessly without making a decision. But if she doesn't make a conscious decision, "fate" will decide. Glasser's use of postponement allows her to stop her vacillating and consider what was missing from her relationship (*excitement*) and allows her to decide what she wants in accord with her values (*freedom*).

Sometimes postponement can also be paired with natural or logical consequences (i.e., you can delay your decision, but if you do, then "*x*" will occur . . ."). Using Motivational Interviewing techniques like "developing discrepancies" can be helpful to tranquilize the client's frenetic behavior. Consider the following brief example with Marsha Linehan.

Master Example 3.3: But Don't Take Our Word for It!

In this example, master clinician *Marsha Linehan,* PhD (developer of Dialectical Behavioral Therapy—DBT), works with a man who is procrastinating about completing a task with a deadline (Alexander Street Press, 2012).

Marsha Linehan: If you don't do it, then you could actually lose 4 whole days of exercise.
Client: Yes.
Marsha Linehan: Alright. And so as long as you are willing to miss the exercise, you don't have to write.
Client: (Nods, laughs) Yes . . . I would be willing to try . . .
Marsha Linehan: Okay, okay. I figure you would . . .
Client: It scares me a little bit, yeah, it's a good consequence, because there's a lot tied up in that.
Marsha Linehan: Yeah, I'm sure, I can tell.
Client: Uh-huh. (laughs)
Marsha Linehan: Okay. This is good, okay.

Again, in this case example, the logic on each level is clear: (1) I want to keep my commitments; (2) I don't want to do the work now; and (3) I have a looming deadline. Linehan uses something that the client *does* like to do (exercise) and leverages it as a consequence. Then the client has the choice of keeping his commitment (and getting his exercise time) or not writing (and not getting his exercise time). This allows the therapist to say to the client: "You can choose to postpone doing your work (keep your commitments), *but* you will have to give up something you value."

Prohibition

Prohibition is a tranquilizing paradoxical intervention that is closely related to permission and postponing; however, in this intervention, the therapist in a friendly way benignly "can't support" a client doing what he has already not been doing. The "rationale" that the therapist gives for prohibiting what a client has already not been doing is that doing something could prove injurious or disastrous in some way. Of course, such a response to a client dilemma assumes a strong therapeutic relationship and alliance. Like the other tranquilizers, it defies *the client's* idea of "common sense." Clients enter counseling or therapy *expecting to be changed or influenced* in some way. Thus, their expectations dictate that a "therapist" would try to reverse "bad" behavior or encourage "good" behavior. This represents clients' *linear thinking,* and doesn't allow for the influence of their ambivalence, emotional factors, or schema dynamics.

Prohibition entails quintessential characteristics of paradoxical interventions because it essentially says that in order to change, you have to *not* change. As a result, on the surface, it is seemingly absurd, but it does create a positive double-bind. Such an injunction either provokes a reaction to go against the therapist's directive (and go toward a positive result), or stops a client's agonizing and vacillation—the client "wins" either way. This produces an emotional reaction that allows a reappraisal of the situation and a reconnection of the emotional system and schema dynamics that provides an opportunity for a more lasting solution to emerge.

A frequent setting for the use of prohibition comes from couples' sex therapy. Performance anxiety is a frequent component in sexual dysfunction. That is, an individual experiences increased anxiety about how "good" he or she is as a lover (i.e., "performance"). As a person worries more about his or her sexual performance, ability to perform suffers more and more. As ability to perform suffers, anxiety increases further and starts a downward cascading spiral of frustration and fear. As a result, a couple will begin to grow distant from one another and find ways to avoid the painful subject of sexual intimacy. This distance begins to strain the relationship further, which can eventually lead to the couple seeking therapy. Many times, even performance-enhancing medications (e.g., Viagra and Cialis) cannot help a couple achieve the intimacy that they desire because of psychological factors.

A standard practice of therapists working with couples experiencing some measure of sexual dysfunction is to teach Masters and Johnson's (1966) technique of "sensate focus," in which each person takes a turn giving and receiving pleasurable stimulation. The receiving partner controls the amount of stimulation being given by telling the partner to start or stop. In the beginning, the couple is required to give only nonerotic pleasurable stimulation. More explicit sexual stimulation is gradually (with each successful episode) introduced. The couple is usually given a directive from the beginning benignly "prohibiting" them from engaging in sexual intercourse. Such "prohibition" is intended to remove the sense of pressure accruing to the couple from "performance anxiety" and the sense of urgency to perform sexually. Instead, they are encouraged to concentrate on the other forms of pleasurable stimulation. Such instruction *disengages* the couple from their struggle with symptomatic behavior and provides them a measure of tranquilizing relief. As a couple experiences a measure of success, they often are unable to comply with the prohibition and come to therapy sheepishly (or proudly) announcing that they "disobeyed" the prohibition against sexual intercourse and had a successful and fulfilling night of lovemaking. In this instance, prohibiting intercourse allows a couple—relieved from the pressure to perform—to relax. They have received a needed psychological tranquilizer. Thus, they can "disobey" the prohibition and be *successful* at the same time (thus breaking the cycle of performance anxiety or inability to perform). In either event, they win. A debriefing of the couple and working through how it was that they were able to achieve their results, what the experience was like, what has been transpiring between them, etc. can follow. Consider the example of prohibition in Clinical Case Example 3.3.

Clinical Case Example 3.3: A Talented Young Musician

A talented young professional concert musician, who previously had been playing successfully in a symphony orchestra, had been unemployed for the last several years. Because of his early learned family role and many other chronic emotional problems, he felt a great deal of discouragement and despaired of ever working again as a professional musician. His work was the highlight of his life. Taking note of an advertisement, he felt compelled to audition for another symphony position while at the same time being terrified at the prospect of either obtaining (not feeling he would be able to "handle it") or being denied the job (hence, another failure and still further discouragement). He felt absolutely certain that he had the technical ability to pass the audition because he was in top form, had continued to practice, was taking a master class, and had a history of successfully auditioning on numerous other occasions. He was no stranger to such a challenge. But, he was nevertheless terrified of the prospects of auditioning and being turned down.

Questions

- Discuss how the client "wins" if he isn't offered a position and if he is offered a position.
- Carefully spell out the ambivalence the young man faced.
- In what way was prohibiting his taking a position tranquilizing to this man?

It was suggested to the client that he was in no position to make a professional decision at this time and should consider not going back to work for the immediate future. On the other hand, he *was encouraged* to perhaps follow his prosocial inclinations and audition for the symphony position *with the idea that he had no intention of accepting the position at this time should it be offered.* He was to think of the audition as merely "practice" for a future time when he would be in a better psychological position to be able to make a professional decision and commitment.

The suggestion took into account both aspects of the client's felt ambivalence, namely, wanting to be successful and simultaneously fearing he would fail while delaying a decision and prolonging a crisis with which he was not prepared to deal at *the present time.* Interestingly, the client embraced the therapist's suggestion. In fact, he auditioned so successfully that he was offered a position with the symphony immediately after his audition. He reported in his next therapy session with thorough glee that he accepted the position on the spot!

Nonlinear listening is helpful, but *listening for inference* (i.e., what the client *doesn't* want) can provide the therapist with the essential clues about what needs to be "prohibited." In Clinical Case Example 3.3, using nonlinear *listening for inference,* the therapist understood what it was that this man didn't want: facing the possibility of failure because he was so discouraged. By introducing the elements of prohibition and choice, the client became much more relaxed (i.e., tranquilized). He believed that he was not in any danger of failing because he was directed to have *no intention of accepting a position.* There could be no failure. The audition was only to be "practice."

Prohibition can also mean that the client doesn't have to "go it alone." Consider this excerpt from "The Case of Ashley:"

Therapist: Ok, do you remember the scene where Scarlett O'Hara comes back to her home after the ravages of the Civil War and there's no food; everyone is starving. At the climactic scene in the first half of the film, she runs out of the garden and digs up some rotted potatoes, and out of desperation, she eats them. She had gone from wealthy and well-to-do Southern Belle, to being desperate and hungry. And crying, humiliated, she shakes her fist at heaven and says "As God as my witness, I will never go hungry again!" I think that everyone has their "Scarlett O'Hara" moment in their lives where they are brought low and shake their fist at heaven and say "As God as my witness, I will never [BLANK], again."

Ashley: Yeah.

Therapist: And do you know what your "blank" is?

Ashley: I'll never be replaced again.

Therapist: I think you are right. And I think you have a "go to" strategy to make sure that doesn't happen. Do you know what that is?

Ashley: Having to be in control all the time?

Therapist: Bingo. And, I think that your fear of "messes," which drives you to clean everything up for everyone, is a sign that you want help. But you are afraid to ask for it because you think they might get rid of you—replace you. SO you adopt a "go-it-alone" strategy. You try to do it all and then kick yourself when you can't live up to that. You wind up getting less of what you want, and more of what you don't want.

Ashley: I never thought of it like that before.

Therapist: And it is the same at home. It's the same pattern. You don't ask for help or togetherness, and instead you just DO, well, everything. And while you don't get kicked out, you also don't feel like you are "on the inside" anywhere. You don't feel secure.

Ashley: No. I haven't felt that way, not for a long time. Maybe never, I don't know . . .

Therapist: Kind of like you did as a girl?

Ashley: Yeah, wishing someone would see me, see that I'm alone . . .

Therapist: And that you need help?

Ashley: [RELUCTANTLY] Yeah.

Therapist: I heard some hesitation in your voice when I suggested that you needed help.

Ashley: Yeah, I just cringed inside. I felt a lump in my throat.

Therapist: What was that lump?

Ashley: What was it? [DOESN'T QUITE GET THE QUESTION]

Therapist: Yeah, where do you think it came from?

Ashley: Fear.

Therapist: Of needing help?

Ashley: Yeah, and asking for it.

Therapist: I see. So just thinking of the possibility of asking for help is enough to bring up the old fear of being replaced?

Ashley: Uh-huh

Therapist: So then to move too fast, and for me to say "OK, so tomorrow you are going to ask everyone at home and at work for help" probably isn't going to feel as good, and probably won't work, right?

Ashley: Probably, yeah.

Therapist: But you can agree with me that it is a goal to work toward

Ashley: Yeah [SLOWLY]

Therapist: OK, I heard the hesitation again. How about if we worked on the goal of helping you lower your fear of being replaced? Help you feel less lonely, would that be better?

Ashley: Yeah [NODDING]

Therapist: OK, the bad news is that you will have to work on all areas of your life, but the good news is that we can take it slowly—a little at a time. But it is going to mean that you have to decide which area you want to work on first: relationship with your husband or work.

Ashley: I think I would like to work on my relationship with my husband.

Therapist: OK, fair enough, but just to let you know, that at a future date, we will address work, OK?

Ashley: OK.

Therapist: Now, for both home and work, we are going to use the same basic strategy. In order to feel included, and actually GAIN more control over your life, you are going to have to give up some control of things. It will bring up the old fears of being replaced, but if you do not do this, you will guarantee that in the future, you will find yourself in the same place you did as a child. So, to avoid this awful thing happening to you, you are going to have to let people help you, and the only way that they will, is if you ask them.

Ashley: Uh-huh.

Therapist: But I guarantee that if you do let people know how overwhelmed you are, and let them help you, that you will find that they want to help you. You won't feel the need to control everything, and you won't feel that your life is so out of control.

So, in this example, Ashley's fear of being replaced is what drives her overachieving. But not being replaced is not the same thing as feeling like she belongs or is connected—which is what she *really* wants. By prohibiting her "go-it-alone" overachievement strategy, she can see (a) where her strategy comes from (family of origin), and (b) how to both *not* be replaced, *and* belong by doing the *opposite* of "going it alone": asking for help. Next, we move on to the last type of tranquilizer, persuasion.

Persuasion

Another of the *P*'s of the paradox is persuasion, namely, urging and advocating for symptomatic behavior. It is perhaps one of the last things (i.e., opposite of expectations) that a client *expects* to hear from his therapist. *When using paradoxical persuasion, a therapist champions the cause of symptom retention and produces a positive, plausible rationale for such advocacy. Like prohibition and other tranquilizers, persuasion is truly paradoxical in nature—it is absurd for a therapist to advocate that a client do the very thing he or she is complaining about or seeking to avoid, but at the same time there is an element of truthfulness in doing so.* The rationale is that the therapist insists that the client is not yet ready to attempt new behaviors and/or responsibilities from which his symptomatic stress has insulated him. There are many implications to making changes that one is not prepared for.

Using persuasion, therapists often "argue" with the client that he hasn't fully considered the implications of making a hasty retreat from symptomatic behavior—getting better too fast can be ill advised. The therapist can further insist—seriously, albeit benignly—that the symptom should be retained due to its considerable benefits to the patient that he may not be able to see at this time. In many respects, such counsel follow Burns' (2010) model of paradoxical agenda setting, namely, advocating for all of the *disadvantages* of making changes. This provides a measure of tranquilizing for the patient regarding his problem, symptom, or behavior and allows the client an opportunity to begin disengaging from his struggle with it or to begin working through the issues in earnest.

Arguing for the symptom/complaint and *joining the resistance* are well-known therapeutic terms that have described this intervention. According to Mozdzierz et al. (2014), when clients are not ready to make changes, they often engage in a variety of different coping strategies, from actively denying that there is a problem (the precontemplation stage) to admitting that there is a problem but that they are not yet willing to take the necessary steps for change (the contemplation stage). Persuasion can help a client to make movements from one stage of change to another. It can be especially useful when a patient is advocating a need to change, but there is no concrete information to suggest that positive movement has taken place (i.e., the preparing for action stage). The therapist *argues, advocates,* and *persuades* for the benefits of the symptom (traits, behaviors, perceptions, etc.) to be retained because it has certain clear protective advantages. The therapist then uses Socratic questioning (like analysis, interpretation, or evaluation questions) to explore how the patient might use the symptom, etc. to her advantage to improve her present and/or future life. Consider the following example from master practitioner, Steven Andreas.

Master Example 3.4: But Don't Take Our Word for It!

In this example of a transcript with a master practitioner, *Steve Andreas* (creator of Neurolingusitic Programming, NLP), works with a woman who is dealing with her anger issues at everyone else, but herself (Alexander Street Press, 2012).

Steven Andreas: Can you do it another way? Can you . . . In here you would express compassion for him, right? What if you talk to him like that? What if you told him about how badly he hurt you, but then in a voice that was not angry and blaming but just talking about yourself, just to let him know, because that's important to you, isn't it, to let him know that? But in such a way that you are telling him about yourself, not blaming him, saying, look, when you lied to me or whatever it was, blah, blah, blah, boy that was like a knife in my heart, or how would you describe it, so that he could know what impact he's having on the world?

Melissa: [silence]

Steven Andreas: My guess is you'd like to protect somebody else from this, wouldn't you?

Melissa: Yeah!

Steven Andreas: In the future, if he's with somebody else, would you want them to go through the same thing you went through?

Melissa: Uh . . . huh . . .

Steven Andreas: So, you'd like to have an impact on him, right, even if you never see him again? Wouldn't it be nice if you could say, "Hey, that didn't work for me, that hurt like hell," or whatever your words would be and make him understand that what he did, didn't fit for you?

Melissa: [silence] I think I can do it.

In the example above, Andreas attempts to persuade Melissa that her anger toward her ex-boyfriend, which has allowed her to frenetically act out in an unproductive manner, can be used to *help* provide him feedback. In this way, the angry behavior is tranquilized, and the client's real issues can emerge. Consider this example from "The Case of Mike":

Therapist: Well, let me ask you, we are not dumb creatures. We don't adopt strategies or "philosophy" that won't work for us. We do things that help us to be successful. So tell me how this "philosophy" is helpful or useful to you?

Mike: What? Losing my temper? Being stubborn?

Therapist: Yes.

Mike: Hmmm. It doesn't seem to help me. Most people avoid me, it pushes people away.

Therapist:	So it does help you by keeping you from having to deal with other people?
Mike:	Yeah.
Therapist:	And that is good when you want to avoid some people [Mike nods head yes], but it also spills over to people that you care about, like your fiancée?
Mike:	Yeah, I guess it does.
Therapist:	Is that something that you would like to change?

In persuading a client, the therapist does not insist that the client practice his trait, symptom, behavior, complaint, or the like—only that he considers its advantages and long-term benefits. In therapy, persuasive rationales might be initiated by the therapist asking herself, "Why *should* this particular client *not* be depressed, or why should he stop drinking, trust people, become more active, express feelings more openly, etc.?" They are not persuaded by linear commonsense thinking because their experience (long embedded in schema dynamics) has taught them that they can't trust the world and its inhabitants—that has been their lifelong experience. Instead, strategies like "rolling with the resistance" and persuasion in favor of a symptom can help to facilitate a therapeutic alliance, as well as facilitate a more rapid disengagement from the problematic behavior. Clinical Case Example 3.4 further illustrates persuasion.

Clinical Case Example 3.4: Distraught Woman Whose World Has Collapsed

In another example, an extremely distraught woman sought help because her husband had cheated on her. She described a "perfect" family upbringing and what she thought was a "perfect" marriage. The more she delved into her husband's behavior, the more reprehensible things she found, such as his frequenting massage parlors, using Internet porn sites, and so forth. She was devastated, as well as her "perfect" world and "perfect" children, because in her rage she had blatantly divulged his behavior to her children, who found themselves tormented and torn over loyalties to their victimized mother and still wanting to have a connection to their father.

After having "kicked" her husband out of the house and forbidden him from reentering without her permission, whenever they would plan to meet to discuss their predicament and possible options, she found herself verbally assaulting him. As several months passed, the wife found herself calming down and becoming more "rational." She did not appear to want a divorce, perceiving such an alternative as turning her into a "loser." On the other hand, she did not appear enthusiastic about taking her husband back because that would make *him* a "winner" (i.e., he had everything to gain, namely, his wife, his children, and his home) and her a "loser" (i.e., she would be taking a "cheater" back, and her husband was getting the better "deal"). In the process of constantly reevaluating her circumstances and alternatives, she found herself wanting to "punish" him. She also believed that periodically "punishing" him "forever" by rubbing his face in his misdeeds was her way of reminding herself that he was not going to get a "better deal" if she took him back.

Questions

- What are the poles of the client's dilemma? What kind of dilemma is it?
- What is the behavior that needs to be tranquilized? How is it creating problems for the client and getting in the way of therapeutic progress?
- Discuss the paradoxical nature of the reframe for the client (i.e., two true elements that were mutually incompatible, yet true) and the counselor (an absurd or contradictory statement that contains truth).

In Clinical Case Example 3.4, the client talked about her strategy and what her options might be, and she related that she had better begin finding more positive things to say about him. The therapist persuasively advocated that finding positive things about him was not necessarily in her interests! In this way, the therapist uses one of the injunctions of the double-bind to make the "case," but while it is logically sound, the conclusion is not valid for the client. As a result, she expressed disbelief. If she was going to take him back, she maintained that her periodic harangues couldn't go on forever. Again, the therapist pleaded his case that it was not in her interests to see good things about her husband because she was, at the core, interested in who was getting a "better deal." As Miller and Rose (2009) and Miller and Rollnick (2002, 2012) advocate, "change talk" had already begun, stimulated by the therapist's persuading for maintenance of not finding anything positive to say about her husband. As long as she maintained that posture, it *wasn't* in her interests to find positive things about him. Part of her "view of self" schema dynamic was that she believed that she could only feel good about herself if she was doing better than others and was "top dog." That nonlinear, schema-based value had to be addressed in a nonlinear way. Persuading her *not* to abandon her long-held beliefs about her husband's imperfection and unsuitability was an absurd paradoxical statement that nevertheless contained elements of truth *for her*. When the client absorbed the two incompatible concepts of the double-bind (i.e., "He's a loser" and "I'm better than him") while also finding that she still cared for him, she was able to choose with clarity, according to her values, and disengaged from her struggle and moved the therapy forward.

Master Example 3.5: But Don't Take Our Word for It!

This excerpt is taken from a session with *Robert Wubbolding* (master clinician and author in Reality Therapy), as he works with a man who is facing a life-threatening illness. Notice how he gently *persuades* the client to help manage his worry over his health (Alexander Street Press, 2012).

Dr. Robert Wubbolding: ... and, my goodness, look at all the things you're doing to, to confront it. But the, but maybe it's just real, more realistic to have a pause and to increase that pause from an hour to an hour and 15 minutes to an hour and a half. So that, it makes those moments and hours that you, that you talk, think about it more bearable.

John: A tough thing to say. It's like I don't know if I can make it to the end of the road on this thing. (crosstalk)

Dr. Robert Wubbolding: Yeah, uh hmm.

John: You know?

Dr. Robert Wubbolding: Well, who does have the coping mechanisms?

John: I don't know. I mean, we, we, we tend to, like in society like glorify death that, you know, everybody goes out and just this wonderful, you know sunny little way with, you know, with, surrounded by family. I just don't see that happening. You know, and I'm scared to death of this thing.

Dr. Robert Wubbolding: Yeah.

John: Uhm.

Dr. Robert Wubbolding: Well, what, what I'd like to, to, to ask you about is, and talk about is some ways to lessen the fear. I don't think, I don't think there, the fear is gonna go vanish and, and, you know, you're gonna just be eager to, to, to face all of this but I think that it might be less painful. And, and ah, the way I look at it is that the more you do things and you've identified a number of those things, the more you do those things, the more pause you get. And can put this on hold. I mean, you're not one to deny it, the, the sweep it under the rug . . . (crosstalk)

John: No.

In the example above, Wubbolding understands that the client is afraid to face his circumstances, and has been trying to avoid them. His suggestion that he find ways to continue to avoid them ("brief pauses") actually creates a way of appropriately facing what is making him afraid. This is the powerful nature of tranquilizers (like persuasion). In each of these instances, the client is in a heightened, agitated state. As with the other tranquilizer "P's", the client is expecting a fight. Paradoxical persuasion takes the therapist out of the position of being the "opposite" or "antithesis," and helps avoid a power struggle with the client by advocating for what she is already doing. Instead, the use of persuasion suggests to the client that her complaint isn't so problematic—as a matter of fact, there are advantages to it. The end result is that the client is no longer struggling with attempting to rid herself of the complaint. In the process, the client's ambivalence begins to resolve, and the real issues to be dealt with can emerge.

Summary

There are a number of similarities and a good deal of overlapping among the various paradoxical tranquilizers that we have described. We would like to clarify at this point that there are subtle differences in the use of these interventions. Those differences are based upon several factors: the distress, excitability, anguish, and so on of a particular client; the amount of duress the client is experiencing to do something about his or her circumstances; as well as what it is that the therapist is attempting to accomplish on behalf of the client. For instance, prohibition and postponement are meant to tranquilize because the client with whom they are working is in a high degree of emotional excitement and stress. The difference in these two interventions would be the degree of emphasis on the part of the therapist. Postponement generally entails more of a time dimension and allows a client to delay a decision in which they are highly conflicted and ambivalent. Prohibition benignly and empathically but formally discourages a particular activity or decision as not being in the client's interests at the present time. Each of these tranquilizers is meant to stimulate the resolution of a client's ambivalences regarding his or her problematic life circumstances. In the next chapter, we will present the next type of paradoxical intervention, which are the opposite of tranquilizers (at least on the surface!): the *energizers*.

Note

1. "Successful" from the client's perspective because it allows him or her to avoid making a decision.

4 The Use of Energizer Paradoxical Interventions

Earlier, we introduced paradoxical interventions and demonstrated how they can be used to neutralize and tranquilize client behavior. However, many times, clients demonstrate complacency, pessimism, or overt discouragement regarding their circumstances. They find it difficult to make efforts to participate fully in treatment and are often categorized as "resistant." Perhaps the best way of describing such clients is that they are "stuck." In many ways, they are like the character Eeyore from the Winnie-the-Pooh stories by A. A. Milne. They are generally pessimistic and (from their experiences) feel rightly so! Frequently, there is a disconnect between (a) their stated needs (i.e., symptom relief); (b) the underlying purpose those symptoms may serve (e.g., protection from failure, or avoidance); and (c) what they are willing to do or feel they can do about their situation. As with many clients, they appear to be reacting to their schemas and feelings of ambivalence by endlessly vacillating, being immobilized, trying to escape, or letting fate decide. The result is that they feel powerless and become immobilized.

Well-meaning *linear-thinking* therapists who overtly attempt to encourage clients to change (e.g., by using empathy, or taking one side of the problem) are quickly frustrated when the client does not change. If it is not a chronic problem already at the beginning of treatment, unresolved ambivalences can soon develop characteristics of being chronic and intractable. At times, clinicians will yield and accept a client's explanation that his or her condition is beyond help. We have suggested that the assessment process requires determining what is motivating a client to come into therapy at this particular time (see Mozdzierz, Peluso, & Lisiecki, 2014). That process helps to determine what direction therapeutic interventions will take. For example, a therapist's interventions need to be directed toward dealing with a client's ambivalence or those behaviors, feelings, symptoms, behaviors, complaints, and so on that interfere with dealing with the ambivalence. There is a class of paradoxical interventions that we have labeled *energizers* to deal with such circumstances.

The Energizers

Energizers represent a class of nonlinear paradoxical interventions designed to encourage, stimulate, and mobilize clients who, as a result of their experience of ambivalence (i.e., dilemma), have either become immobilized or are endlessly vacillating despite the best efforts to implement the marshalling properties of Motivational Interviewing. Energizers prompt new behaviors that are contrary to the more rigid and maladaptive perceptual and behavioral entrapments of what they have been doing (i.e., "more of the same").

By proposing an energizing paradoxical intervention, the therapist is trying to "disturb" clients' defensive and rigid perception of the situation and their behavior in it, in order to mobilize resources that a client has simply been unable to access, either because of faulty and appraisal processes (e.g., deletions and distortions) and very skewed schema dynamics that prevent action or because of feelings of ambivalence. The results of altering a clients' perceptual system make it difficult for them to return to the way they previously were seeing things. We cite Clinical Case Example 4.1 as an illustration.

Clinical Case Example 4.1: Chronic Distress Over Bad Thoughts

A young, frail-looking woman in her late 20s sought counseling as a result of her husband being placed in a nursing home 2 weeks earlier. She stated that she felt like a failure for no longer being able to care for him at home. He was in his early 30s and the victim of a fulminating multiple sclerosis,[1] a terrible illness that affects all body motor movements but leaves awareness intact. For 2 years prior to the placement of her husband in the nursing home, she had cared for him at home, even though for much of that time he had been confined to a wheelchair. When his bowel and bladder control failed as well as many other voluntary muscle movements, it became physically impossible for her to care for her husband at home even with professional nursing support on a daily basis. She was truly grief-stricken at the fact that he was "stuck in a nursing home for the rest of his life." Her husband, whom she repeatedly emphasized was such a good person, faced a dim future.

She sobbed movingly about the lack of support from some family members and felt disloyal to her husband when friends and family would tell her to forget about him and get on with her life. The same people advised her to seek another life with someone else because she was still young. She admitted that the future looked bleak for herself and her husband. Although she teetered back and forth with thoughts of suicide, she discounted them because she felt that her husband needed her.

During one session, she asked, "Is it wrong to wish that he would die?" She had been struggling with this question over and over again and could not stop feeling guilty over entertaining such thoughts. Because of these thoughts, she found herself visiting her husband less frequently: The thoughts were very intrusive, which, in turn, made her feel *more* guilty.

Questions

- What is the woman's dilemma?
- From the information available, describe more fully some of this woman's schema dynamics.
- How might you help the client by "energizing" her?

Implicit in her question was a double-bind dilemma for the therapist: To tell her it was wrong to wish her husband to die would only make a very courageous young woman feel even guiltier than she already did. On the other hand, to give her permission to wish her husband dead would only make her feel guilty and disloyal. After all, if she did not feel that it was wrong to begin with, she wouldn't have brought the issue up in the first place. Thus, if the therapist told her it was not wrong, she would not have found much comfort. It follows that her schema dynamics did not allow her to comfortably entertain thoughts about wishing him to die. Her schema dynamics also would not permit her to feel good about herself because she felt that she failed her husband by having to place him in a nursing home. Again, we see a client in a chronic double-bind, with two conflicting injunctions. The therapist's response was, "For whose benefit do you want such a seriously and hopelessly ill man to linger on? If you wished him to stay alive as long as possible, perhaps it was to help postpone your own loss and grief? To wish a loved one to continue to linger may be for *our* benefit. On the other hand, to wish him dead may in the final analysis be an act of love and courage in that he would no longer have to deal with his suffering, helplessness, and hopelessness." Thus, employing the Socratic method to create universal definitions and clarify her values through the use of a paradoxical intervention allowed her to see her feelings as a kind of expression of love and sadness at the same time.

Nonlinear Thinking Exercise: Schrödinger's Cat and Newcomb's Paradox

Double-binds and ambivalence require nonlinear thinking, particularly when clients are bound-up or paralyzed by their particular circumstances. Nonlinear thinking, and paradoxical interventions, opens the client up to new possibilities. As an exercise in this, we will consider two similar paradoxes. The first is the problem of Schrödinger's cat. Austrian physicist Erwin Schrödinger put forth the following hypothetical scenario to demonstrate how two opposite realities could simultaneously exist. In his scenario, a cat is sealed in a box. In the box is a flask of poison and a hammer. The hammer is held in place over the flask by a mechanism that will release it if radiation is detected. There is also a source of radiation that will randomly emit a radioactive particle at some point in time (which will release the hammer and break the flask, thus poisoning the cat). After 1 hour, you come back to the box and check on the cat. You cannot know if the cat is alive or dead, because you cannot know if the poison has been released. At that moment in time, the cat is both alive and dead at the same time (since the odds are 50–50 for each)! The question at that moment in time is "What do you *believe?*" Is the cat alive or dead? Whichever reality you choose at that moment is equally valid. It is only when you open the box can you know *for certain* what the cat's condition is (and if your reality is right or wrong!).

Now, consider the following, similar paradox that was created by physicist William Newcomb:

Suppose you are presented with two boxes: A and B. You can't see what is inside, but you are reliably informed that box A contains $1,000 and that box B contains either $1,000,000 or nothing. You are given a choice. You can open both boxes and keep the contents; or you can open just box B and keep its contents.

(Hayden & Picard, 2009, p. 140)

Now, before you answer, consider this additional information. What if you were told that both boxes were filled according to a computerized prediction program that operated according to the following rules: If it predicted that you would only open box B, then it would put $1,000,000. BUT if it predicted that you would open both boxes, it left box B blank. So the question is, what do you decide to do? Choose your answer, then read on.

If you decide to open box B, then the prediction program should have anticipated it and put the $1,000,000 in it, so that should be easy, right? Why would anyone choose opening both boxes? If you did, then the prediction program would have anticipated that and left box B empty. Therefore, you would only get $1,000. Well, here is where it gets interesting, because the program has already chosen and filled the boxes before you ever came into the picture, and you have no way of influencing the outcome. The only influence is by what you would do. You would have to hope that the prediction program is *right*. If it is and you chose box B, you are a millionaire, and if you chose both, you would only get a thousand dollars.

But what if it is wrong in predicting your decision? If it predicted you would open both and you only open box B, then you get NOTHING (because box B would be empty and box A would have $1,000 that you missed out on). BUT if it predicted you would choose B and you chose to open both, you get $1,001,000 (the biggest possible payout). So the easy choice (just box B) gets you a big payout, but risks getting nothing, and opening both boxes guarantees you something and you have a chance for the BIGGEST payout. How is THAT for nonlinear? (By the way, what did you choose? And would you change your answer now that you read more?)

Now what does this have to do with clients? Well like the "Monty Hall Paradox" (see Mozdzierz, Peluso, & Lisiecki, 2014), people often choose what seems like the best option without fully thinking it through. Furthermore, they often stubbornly cling to their belief. The therapist's job is to help the client see that rigidly clinging to a losing strategy is not in their best interest, even when they are convinced that they have a winning strategy. Or convincing a client that the *opposite* of their particular belief about something is just as true when faced with an ambiguous situation (like Schrödinger's cat). That often requires advanced nonlinear thinking, and paradoxical interventions!

Advanced Nonlinear Thinking and Energizers

In Clinical Case Example 4.1, the young woman felt and expressed relief on hearing this particular perspective that she had never considered. Although it did not mitigate the grim realities she still faced, she derived a sense of comfort and encouragement from feeling understood and having "an answer." She felt "energized" (i.e., not euphoric, but more capable of facing the realities of her life circumstances), more hopeful, began visiting her husband with more regularity, and no longer complained of being troubled by thoughts of wishing him dead.

Practitioners in the earlier stages of their development, e.g., at Level 1 and 2, frequently encounter difficulty with energizing interventions because they often contravene more "logical" (i.e., *linear*) notions of what it is to be a "helper." For therapists and counselors, the concepts of helping and forging a therapeutic alliance clearly necessitate empathy. Although empathy is a necessary condition for addressing the suffering component of our clients, it is not necessarily sufficient to stimulate the resolution of ambivalence, change, and growth.

Master Example 4.1: But Don't Take Our Word for It!

This excerpt is taken from a session with *Judith Beck* (master clinician and author in Cognitive-Behavioral Therapy) as she works with a woman who worried about failing in life as an adult (Alexander Street Press, 2012).

Judith Beck: Um, now let's take the same picture where you're back in that room, and looking out at that room. Is there some way to figure out how to change the, that picture in your mind. So that actually you're feeling stronger? And feel as if you're moving ahead in life?
Latrice: Put some furniture in . . .
Judith Beck: Put some furniture in, that's one thing . . .
Latrice: Yeah, uh, yeah I think I could change the picture. Um.
Judith Beck: What kind of furniture would you put in that room?
Latrice: Um, a bed, and family pictures.
Judith Beck: Would you like to imagine your kids jumping on the bed or something?
Latrice: Yeah.
Judith Beck: Having fun in the room?
Latrice: Yeah.
Judith Beck: What do you see them doing? You know them, I don't know them.
Latrice: They're jumping in the bed.
Judith Beck: Jumping on the bed. I guess I do know them. [BOTH LAUGH]
Latrice: That's what they would probably be doing, jumping on the bed.
Judith Beck: Okay, so now when you have this picture in your head, and the room is furnished and it's got pictures on the wall. And there's a couch and

> a bed and you see that you got your three kids and they're jumping on the bed. How does that make you feel emotionally?
>
> *Latrice:* Better.
>
> *Judith Beck:* Does it?
>
> *Latrice:* Yeah it does.
>
> *Judith Beck:* Now the fact of the matter is that we don't know whether or not you're going to end up in that room again.
>
> *Latrice:* Right.
>
> *Judith Beck:* My guess is somebody else probably lives there now, is that right?
>
> *Latrice:* Yeah.
>
> *Judith Beck:* So it's not likely that you're going to end up in the room.
>
> *Latrice:* Yeah.
>
> *Judith Beck:* So it's just something that you had a fantasy about.
>
> *Latrice:* Right.
>
> *Judith Beck:* So what I'm suggesting is, since it's just a fantasy, it's not true anyway . . .
>
> *Latrice:* Okay.
>
> *Judith Beck:* Take that fantasy and improve it in a way that makes you feel better.
>
> *Latrice:* Okay.

In the example above, Beck uses simple, Socratic questioning to work with the client's negative fantasy and make it more positive. In this way, Latrice doesn't have to be paralyzed by her fear of "going back" to her childhood room (which was a symbol of failure), and she instead could find the energy to move *forward*. Clients who are in need of energizing frequently require a therapeutic response that does the opposite of what they expect. While energizers are designed to stimulate client movement along the spectrum of change, they are always implemented within a climate of deep respect for the client and a maintenance of the therapeutic relationship. *It is important to remember that although energizers present two statements about the client's problem that are contradictory, they still contain an element of truth.* When done effectively, such interventions produce what Watzlawick, Weakland, and Fisch (1974) and Fraser and Solovey (2007) discussed as "second-order change." As mentioned in Chapter 1, there is no "room" for the problem when the second-order change is made, and so the problem behavior (in this case, fear) disappears or is able to be dismissed by the client.

Nonlinear Listening and Energizers

As with other elements in this text, *nonlinear* listening is important in determining what clients need to help move them along. In therapy, clients who need energizing may complain that they are "tired": "I'm doing all that I can just to stay afloat and have no time or energy to think about doing anything different." The therapist recognizes that these clients are stuck between their schema dynamics (view of self, others, or the world) and circumstances that they face (or don't *want* to face). They cannot derive a way of contending with whatever issue that they face without sensing "defeat." Energizers alter a symptom or complaint so that it no longer has the negative impact on treatment it previously had. In each case, a clinician must listen for the following:

- *Congruence* (Does the client *act in a manner consistent* with the help that he says he is seeking?)
- *Absence* (Is a client's inactivity a distraction from working on issues of ambivalence?)
- *Presence* (What does a client's behavior tell me that the client is not expressing verbally?)
- *Inference* (What is the client telling me she *doesn't* want?)
- *Resistance* (When recommendation for change is made, the response is "Yes, but . . .")
- *Listening for beliefs,* as a source of information about schema dynamics
- *Listening for feelings,* as a valuable source of information about a client's emotional system
- *Understanding* the circumstance of a client's dilemma, the double-bind that they face, and the ambivalence that results from it

Each of these methods of listening provides the nonlinear-thinking clinician with *potential* information about what the client needs from therapy.

Types of Energizers

We present three types ("*P*'s") of paradoxical energizer interventions: prosocial redefinition, practice, and pedagogism. Each of them stimulates an emotional response that (hopefully) encourages a client to reappraise his or her circumstances and move toward new solutions. In turn, this reappraisal simultaneously allows a client to disengage even slightly from problematic behavioral solutions. As a result, a client develops a new sense of possibility. The clinical examples of energizers that follow represent therapeutic efforts designed at invigorating feelings, behaviors, or movement in relationship to others in the client's life or in relationship to the world. The possibilities for utilizing energizers are enormous depending on the creativity, sensitivity, and flexibility of the practitioner. We reiterate that the categories of paradox are guides, and not an exhaustive list of energizers.

Prosocial Redefinition

Prosocial redefinition is an energizer—a paradoxical intervention that seeks to capture the essence of a client's problematic behavior that pushes others away, and finds a positive aspect to it. As described earlier, prosocial redefinition reconstructs and reframes problematic behavior in a way that reveals it to have a *prosocial* dimension. Consider clients who develop agoraphobia—a most debilitating condition. They fear the outside world *so* much that they confine themselves to the safety of their home. Their schematized appraisal of the world is pessimistic and inflexible (i.e., "There is danger *everywhere*"), and they react emotionally in a volatile way as a result of such appraisals. Now imagine that you are a friend, relative, spouse, or child of this person. The quality of your relationship might be quite strained. Further complicating matters, a phobic individual can wield great power as a means of controlling a relationship(s) while denying that he is doing so—"It is the *phobia* that is controlling, not me! I just can't help it!" Unless someone is willing to conform to the agoraphobic person's "rules" of fear, a relationship is destined for difficulties. All of this can lead to such clients feeling more isolated and alone as individuals affected by their behavior feel unable to be constrained by the agoraphobic's behavior. To illustrate prosocial redefinition, we present an excerpt from master clinician Bradford Keeney.

Master Example 4.2: But Don't Take Our Word for It!

In this transcript, master clinician and author *Bradford Keeney* is interviewing a female client who is struggling with her relationship with her husband. In this brief exchange, he begins to uncover some hidden talents (and power) that the client has (Alexander Street Press, 2012).

Bradford Keeney: So you're good at shocking?
Client: Oh, very good in shocking. My husband says I am the queen of shock value.
Bradford Keeney: Oh, really? And you're telling me now that you can't come up with another word I think you're holding back. How have you shocked him in the past? If you are the "master of shock."
Client: Probably just things I've beeped into his beeper.
Bradford Keeney: Yeah.
Client: Yeah.
Bradford Keeney: So, this is some . . . you are skilled at this.
Client: Oh, I'm very skilled at this.
Bradford Keeney: I want to hear more about this. Tell me more about this ability to shock. What kind of things . . . what kind of things are shocking things in the beeper are they, things you could say?
Client: When my friends taught me how to put a code like figure out the number in the letter and put it on the beeper like if I was going to say I love you I would put the numbers for I love you and the letters for I love you, the numbers, I always get numbers almost confusing. For I love you, and then he call me back and he goes did you beep me I said, yes I beeped you. He said, what did you say, I go look at the phone and figure it out.
Bradford Keeney: Ah . . . Code. So when is the last time you exercised this communication?
Client: I did it today. I did that today.
Bradford Keeney: And did he like it?
Client: He was very surprised. This morning he called me and told me that he did not think this marriage was going to work. So this afternoon, with a tear in my eye I beeped that, I so love you.
Bradford Keeney: So you do have this special talent and resource of a . . . of shocking that's proven to be something wonderful for the relationship.
Client: Yeah.

Assessing in a way that looks for strengths and unused resources, however, reveals other possibilities. Furthermore, knowing a client's schema dynamics also allows a therapist to see other possibilities. In the example above, Keeney redefines the client's ability to "shock" as a resource to be used to reconnect with her husband. So even though she feels powerless against his drinking behavior, which had paralyzed her, the prosocial redefinition of her "shock" value gives her a path to making a difference in her relationship. Looking at the situation in such a manner doesn't change the reality or "facts" of the situation. But it constructs a prosocial and potentially *energizing reappraisal* of her circumstances, which invites the client to find new ways to think about her problem and change it. Even if it doesn't lead to immediate change, it is encouraging to the client and strengthens the therapeutic alliance.

Prosocial redefinitions are enormously useful in helping clients make sense of negative emotions as well. For example, anger as an emotion of power and wanting to overwhelm others can be reinterpreted dialectically as representing an expression of helplessness—someone cannot influence or achieve what it is that he or she wants in transactions with others, so the person attempts to overwhelm them with a display of anger. Such reinterpretation can be useful in helping clients to make sense of their internal feeling states as well as future instances in which they feel angry—they can look for other means of influencing, reappraise the situation, and so on. Without such alternate understandings (i.e., a spectrum of meanings), clients can continue to feel guilty about negative emotions that they experience and express. This often leaves clients feeling "stuck."

Another category of clients who often need energizing are those who become entangled with the criminal justice system. The linear thinking of conventional therapeutic and counseling wisdom is based on the idea that successful treatment outcomes are made when the client admits that what he or she has done is wrong and demonstrates some remorse. Of course, such thinking often leads to a nonproductive power struggle. This is just as true for people who stringently maintain their innocence as it is for those people who "wallow" aimlessly in their guilt in order to atone for their "sins" (reluctant and resigned precontemplators, respectively). Mozdzierz et al. (2014) discussed the nonlinear concept of *listening for absence* (or what the client is *not* saying) and the discussion of conversations that seem to go nowhere (like "rabbit holes" and useless "war stories") and how some clients believe that they are making progress with these, when they are not. More likely, they are stuck in the repetitive cycle of doing penance and never being quite finished with making amends (i.e., the "preparation for action" stage of change). What they share in common with other clients is that their behavior prevents them from doing any constructive therapeutic work. Finding a way to disentangle such people from their useless solutions and bring them and their behavior back into the mainstream of human society becomes an essential therapeutic task (i.e., helping to get them *out of the hole they have dug for themselves*). Therapists frequently find it problematic knowing exactly how to do this. On the one hand, to minimize a client's feelings is tantamount to approving of his or her crime, whereas to agree with the client's unrelenting need to express repentance is to give permission to continue wallowing. Instead, a paradoxical intervention can be quite helpful in freeing the person from the negative useless behavior and toward a more therapeutic resolution. We present Clinical Case Example 4.2 as an example.

Clinical Case Example 4.2: A Stalker

A male college-aged client was convicted of stalking his ex-girlfriend.[2] In treatment, the client described how he met his ex-girlfriend in a bar where she had approached and pursued him and engaged in a night of dancing. From there, the relationship became very intense very fast. He believed that things between them were good and was shocked when she suddenly and unexpectedly broke up with him. As a result of the breakup, he felt empty and confused and tried to contact her several times to find out about what happened. According to the client, it was his persistent attempts to confront his ex-girlfriend to find out why she left him that led to the stalking complaints and his ultimate conviction. In one specific episode, he admitted that he went over to his ex-girlfriend's house, but found that someone was with her. He decided to hide in the shrubs to see who would come out, but did not intend to be discovered. Unfortunately, she found him, became understandably upset, and pressed charges against him. When he was asked why he went to her home and what he was intending to do, he said, looking lost and sad, "I don't know." It was clear, however, that he felt stupid, guilty, sad, and endlessly remorseful.

Questions

- What is the client's dilemma in this scenario?
- What is the "stuck" behavior that needs to be energized? How is it creating problems for the clients and getting in the way of therapeutic progress?
- How would you use a paradoxical prosocial redefinition with this client?
- Discuss the paradoxical nature of the intervention for the client (i.e., two elements that are mutually incompatible, yet true) and the counselor (i.e., an absurd or contradictory statement that contains truth).

In Clinical Case Example 4.2, the therapist's assessment of this sad young man was that he was in mourning over the sudden and unexpected loss of the relationship and that the stalking was a way of expressing his grief, albeit in a nonproductive, socially useless way. In fact, his behavior had many characteristics of mourning: denial regarding the loss, behaving as though she was still a part of his life, and so on. The therapist reflected this to the client and added, "Most people when they grieve have a gravesite or memorial place to go to if they want to mourn over the resting place of their loved one. Maybe that is what you were trying to do when you were stalking your ex-girlfriend; finding the 'resting place' of your relationship so that you could grieve and move forward with your life."

Immediately, the young man agreed with the unexpected interpretation. He began to see *what* he did in light of *why* he did it, and he began the mourning process and moving forward. At termination, when asked what the most helpful part of his counseling was, he stated that it was the "cemetery" metaphor—"because it made me seem 'normal' and not the 'monster' that they made me out to be in court." Developing a prosocial explanation that was clearly plausible given the man's personal history and the circumstances of his situation, he could acknowledge that he *had* been wrong but that he was not irredeemable. This paradoxical intervention helped him to reappraise the situation as much more benign than he had been feeling and make a choice to change his behavior. Subsequently, he developed a way of saying farewell to the relationship and disengaging from the pain he felt. Prosocial redefinition helps clients to break away from the self-imposed exiles and old (mistaken) ways of behaving. This "liberation" gives them the energizing they require to reengage in resuming a productive life.

Another time when prosocial redefinition is helpful is when clients begin to make progress in therapy, but then become fearful of the change and begin to revert to their old ways. Take, for example, from master family practitioner Monica McGoldrick, where a setback in therapy, is really progress.

Master Example 4.3: But Don't Take Our Word for It!

This excerpt is taken from a family therapy session with *Monica McGoldrick* (author of *Genograms* and *Ethnicity and Family Therapy*) as she works with a teenage daughter, her father, and her step-mother (Alexander Street Press, 2012).

Monica McGoldrick: Listen, I think we need to get this whole situation into some kind of perspective, you know? If you think about Michelle in terms of what's happening, she really is a good kid, you know? There is a lot to worry about, and she's like, terrific, actually. For her to stay out late by herself is serious, because whatever kind of a good kid she is, it's dangerous. So believe me, I'm not saying, "Hey, yo! Let her, let her decide her own curfew. That's fine." I'm not saying that at all. She needs to know from you that you really mean it. That you're going to know when she doesn't come in at night. That you really mean it when you say, "Call," no ifs, ands, or buts—and that there really are consequences. She loves you. She needs you. And I don't think you really get that. And honestly, that's why I think you're flipping out about this, because I think emotionally you're much more in touch with the real dangers, with what's really going on with teenagers, with, with what's really going on around, and that you're the one who's gonna be able to reassure her, not me, by making sure you really follow through.

David: You know, I, I think I understand you, but ah, ah, ah, I just feel like I can only do this within limits. I mean, I am, I feel in some ways that I'm being drawn and quartered, because I, ah, I have a very, very stressful job right now and, ah.

Monica McGoldrick: But you can't just do it to a certain extent. Because Kathleen is right, she could be lost if you do not connect with her. She could well get lost. She's not lost now; she's terrific. I'm saying this 'coz I, I'm trying to really get through to you, but I don't think you understand this. The fact that she connected with me as well as she has in so few sessions is remarkable. She is really seeking to be connected, but you've got to take the opportunity. She really needs you. You know, she needs you to do more than just, sort of, when you're around, sort of say half-heartedly, you're grounded, or something.

David: I'm under a lot of pressure too, you know. It's ah, ah, ah, I, you know, when you think about what's happened over the last 4 years, you're talking about the death of a wife, you're talking about remarrying. We've just had another child.

Monica McGoldrick: But, but what are you saying, really? Where are you going to go? You know, she's 15. At 18, she's going to be gone. You have 3 years, and she's going to be gone. You can either do it or not do it. Those are the only two options that I can see.

David: Well, all I can say is, I can try to do it to the best of my ability. That's all I can say.

Monica McGoldrick: You know, work is a good excuse, and it's also, frankly, an excuse that a lot of men use to avoid very painful things that men in our society are not socialized to be able to deal with easily. You can use that. I'm urging you to think about doing it a different way. And I think you can do it. I, I was actually very struck at how emotionally present you were last week. That you, I mean, when you were able to recognize what not dealing with Carmen meant for your daughter, I mean, I was really astonished, actually, at your being able to be that in touch with her emotionally to, to realize that. But it matters.

David: It was very upsetting to me because I, I thought we were making some progress.

Monica McGoldrick: What I actually think happened this week, which, it's very common to have, you know, people begin to move with something that's important, and then they get scared and back off, what I think happened is for what reasons, I'm not sure, something triggered Michelle to do something which it is worse than any of the acting out we've talked about before. I suspect it's in reaction to what happened here last week: that she somehow got scared. Now what reason, I don't exactly know, but I think it's very much in relation to what we were talking about: that she really needs to deal with who her mother was for her, that a lot of who she is is tied up with all of that history that she's got to be able to deal with.

So in this example, despite the fact that the client and his daughter have begun to get close, he begins to get worried that it won't last and starts to focus on her recent negative behavior rather than the relationship change that is emerging. He further tries to justify his desire to stop trying by claiming that he is under too much pressure. McGoldrick uses two paradoxical interventions in this scenario, a challenger (see Chapter 5) and an energizer. First, she uses the challenger, positive provocation ("work is a good excuse, and it's also, frankly, an excuse that a lot of men use to avoid very painful things . . .") and follows it with a prosocial redefinition ("I suspect it's in reaction to what happened here last week . . .") to redefine it as an indication of progress. In this instance, she avoids falling into the trap of the auto double-bind that David is suggesting and puts the focus off of her and onto David.

Practice

There is an old joke about a man who arrives in New York and gets lost. He waves down a truck driver and says: "Hey mister, how do you get to Carnegie Hall?" The truck driver says: "Practice, practice, practice!" Anyone who has ever tried to learn to play an instrument or a new sport, or develop any new skill, knows the value of practice (i.e., "Practice makes perfect"). The problem is that human nature being what it is, many people don't follow through with practicing even though they know it is what they need. The same understanding is equally true in a clinical setting as well—it is often difficult to stimulate our clients and patients to practice new ways of doing things.

Obviously, rigid thinking and repeating ineffective solutions don't reflect common sense. But such thinking and solutions do reflect a very particular type of personal and idiosyncratic nonlinear reasoning. Motivating these clients to practice a new way of thinking and dealing with their condition is challenging because they have frequently exhausted themselves with rigid and unproductive thinking and ineffectual solutions. A paradoxical intervention that can sometimes help in dislodging a client from counterproductive activity is the energizer we call *practice*. *Practice defines the "problematic" behavior and encourages a client to "practice" it and become better at it but for benign purposes.* For many clients, such instruction is clearly counterintuitive (like most other paradoxical interventions) because it is *nonlinear,* unusual, and totally unexpected.[3]

Clients are asked to practice their symptoms or demonstrate them during the therapy session in order to demonstrate the client's command over the behavior. When they hesitate to do so or claim that they cannot, clients' schema dynamics, emotional system, or feelings of ambivalence can be revealed. In order to detect those dynamisms, a therapist must rely on nonlinear listening, especially *listening for congruence, listening for absence,* and *listening for resistance.* This can be particularly useful in working with individuals who exhibit two types of personality characteristics: paranoia and perfectionism.

Take, for example, a person with a paranoid disposition toward life, who has a negative and unrealistic or inflexible view of others and the world and cannot afford to let her guard down. These individuals fear being betrayed or taken advantage of by "the enemy," life circumstances, etc. By understanding this, a therapist can paradoxically encourage such clients to practice being even more "vigilant," often suggesting restraint from making decisions until collecting *more* information, even if that is their presenting concern (i.e., "I can't seem to make a decision."). Such a suggestion is thoroughly congruent with the way paranoid individuals see the world. It must be emphasized that this intervention cannot be done mockingly or with amusement. It is only *truly* paradoxical if it is done within the context of a therapeutic alliance, and with a good understanding of the client's schema dynamics. We present Clinical Case Example 4.3 to illustrate.

Clinical Case Example 4.3: A Paranoid Young Woman

A young woman in her mid-20s came to therapy at the insistence of her family because of her increasingly disturbing paranoid behavior. In particular, the client's paranoia fixated around FBI agents. She believed that they were trying to entrap her because they mistakenly believed that she was a terrorist. She claimed that she knew that they were tapping her phone line and trying to frame her. It was only because she was very careful with her personal trash, bank statements, and other identifying information that she had not been caught. She claimed that she has known people who have "disappeared" and have been sent to unknown prisons, never to be heard from again.

The woman was intelligent and lucid and held down a secretarial job that she was good at (because she was so meticulous and cautious); however, she refused to date. Recently, she had begun to share her ideas with coworkers, which had caused her to be the object of some ridicule. The client now believed that those coworkers may be in on the conspiracy and are trying to get rid of her. The client stated that she was in fear of her job because of layoff rumors.

Questions

- What is the client's dilemma in this scenario?
- What is the "stuck" behavior that needs to be energized? How is it creating problems for the clients and getting in the way of therapeutic progress?
- How would you use the therapeutic paradoxical intervention of practice with the client?
- Discuss the paradoxical nature of the intervention for the client (i.e., two elements that are mutually incompatible, yet each is true) and the counselor (i.e., an absurd or contradictory statement that contains truth).

In Clinical Case Example 4.3, the therapist understood that there was no way to dislodge this woman's paranoid belief system. Instead, he intervened by paradoxically (using inductive reasoning) stating, "You know, I can't say if you are right or wrong on this, but what I do know is that sometimes *you can't be too cautious.* What I think you may want to consider doing is to write down a log of instances in the next week when you suspect that you are under surveillance." The client agreed to the assignment. Once the client agreed to the assignment and "practiced" the troublesome behavior, *she had agreed to be cooperative with the therapist.* But when she returned the next week, she stated there were only two entries in her "log." Upon reading them, and using some Socratic questioning, it became obvious that the client was responding to situations when she felt afraid or alone.

Once the client accepted the assignment and the therapist's "help," her schema dynamics could be explored as well as her emotional appraisal processes. The therapist decided to go a step further, stating, "It seems that whoever is pursuing you may be backing off. Let's give it another week, but this time *really* try to come up with some evidence." The client was unable to produce anything, and the therapist began to introduce to her that there might be another explanation for what she felt. The energizer paradoxical intervention mobilized her to go beyond the problematic behavior and take a second look at her behavior.

Understanding the schema dynamics of the truly paranoid person is important. It is *nonlinear thinking and reasoning* that provide guidance in working therapeutically with such clients. Consider the following *inductive reasoning:* For the most part, the paranoid person has had lifelong experiences of feeling disappointed, betrayed, and hurt by others. If a therapist comes along and says, "You can trust me!" the paranoid person's defenses will be elevated because it has simply not been their experience that they can trust anyone. But, if a therapist accepts this conclusion and suggests that the world *is* unpredictable and dangerous, it becomes strangely (i.e., paradoxically) empathic and compatible with how a paranoid person sees the world. Thus, urging that the paranoid person collect more information, go slowly, carry a low profile, and so on becomes a paradoxical directive to be more careful—and paranoid. Of course, such "information" became the basis or premise for a new chain of inductive reasoning, which the therapist will lead to a more valid conclusion.

The paradoxical element of the intervention also comes from encouraging the client to practice *under the direction of the therapist,* which makes it a cooperative act (e.g., if he does go more slowly, or collect more information) and in harmony with the therapist; if he doesn't, he is relinquishing some of the heightened paranoia as unnecessary. The "absurd" element is that the therapist understands the client's point of view and the context in which the behavior is valid.[4] For many clients, the fact that the therapist understands their point of view and doesn't condemn them for it is "energizing." In this way, the therapist is aligned with the client and can use the alliance to begin exploring and understanding the client's emotional system, appraisal processes, and ambivalence.

Another person for whom practice is often a good interventional fit is the perfectionist. Such an individual often spends significant time and energy making certain that he does not make a mistake or do something poorly. In the process, perfectionists often exhaust themselves. They find that they don't enjoy life, friends, family, and the like as much as they might were it not for the curse of their perfectionism. A perfectionist may come for treatment with dysthymia and a host of depressive symptoms because he cannot stop focusing on his own actions and the constant need to make certain of his perfectionism. Clinical Case Example 4.4 illustrates.

Clinical Case Example 4.4: An Unhappy Perfectionist

The client was a happily married man in his late 30s who came to counseling for help in dealing with coworkers whom he supervised. In particular, he felt like a failure because he couldn't get them to take their jobs (or do them, for that matter) as seriously as he did. He was also afraid that their poor performance would reflect badly on him with his superiors. He felt dejected, defeated, and depressed; had lost interest in things that gave him pleasure; was staying later at work; and was beginning to "snap" at his wife. Through the use of *nonlinear listening* during the course of one session, the therapist gauged that he was dealing with a perfectionist and suggested it to the client. The client immediately saw how the theme of perfectionism fit with his behavior and feelings, although he hadn't considered it before. His pursuit of perfectionism was leading to perceived failures; the perceived failures were leading to more useless pursuits of perfectionism.

When all was said and done, this likable but perplexed young man found himself in a "catch 22" (i.e., a double-bind). He admitted to staying late at work on a regular basis, redoing his subordinates' paperwork to make sure that it was free of errors and up to his standards. Embarrassed, he also reported it was seldom that he gave feedback to these individuals about what he was doing for fear of looking "weak" to them. As he explored his feelings about this, he admitted that he did not want to act like this anymore but that he didn't know what to do.

Questions

- What is the client's dilemma in this scenario?
- What is the "stuck" behavior that needs to be energized? How is it creating problems for the client and getting in the way of therapeutic progress?
- How would you use the therapeutic paradoxical intervention of practice with the client?
- Discuss the paradoxical nature of the intervention for the client (i.e., two elements that are mutually incompatible, yet both true) and the counselor (i.e., an absurd or contradictory statement that contains a truth).

Because the client in Clinical Case Example 4.4 spent so much time trying to catch errors or prevent them, the therapist recommended that every day the young man should "practice" deliberately making an error, do something wrong, or do something incorrectly. The rationale given to him for this suggestion was simple enough: It didn't matter what he chose to "screw up" as long as he agreed to practice this habit and allow the natural consequences to result. In addition, he was told that if he found himself worrying about making a mistake, he would remind himself that he already made his mistake for the day and that he didn't have to worry about making another one. The young man agreed to "practice." Remember the irony of the present instance: someone with perfectionistic qualities wants to "practice" because, as we all know, "Practice makes perfect!"

The next week, the young man returned much more energized and more at ease. He reported being able to carry out the suggestion to practice "screwing up" and that he felt "totally different" about himself and his situation at work. Using inductive reasoning, the therapist guided him to see that the world wasn't "going to end" for him if he was less than perfect. In addition, he was (for the most part) able to put aside chronic worrying about his performance. As a result, he found himself better able to interact with coworkers without the tension that had been permeating his professional relationships. The paradoxical interaction had the effect of creating a second-order change in the client by offering another perspective on his behavior that allowed him to *get out of the hole that he dug for himself.* In subsequent sessions, he was able to work on some of the underlying issues prompting his perfectionistic tendencies as well as develop assertiveness skills in order to ask others for appropriate help in getting his needs met.

In the previous example, knowing the client's schema dynamics (unrealistic view of self) allowed the therapist to strategically use practice as a paradoxical intervention to help free some of the client's energy and showed him how to be a success. By contrast, a different therapeutic route could have been chosen such as a more traditional (i.e., linear) cognitive-behavioral approach. In such an approach, the client is instructed and encouraged to track thoughts that go with the perfectionistic tendencies. But, such linear-thinking interventions would probably take more time. By requesting him to practice being imperfect, he discovered a means of disengagement from the more useless method of dealing with work-related problems (i.e., living in fear of making a mistake). In other words, the paradoxical intervention has effects on the cognitive, relational, and emotional levels all *at the same time!* His disengagement from concern about making mistakes subsequently allowed him to discover the energy to recognize his own value as well as the value of working with others.

Pedagogism

As the saying goes, "Teaching is learning twice." *Pedagogism is a gentle but energizing paradoxical intervention in which a client walks a therapist through the processes and the logic underlying what others have often times defined as problematic.* As a case in point, defiant adolescents, precontemplators, and mandated clients find themselves in difficulty because of the impact of their behaviors on others, although they may not see their behavior as particularly problematic. Pedagogism is considered a particularly useful intervention to use with such clients, who seem to "dare" a therapist to make them change. Attempts to *make* a defiant client change appear doomed before they begin. But, by using *nonlinear thinking,* a therapist may request such a defiant client to explain the "secret" of her success, namely, a positive framing of what has been defined as troublesome (for others) behavior. More specifically, a defiant adolescent may be asked in an admiring way how she is able to "keep everything together so well" with her parents, school officials, and so on "harping" on her. Such behavior (i.e., apparently not letting anything bother her) is defined and reported to the client as a valuable skill that the therapist would like to know more about and learn from the client so that he might teach it to others.

The paradoxical energizer of pedagogism takes the "problem" behavior, finds its dialectical opposite, and, in a *nonlinear* fashion, "turns it on its head." Using *nonlinear thinking,* the therapist does not attempt to convince the client that his behavior is wrong or maladaptive, which is what the client expects. Obviously, if the defiant adolescent begins relating how he manages to keep things together and not be bothered, he is cooperating with the therapist—previously defiant behavior has been transformed into a cooperative venture between client and therapist. Instead, adopting "Socratic ignorance" and intellectual modesty (see Chapter 1) has the effect of placing the client in the role of "knowledgeable expert" rather than helpless victim (Mozdzierz, Macchitelli, & Lisiecki, 1976). After a while, maintaining such a defiant posture in treatment becomes difficult for the adolescent, and she begins to engage more in the therapeutic endeavor. In a series of classical articles, Marshall (1972, 1974, 1976) suggested this method of intervention for dealing with a variety of child and adolescent problems. Pedagogism can also be used in other contexts, as Clinical Case Example 4.5 illustrates.

Clinical Case Example 4.5: Design a Plan for the Wife to Follow

The following illustration of this comes from a couples' therapy session. The husband initiated the therapy, complaining, among other things, that his wife never picked up around the house as he expected. The husband made it very clear to his wife that because he earned enough money for her to stay at home, the very least that she could do (in his opinion) was to keep the house clean. Upon further assessment, it was discovered that they had three children under the age of 0 and that the wife did actually keep the house fairly clean. The husband, it seemed, was not reacting to filth, but to the "mess" of toys that would be used by the kids and the occasional dirty diaper left in the garbage pail that his wife had not been able to empty before he came home. The exasperated wife defensively explained how she spent most of her time keeping the house clean for her husband, but that he never seemed to appreciate or notice all that she had done but instead chose to focus on the few things that the children had left out.

The therapist intervened paradoxically. He instructed the husband to write up a plan—a set of instructions for teaching—to keep the house the way he expected and bring it back the next week to discuss with his wife. He gladly accepted, and the next week he came in with a five-page document on what he expected from his wife's cleaning efforts, and how to implement them. The therapist then, with a completely straight face, asked the husband if he had "field-tested" his plan. The husband first said that he had, and that these were the rules that he had used all his life. When asked, however, if he had actually performed them under the same conditions that his wife encountered daily, he answered no. The therapist, knowing that the husband had some training as an engineer, stated that any project or plan must surely be pilot-tested before being implemented. The husband reluctantly agreed, and the therapist then asked the wife to take a day, leave the house and the children, and do whatever she wanted. In the meantime, the husband was to apply his manual for an entire day with the kids, to see how well it worked out. The husband tried to protest, but he agreed to put it to the test, with both spouses to report back. The therapist even said that he would be interested in a copy because he had difficulty keeping his house tidy. This is considered central to a pedagogically paradoxical intervention: The client's insistent investment in his complaint is used as something that can be taught—in this instance, even to the therapist!

The next week, the couple reported that they had tried to implement the plan, and when the wife came home, she found that half the things on the husband's list were not accomplished. The husband admitted that he really didn't know how much work his wife did with the children, calling it a "full- AND part-time job." At this point, the husband began to admit to having some feelings of jealousy and neglect from his wife that ultimately led to his devaluing her work and leading to his attention-seeking complaint behavior (i.e., the heart of the problem all along). The wife protested that she had told the husband that this was the case, but that he had always denied it. "That is because," the therapist said, "until now he didn't really *know* it. The point is that now that he does, you have to decide what the two of you want to do about it." At this point, the couple was ready to begin to work, whereas before the paradoxical intervention, criticism of the wife's ability to clean would have dominated the conversation and sandbagged the therapy. Not only weren't his unrealistic "complaints" and demands unchallenged, but also they were elicited as a source of expertise that could be taught to others; however, in the process, he would have to acknowledge and learn some important things about running a household with little children.

Pedagogism also works effectively in energizing clients who have been victims of difficult life circumstances. Whether the victim of crime, illness, defective genes, or a random unfortunate event in life, many clients are overwhelmed, are preoccupied with having been victimized, and find it difficult to focus on other areas of strength or resilience in their lives. In addition, their negative focus (i.e., preoccupied, feeling victimized, etc.) leaves them de-energized and can often continue to make them feel stuck. Part of the sense of feeling stuck stems from the legitimate sense of being overwhelmed by the events that such clients have experienced. Their customary templates for understanding life (i.e., their schematized views) have little frame of reference to cope with such circumstances. As a result, they may understandably overestimate threats in their environment, or underestimate their ability (e.g., strengths and resources) to cope with these threats. Pedagogism in this instance is a method to energize such clients by helping them to focus on how their experience as a victim has created significant resilience.

Summary

Energizer paradoxical interventions are best used for clients who are immobilized by their particular circumstances or by their ambivalence. According to the stages of change model (i.e., Prochaska & DiClemente, 1982, 1984, 2005), such individuals may be in the contemplation stage (i.e., aware that they have a problem, but not ready to face it) or in the preparing for action stage (i.e., getting ready to make a change, but not taking action yet). For one reason or another, they seem to be stuck in a hole (their problem behavior) and they cannot get out (cannot become energized). Clinicians can figure out that this is happening by paying attention to their own countertransference feelings and subsequently conclude that the client needs an energizer. For example, the therapist feeling very tired and weary in the session (like she is doing all of the work) or feeling that the client or the therapy is stuck may be indicators that the client feels like he is in a hole that he cannot get out of (because of fear, etc.). Therefore, the client needs to be motivated or energized to see that he has the ability to stop the problem behavior and move forward with therapy. Next, we present one of the more complex classes of paradoxical interventions: the challengers.

Notes

1. Fulminating multiple sclerosis is a particularly devastating and rapidly progressing neurological disorder in which the covering of the body's nerves are destroyed, resulting in a scarring of the nerves, rendering them inoperative, and thus leading to greater and greater paralysis.
2. Although stalking is clearly an issue that can reveal serious psychopathology and require thorough investigation, in this instance, it should be noted that the young man was not considered to be a danger to his ex-girlfriend. He lived several hundred miles from her and was under a strict court-ordered "order of protection" not to enter the town where the infraction took place or go anywhere near her, which he was abiding by (although many times individuals convicted of similar crimes do not).
3. Perhaps the most common expectation that clients have is to be told to "stop" doing what it is that is problematic. They already know they should stop, and not being able to do so is often what prompts their coming for treatment.
4. This is not to say that the therapist needs to agree with or condone the client's behavior to use this intervention. The therapist does need to believe in the nature of the nonlinear intervention.

5 The Use of Challenger Paradoxical Interventions

The final classification of paradoxical interventions is probably the most difficult to master. They are reserved for those clinicians who have truly grasped the elements of advanced *nonlinear* thought processes demonstrated by master clinicians (such as inductive reasoning, Socratic questioning, double-binds, second-order change, etc.), have a firm understanding of the other domains of competence, and also feel comfortable using paradoxical interventions.

The challengers are a class of paradoxical interventions that are unsettling to a client's status quo; in short, they are provocative. In much the same way that a grain of sand causes an irritating challenge to an oyster (thus causing the creation of a pearl), so, too, the challengers provide a positive unsettling feeling to a client in the name of therapeutic movement. As "disturbing" as they are to the client's (maladaptive) status quo, challengers are meant to provoke positive therapeutic movement or prompt a greater sense of *prosocial equilibrium* to a client in maintaining his or her symptoms.

Just as with the energizers (discussed in Chapter 4), clients who require challengers feel burdened and stuck. The circumstances of their life generally require them to do more than they feel capable of doing, and their behavior (even though it is problematic) is the "best" that they can do. Unlike clients who require energizers and are immobilized and are (for the most part) unable to move forward, clients who require challengers are acting in a way that is (at best) not in their interests, and (at worst) dangerous. Put simply, the client truly believes that, given his circumstance, he is doing all that he possibly can and that it is the *right* thing to do. Often, clients' schema dynamics (generally, the view of self) contain unrealistic expectations of what they "ought" to be able to do. Their limited resources or fear of failure, however, forces them to "fall short" of what they should or could do. Or, their schema dynamics may dictate that if they do not foresee being able to "get" what it is that they want, they must retreat. As a result, such clients are caught in a dilemma and have intense feelings of ambivalence. They become entrenched in their positions with a discouraging, reactionary, and defensive stance toward others and life, and in addition engage in maladaptive (or even dangerous) behavior patterns. They convince themselves, "No one understands what I am going through," and such internal dialogue helps them justify their actions. Such clients never seem to make it into the textbooks and practice cases, and yet they appear in the practitioner's office every day. In fact, it is precisely because such clients are so typical of those who appear in clinicians' offices that we include them here.

Nonlinear Listening and Challengers

As always, *nonlinear listening* is especially important in determining whether challenging paradoxical interventions may be needed to mobilize a client. In therapy, clients who need challenging may complain that they are "tired": "I'm doing all that I can just to stay afloat and have no time or energy to think about doing anything more or different." It is clear that they are stuck in a double-bind, *and* they often try to ensnare the therapist in one as well (the auto "double-bind" see Chapter 1). So they don't have to change. The master therapist recognizes that such clients are stuck between their schema dynamics (view of self, others, or life or the world) and circumstances that they face (or don't *want* to face). When a therapist intervenes by using one of the challengers, however, a client's symptom is transformed so that it no longer does what it has been doing. In order to effectively set the stage for such a transformation, a therapist must listen for *congruence* (i.e., is the client really wanting the help he is seeking?), *absence* (i.e., is all this behavior distracting from the *real* issue?), *inference* (what is the client telling me he *doesn't* want to happen?), *presence* (i.e., what is his behavior saying that the client is not telling me verbally?), and *resistance* (when I recommend that he changes, does he "Yes, but . . ." me?). Such *nonlinear listening* provides a therapist the guidance that she needs in stimulating a client from his lethargy or retreat by appropriate challenging.

Advanced Nonlinear Thinking and Challengers

With challengers, a master clinician must use all of the linear and nonlinear thinking tools at his or her disposal. A firm understanding of the nature of double-binds and the role that schema dynamics play is essential. The clinician must be able to recognize faulty conclusions derived from deductive reasoning and counter it with inductive reasoning. In addition, clinicians using challenger paradoxical interventions realize that in order to point out the fallacy of the client's thinking, the challenging paradoxical intervention will require elements of the Socratic method in order to achieve second-order change. Each of these will be demonstrated in the examples to come in this chapter. We encourage the reader to consider the elements of advanced nonlinear thinking when reading the case studies *and* the paradoxical intervention used.

Types of Challengers

There are four types (or "*P's*") of paradoxical challenger interventions: proportionality, prediction, prescription, and positive provocation. Each of them prompts a client to react and (hopefully) *disengage* even slightly from his or her problematic behavioral solutions with at least a partial restoration of more adaptive functioning. This is perhaps one of the most difficult of the classes of paradoxical interventions for many clinicians because it entails some level of directness. Caution is recommended, however, about being "direct": If challengers are presented too passively, the intervention can be easily dismissed by a client ("Oh, what do you know? You're not going through what I am going through!"). Likewise, if such interventions are done too aggressively, a client will feel that the counselor is unjustly attacking him or her. Perhaps the most cogent suggestion that we can make is that challengers should be presented with respect and with confidence in their being appropriate in a matter-of-fact manner. The use of Socratic questioning is also useful in presenting "challengers" to clients. Again, like all paradoxical interventions, therapists must be aware of all the other domains to be able to help a client with a challenger paradoxical intervention. We now present the "*P*'s" of the challengers, as well as case examples to illustrate the principles underlying these paradoxical interventions.

Proportionality

The concept of proportionality refers to the universal and natural striving for balance found in all of life and the universe. There is an inherent sense of this harmony when one leads a "balanced" life. In family systems theory, this is referred to as *equilibrium*. Unfortunately, for one reason or another (e.g., willfulness, misunderstanding, oversensitivity, faulty genes, brain chemistry gone awry, or misinterpretation), human beings seem to have considerable difficulty in achieving balance.

In daily living, individuals must rely on their constant automatic appraisals of life's events (i.e., the capacity for a "blink"—thinking without thinking—response—see Gladwell, 2005) to inform them of the possibility of threats and/or the possibility of achieving things desirable. Unfortunately, because such automatic appraisals are so incredibly rapid, they come with inherent biases or distortions. Although it may be oversimplified, the extent of the distortion provided by automatic appraisals is contingent upon how far removed from common sense they are. It is quite common that clients seeking treatment have developed *disproportionate appraisals and responses* to perceived threats, failures, and so on in their lives.

When things are distorted, in many ways it's like looking at an old "funhouse" mirror that distorts a person's reflection. The appraisal acts like the warped mirror, which makes the head and body seem to be either too big or small and doesn't fit with reality. In times of stress, which are regular occurrences in today's complicated world, the images we have of ourselves (or situations in which we find ourselves) may become warped or out of proportion due to our distorted appraisals. During particularly stressful times, most people make efforts to bring things back into their proper proportion (e.g., the time spent on work and family life), just like people try to do with their reflections in the funhouse mirror by moving up or down to get a more realistic image. Some individuals, however, get things terribly out of proportion and out of balance and don't seem to be able to get them in proper balance. They make the best effort that they can to bring things back into proportion, but cannot do it in constructive ways, so they live with "warped" solutions. This is indicative of being in a double-bind. Eventually, these individuals become stuck in maladaptive and even absurd "solutions," behaviors, strategies, and so on (i.e., distorted responses to distorted appraisals) and are unable to extract themselves from those solutions. The out-of-balance situation becomes "typical" and automatic, which becomes a "problem." Most often, their maladaptive disproportionate responses to life circumstances become problematic for other people.

Rather than using logic, reasoning, commonsense reality, or consensual validation (i.e., linear approaches) to deal with all manner of human absurdities, a therapist, using paradoxical interventions, takes a nonlinear approach, *joins* with the client's disproportionate appraisal and response, and extends them even further than the client had (i.e., "hyperextends" them). Nonlinear thinking is crucial in this process: The therapist knows that the client's "out-of-balance" behavior appears to make sense to *him* or *her.* Proportionality consists of taking a patient's unbalanced (i.e., out-of-proportion) position and exaggerating it, taking it to a greater extent than the patient (much like Miller and Rollnick's [2012] "agreeing with a twist" or "developing discrepancies"). In effect, when a therapist exaggerates the behavior in such a way, it often times renders the patient's out-of-balance position much less palatable or tenable. Clinical Case Example 5.1 may help to illustrate this.

Clinical Case Example 5.1: A Sad Mother's Visit With Her Adult Children

A very accomplished professional woman sought brief therapy because her oldest adult sons had chosen careers that took them far from home after graduating from college. She quietly lamented how much she missed them, how emotionally close they had once been, and how she relished their confiding in her. On one particular occasion, as tears welled in her eyes, she described how they came home for a visit, but would decide to spend most of their time staying over at a friend's apartment in the downtown area, where they could reconnect with their childhood buddies and "party."

The therapist stood up from his desk chair and said, as though pondering something very difficult to figure out, "Let me see if I have this right. (Gesturing with his right hand as though he were weighing what he was saying.) The boys could spend time with Mom (gesturing with his left hand as though he were weighing and comparing it against what was in his right hand)—or, they could spend time with their friends, drink, party, and enjoy their girlfriends. (Obviously exaggerating, with his hands going up and down as though he were continuing to weigh those options.) They could spend time with Mom, or they could party with their friends. Let's see: Young, energetic men with lots of good friends that they haven't seen in a long time could spend time with Mom (continuing to move his hands up and down, as though he were continuing to weigh something), or they could party with their friends."

The woman instantly broke into a broad, knowing smile and laughed, recognizing that she had "exaggerated" her position (i.e., consensually nonlinear thinking) toward her children. Almost instantaneously, she had put things back into balance. It is common sense that young men and women would want to spend free time with their friends, thus establishing a normal life pattern while not meaning to "reject" their parents. The paradoxical intervention allowed the client to reappraise her situation and decide to change her behavior.

This is a good example of how using paradoxical interventions can develop discrepancies in the client's attitude or behavior. The practitioner uses the client's "power" and position to his own (and ultimately) to the client's therapeutic advantage. That is, the person's natural inclination toward balance is engaged once the therapist hyper-extends and exaggerates the client's behaviors. Timing and sensitivity in the application of the concept of proportionality are extremely important considerations, as is the manner of presentation. Developing skill at executing such timing and sensitivity is a hallmark of the master practitioner. As such, we hope the reader will see that at times, a somewhat humorous presentation (as in Clinical Case Example 5.1) is called for, and at times, a more serious one is needed. In either event, the therapist extends the client's symptoms or complaints to the point of exaggerating something already out of proportion and carrying it to the point of a *reductio ad absurdum* (reduction to the absurd).

Some readers might be thinking, "Well, that's fine for the kind of people you see in your practice, but I work for an agency where the clients aren't at a very high level of functioning. Such things wouldn't work with my clients!" It is with this reader in mind that we describe our final example of positive provocation in Clinical Case Example 5.2.

Clinical Case Example 5.2: Too Weak to Get Up and . . .?

A fast-aging woman recovering from substance abuse and a recent brief depression that required hospitalization in a state facility was complaining of her teenage son. As a single parent, she lived in poverty on public assistance with her other adult children, all of whom demonstrated psychiatric symptoms of one sort or another. She did not complete high school (which she regretted), had never held a job for more than a few months, but was able to maintain a marginal existence in the community with the help of her day treatment program and appropriate medications. Although she suffered from a variety of psychiatric symptoms, she was determined to be a "good mother." She sought specialized counseling for a problem that she was having with her 16-year-old son.

Mostly due to a lack of supervision, no father in his life, and little motivation, the boy dropped out of school in 9th grade. His mother would beg him to go back to school and get a GED, but he continually defied his mother's pleas for him to go to school. His excuse when she would bother him about it was to say that he was too "weak and tired" to go to school.

As part of the evaluation, the boy and his mother were interviewed together. The mother complained of the boy's lack of activity and openly "shamed" her son in front of the therapist by revealing his "laziness." As an example of his laziness, she cited the fact that he refused to get up in the middle of the night and go to the bathroom. Instead, she explained, he would urinate in a 5-gallon "pee bucket" that she complained smelled "terrible"—especially in the summer because they did not have air conditioning. The boy seemed ashamed at this, but simply shrugged his shoulders and said that he didn't feel good. He expressed being interested in getting a job, to which his mother countered that he should go to school instead. At the same time, he insisted that he didn't want to go to school.

In Clinical Case Example 5.2, the therapist entered the impasse by insisting to the boy's mother that her son was obviously "too weak and sickly" to be able to sustain any type of work (in point of fact, the boy was a model of youthful physical fitness). To further support his position, the therapist noted, "Aren't you too weak to be able to go all the way to the bathroom in the middle of the night? Aren't you too weak to be able to empty the pee bucket?" (essentially taking one side of the client's double-bind and blowing it out of proportion). The boy appeared to absorb the challenge and promptly replied, "I am strong enough to get a job." To this, the therapist replied, "That appears to be nonsense. You should be at home taking care of yourself! You are definitely too weak to go to school or get a job!" The boy insisted that there was a job available at the local fast-food restaurant that he wanted to investigate. He and his mother left the interview with him muttering that he was going to "show" the therapist that he wasn't "too weak to get a job." At the next appointment, the mother told the therapist that her son was now employed. Apparently, the boy's need to take an oppositional stance against his mother was satisfied in a more constructive way by getting (and keeping) a job. The boy was positively provoked and mobilized into therapeutic movement when other motivations offered by his mother apparently carried no weight.[1]

This was a good example of using elements of the double-bind to *get out* of the double-bind. Regarding this case, we hasten to add that, obviously, for a Level 1 or 2 practitioner to offer an apparently irreverent challenging comment to a patient (or client) is fraught with *caveats*. First, the comment must be made with the intention of helping the client to disengage from unproductive behavior (e.g., refusing to talk, withdrawing, and being depressed as a silent protest and an expression of stubbornness). Second, the comment must be made within an atmosphere of respect for the client without malice and certainly without sarcasm (Horvath & Bedi, 2002). To do this effectively, the therapist must understand the client's schema dynamics and show (through an absurd comment) how his behavior is disproportionate in some way. In this example, the client was invited to see how his behavior was out of balance, struggling with something that was inevitable. The antidote was to "challenge" him (i.e., provide an *unexpected disproportionate response*) by arguing that he was too weak, which both supported his argument and challenged his position at the same time. The unexpectedness of the therapeutic response in containing such disproportionality is demonstrated in this excerpt from The Case of Mike:

Mike: I feel so . . . weak. I shouldn't need to do this.
Therapist: And you are worried . . . that "weakness" sounds like some of your father's "philosophy;" is that where it comes from?
Mike: I don't want him to be disappointed in me. I screwed up before, and I want him to be proud.
Therapist: So if you are weak, you feel like you'd disappoint Dad, but if you don't find a way to deal with your feelings, and not lash out in a wounded way, you'll lose your job and fiancée. How would your dad feel about that?
Mike: Disappointed. [QUICKLY] But I don't want to be weak, and I don't want to lose!

Therapist:	What if I told you there was a way to be strong and win at the same time?
Mike:	That'd be great.
Therapist:	Well, what do you think takes more strength, lashing out or holding back when you want to?
Mike:	Holding back.
Therapist:	And what do you think takes more strength, running away from pain or taking the pain?
Mike:	Taking the pain.
Therapist:	So then, everything else you have done in the past was really weakness. That's the mystery of why your anger problem can't be solved by other people. It's because you aren't chiefly angry at them. A big part of this is that you are really angry at yourself. That is why you get so angry with other people when they don't do what you want. It makes you feel unsuccessful and weak, which hurts. Then, you lash out at others. But that doesn't persuade them, it makes them want to do the opposite (just to spite you). That only gets you MORE frustrated and angry. However, if you hold back your anger and confront the pain you feel instead of lashing out and running away, you will be showing strength. You will be the winner, and I bet you'd make your father proud.

In the example above, the therapist takes the concepts of "strength" and "weakness" and reverses them in order to challenge Mike's beliefs about what it means to be strong and weak. By changing the proportions of these concepts, the paradox reveals to the client that his original view of things may be mistaken, and that he is really acting in the *opposite* way than he thinks he is. It allows him to reappraise and make a *second-order* change to his behavior and his way of viewing himself and others (which is a good example of "accommodation" of schema dynamics from Domain 4).

In all of the above examples, proportionality was used to make a point by overstating the client's exaggerated and disproportionate (i.e., nonlinear) position. Simultaneously, using inductive reasoning, critical flaws in the client's thinking and behaving were exposed (or overexposed). As a result, the client disengaged from a nonproductive disproportionate solution to a set of life circumstances. That disengagement fostered a more "commonsense" approach to that set of circumstances and a more natural inclination toward balance. Sometimes, it is by challenging a client's exaggerated perception and position that one is able to help her leave the "funhouse" of wavy mirrors and strange solutions (i.e., nonlinear thinking).

Prescription

Prescription (or "prescribing the symptom") is perhaps what most people think of when they hear the term "paradoxical interventions." *Prescription refers to a therapist encouraging the continuation of disruptive behaviors, but under the direction of (and in cooperation with) the therapist.* While it is a powerful nonlinear tool, it doesn't represent the entirety of paradoxical thinking. In fact, prescription should be used only when appropriate (i.e., *not* for someone who is actively suicidal because of the risk to the individual). Again, from our perspective, to arbitrarily use prescription in order to "*be* paradoxical" is gimmicky, risky, thoughtless, and not at all reflective of a true understanding of the nature of this challenger. Any intervention that takes on the characteristics of being simply a "technique" that seeks to manipulate a client devoid of consideration of the therapeutic relationship, context, advanced nonlinear thinking, and client understanding will only rupture the therapeutic relationship and is not recommended. We provide an example of paradoxically prescribing the symptom in Clinical Case Example 5.3.

Clinical Case Example 5.3: Divorced, Lonely, and Frightened

A prime example of what we mean by the "prescription of a symptom" or complaint comes from the case of a middle-aged, mildly depressed man who had recently received his final divorce papers just before coming for help. He had been married for a long time, and after his divorce, he was lonely, depressed, and leading a rather spectacularly uneventful and reclusive life. He worked long regular hours and occasionally visited his grown children, but otherwise, he mostly stayed at home watching TV or repairing his car. He reported that some friends in a neighboring state had invited him for a holiday weekend and offered to arrange a date for him with a widow they knew. The patient told the therapist about this invitation and expressed a desire to accept his friends' invitation because it would probably be good for him, while simultaneously expressing grave doubts about getting "fixed up" with a blind date that "wouldn't work out" and thereby having a bad time.

Sensing the patient's ambivalence, the therapist commented on the man's simultaneous desire to go and his doubts about how disappointed he might be. It was then suggested to the man that he might as well "go with" his desire to accept the invitation to visit with his friends but keep his distance from the blind date and expect *not* to have a very good time. This would allow him to *have his cake and eat it too* by allowing him to accept the invitation *and* honor his legitimate desire not to get hurt. The paradoxical intervention prescribes that the client should do both things: Go on the trip *and* expect to have a bad time, rather than the either/or dichotomy of "I really want to share my life with someone" but "Because I don't want to get hurt again, I lack the courage that it takes to go out" that the client was wrestling with. Basically, then, his complaint had been prescribed for him as the antidote.

At the following session, the patient reported that he went for the weekend visit and "I didn't have a bad time." He also announced that he expected to make a return visit the following month.

One thing that Clinical Case Example 5.3 demonstrates is that sometimes both poles of a dilemma are legitimate and must be honored. At the same time, clients sometimes create more of a problem than really exists. Prescription (like proportionality) has the effect of hyperextending a client's logic to the point that she is challenged and feels uncomfortable with the implications of her activities. This is similar to the motivational interviewing method of "agreeing with a twist," whereby a therapist agrees with the client's perspective *too much,* and the client begins to back away from her original position.

Prescription takes the client's solution and gives the client the "authorization" to keep on doing what she is doing. When these ambivalent clients find themselves still in the same place, however, they interpret the therapist's intervention paradoxically because it contains two true statements that should not be able to coexist, but do. Generally, these statements are (a) You don't like what you are doing (or what happens to you when you do it), and you want to stop; and (b) given the chance, you will keep doing it. By explicitly feeding into the second statement (giving permission), the implication of the first statement becomes more pronounced for the client. This imbalances the double-bind and allows the client to take a new look at his or her situation. This is the "absurd" aspect underlying the nature of the paradoxical intervention. We present Clinical Case Example 5.4 to demonstrate this further.

Clinical Case Example 5.4: A Woman Complaining of Dizziness

A 50-year-old single woman with multiple chronic medical problems (i.e., COPD, diabetes, heart condition, hypotension, etc.) who was semi-retired from her work in the health care industry found herself unexplainably depressed after two brief successful outpatient surgical procedures. Her depression led to a brief stay in a psychiatric hospital and referral for outpatient medication and therapy follow-up. She described that she felt depressed because she had no interest in doing anything, nothing gave her satisfaction, and she had "no life." She had no relatives and no friends other than at her place of part-time employment, which she couldn't return to until she obtained medical authorization. She was bored at home with "nothing to do but watch TV" and complained of insomnia and chronic anxiety that she had never experienced before. Her antidepressant medications, however, seemed to provide no relief.

Toward the end of the first session, she bitterly complained that she had always been productive, busy, and a generally neat and thorough housekeeper all of her life but that her home was now looking shabby with laundry undone, dishes piling up, and no desire to address any of it. She could not address any household tasks because of one of her medical problems. That is, she suffered from hypotension: "Any time that I get up to do anything for more than 10 minutes, I have to go back and lay down because I get dizzy." Her "solution" was to return to bed, which she found intolerable. Despite her conditions, her physicians felt that she was able to do light housework and other activities of daily living (ADLs) had put no restrictions on her.

After listening to the woman's description of her inactivity and her quite extensive list of medical problems, the therapist suggested that it seemed important for her to be busy, but it was also necessary for her to be cautious— namely, she did not want to provoke an episode of passing out, which could have serious complications. The therapist then suggested that if she was going to do anything around the house, it was important for her to limit her activities to no more than 10 minutes. She was then to return to bed and lay down.

At the very beginning of the next therapy session, the woman somewhat smugly reported that for some reason within a day of her last session, she cleaned the entire house, vacuumed, had done all her dishes, and finished numerous loads of laundry, all with no ill effects! Although she continued to complain of her depression and unrelenting anxiety, from that point on, she continued to be more active. She joined a support group, went shopping for groceries, began searching for a new church affiliation, and so on, also with no ill effects.

In Clinical Case Example 5.4, there were many "complaints" that the client was making: Being bored, having much to do but being unable to do it for more than 10 minutes. One "solution" that this woman seemed to apply to her dilemma and circumstances involved trying to do things but becoming discouraged, frightened, bored, or perhaps a combination of those reactions, which thus became the injunctions in the double-bind. When benignly encouraged to maintain the status quo (i.e., *limit her activities to no more than 10 minutes*) and then return to bed, the woman responded with a somewhat prolific burst of activity that seemed to continue. Her movement *toward* housework was abhorrent; the therapist suggested moving *away* from her housework by engaging in only a few minutes of such activity and then returning to bed *for safety reasons* (i.e., benign purposes). Also important in Clinical Case Example 5.4, the woman demonstrated disdain toward several of her physicians and, by extrapolation, other authority figures (e.g., supervisors). Nonlinear listening for congruence revealed the discrepancy between her physicians' treatment and the client's lack of progress, suggesting that she may harbor a hidden agenda and have considerable ambivalence (i.e., "secondary gains," see Chapter 1). Detecting and understanding such a personal characteristic helped guide the therapist's intervention by posing a suggestion that would have one of the following outcomes: Either the woman was likely to disregard it, or it would help keep her functioning within the safe boundaries of "10 minutes" of physical activity.

As a result of this understanding, the therapist was able to construct a "positive" double-bind in the form of an absurd paradoxical intervention ("Do no more than

10 minutes 'work' and return to bed"—something that she was already doing). From the client's perspective, she receives two true messages that cannot coexist (for her): "You shouldn't try so hard" and "Listen to me; I know what is best for you." The first message was a comfort (in a way) because it didn't challenge her to do anything other than what she already had been doing. But the second message made the comfort in the first statement intolerable because her view of herself was that she was *always* capable of doing things and her view of others was that "they" didn't know what was best for her (especially doctors).

Master Example 5.1: But Don't Take Our Word for It!

In this example, master clinician *Marsha Linehan*, PhD (developer of Dialectical Behavioral Therapy—DBT), works with a woman who is struggling to be on time for service at the church where her husband is a pastor (Alexander Street Press, 2012).

Client: I think he does (laughs).
Marsha Linehan: Well, why do you think that, when he hasn't said anything?
Client: I just think he's trying to be nice, and not put pressure on me, but I don't think it's good for him, for his congregants to be noticing that I'm late for church.
Marsha Linehan: So what would happen if you asked him, don't you think it would help you get yourself there on time if he actually told you he cared?
Client: Yeah, maybe.
Marsha Linehan: Because that would make it more visible to you.
Client: That's true.
Marsha Linehan: So one thing I would suggest is asking him if he cares.
Client: Mmhmm.
Marsha Linehan: Okay? Um. The only other thing, right now, it seems to me that the only way to get yourself to be on time is to give yourself a series of rules for yourself where you say, you're not allowed anymore to believe that you can wash your hair and get ready faster.
Client: Mmhmm.
Marsha Linehan: Because that seems to be the one area that you're unlikely to cut back on no matter what.
Client: Mmhmm.
Marsha Linehan: *And* the real problem has been, is that, you get yourself in the shower too late, and you're not willing to not wash your hair and not do all the things to get dressed. In other words, you're not willing to not look attractive at church.
Client: Mmhmm. So, should I just talk back to myself? So . . .
Marsha Linehan: One thing you can do is ask your husband whether he would rather have you on time and unattractive, or late, attractive?
Client: (laughs)

Linehan uses Socratic questioning to clarify the underlying issues and values of the client's behavior. Ultimately, she challenges her with the prescription to "ask your husband whether he would rather have you on time and unattractive, or late, attractive?" In each of the cases above, the clients (who were arguably capable enough) were unable to accomplish their goals because they were trapped by feelings of ambivalence caused by the rigid and unrealistic schema dynamics and/or by being caught in a double-bind. In their minds, this limited their behavioral choices and got them stuck in their circumstance, or problem, and made alternatives difficult to see. The challengers, and prescription in particular, afforded them an opportunity to disengage from a maladaptive and self-defeating pattern that frustrated their verbalized desires. Only after relinquishing the maladaptive pattern can an individual grasp a new solution.

Prediction

In the paradoxical intervention of prediction, a therapist uses knowledge of a client's schema dynamics, emotional system, and current situation, and any feelings of ambivalence on the client's part, to "prophesy" that certain "events" (e.g., behaviors, ideas, thoughts, and communication patterns) will "probably" occur under certain conditions the client is about to encounter. This is not as "gimmicky" as it may seem. It actually requires that a therapist have a solid informational grounding from which to base a prediction. It also requires an equally sound case conceptualization that allows the therapist to identify the client's particular dilemma and characteristic behavior responses to certain circumstances and then make a prediction. Specifically, the therapist has to be accurate about the client's schema dynamics and recognize the patterns underlying the client's behavior. The therapist "prophesizes" a client's behavior based upon what the client would "probably do anyway" in a given situation. The client then can engage in his maladaptive and repetitive behavior, but because it was "predicted," it will not provide the patient with any "payoff" (i.e., secondary gain) if the predicted outcome occurs. If the predicted outcome does not occur, then although the therapist was proven "wrong," the client has been helped to move in a more prosocial and constructive direction. Clinical Case Example 5.5 is suggested as an example.

Clinical Case Example 5.5: Parenting Issues

A 38-year-old recently divorced mother comes to therapy for help in handling her "hyperactive" 6-year-old son. According to her, "He is out of control and won't ever pay attention to anything that I say!" She continued to say that he will not dress himself without her constant help, often refuses to eat meals that he asks for, and will not sleep in his own bed (preferring to sleep in her bed). An analysis of her lifestyle revealed that she had a highly critical and rejecting mother as well as an absent father. Therefore, she decided that she was going to do what she could to "give my son everything." As a result, she feels guilty saying no or setting any appropriate boundaries with him. The clinician suggested that she was motivated out of a sincere desire to give her son more affection than she got as a child, and recommended some simple parenting skills (setting limits, natural and logical consequences) that would help with her son's behaviors. The client replied by saying, "Oh, that sounds like a good idea, but I am not sure if it will work." At which point, the clinician identified that she was using a "yes . . . but" response and was rejecting his suggestion. The counselor determined that neither his interpretation nor his understanding of the presenting problem was wrong, so he decided to use a paradoxical intervention to help the client see her role in her son's behavior (as well as her role in ending it). The therapist said "Well, I can see how you are concerned about how your actions will be perceived by your son if you try to set some limits, but I wonder what is more cruel as a parent: being cold and rejecting like your parents, or purposely denying the child the skills for making friends and getting along with others as you are doing? While I believe that you feel that you are doing the right thing, I am afraid that it may have some unintended consequences, and all the things that you think are helping are really hurting him." Somewhat indignant, the client challenged the therapist: "What do you mean? How can what I am doing *hurt* him? I am a loving mother!" The therapist responded: "Well let's look at it this way, I mean, if he never learns that there are consequences for his behavior, he will always demand his way. His friends, teachers, coworkers, and others won't treat him the way you do. By denying him the skills to work with other people, he will probably go through life feeling pretty miserable. However, it is your decision about how you want to handle this situation: feel comfortable by not setting limits and denying him these skills, or face your discomfort, help him learn skills for negotiating, and maybe even improve his behavior. But I am not sure you are ready to hear this right now. I suspect that you will ignore my comments here, but in the long run, it's your choice about what you will do."

In the case example above, the paradoxical intervention revealed the double-bind by (a) describing the behavior (not wanting to set limits); (b) the purpose of the behavior (avoid discomfort of son being disappointed and rejecting her); (c) the likely consequence of her maintaining the behavior (son is unable to learn to work with others and leads a miserable life because she won't parent him); and (d) that it was ultimately her choice and that she cannot go back to being ignorant (i.e., if she decides to keep doing what she has always done, she now knows that it is detrimental to her son, and not loving as she once thought).

Regarding Clinical Case Example 5.5, how is it that the therapist can make these "predictions," and what is the therapeutic benefit of doing so? First, the therapist reasonably knew something about the general dynamics of an overprotective mother. Being perfectionistic by nature, she wanted to be "right" and make the "right" decisions and choices for her son. The problem was that *what* she was doing and the way that she saw the situation was making things potentially worse! Second, the therapist drew on the strength of the solid therapeutic alliance and an understanding of the client's schema dynamics. Because the client has been told ("predicted") that she would probably ignore his suggestion, she can either prove the therapist correct and continue to be overprotective or "prove" the therapist wrong by beginning to set limits with the son and letting him experience negative consequences. In effect, this would represent a new experience (on the emotional level) for the client and would be a change in her inflexible response to her son. In addition, she will know that the therapist understands her and her problem, thus enhancing the relationship (an example of "tuning forks" vibrating in synch with one another, see Mozdzierz, Peluso, & Lisiecki, 2014, for details).

Master Example 5.2: But Don't Take Our Word for It!

In this transcript, master clinician and author *Bradford Keeney* is interviewing a female client who is struggling with her relationship with her husband. In this brief exchange, he begins to uncover some hidden talents (and power) that the client has (Alexander Street Press, 2012).

Bradford Keeney: Okay, have you made a decision what you're gonna do or you still . . .
Client: Oh, no I haven't made any decisions.
Bradford Keeney: So you're just really just wondering.
Client: . . . I used to take him to work to the train because I want him to go to work because I need that money right now. He said "I don't know what's going to happen." I can't have him losing his job, you know I mean like he is . . . doesn't make really good money, my money is I don't know what happens to it . . . it goes to the babysitter actually, she makes (inaudible) more than I do, but I like what I do, I work with handicapped people. I totally get into that.
Bradford Keeney: So everything in your life is being this wonderful mother.
Client: Well, I don't want to seem to put myself all up and push him down.
Bradford Keeney: But you see the dilemma, can you see the dilemma that's shaping itself up, and clearly everything you say confirms my hypothesis that . . . that you have fabulous mothering skills working with handicapped people, the concern you have about your own daughter, the . . . the ways in which I think he behaves are not only bringing a lot of pain and suffering to you, but in a crazy way, it's his way of . . . of acknowledging that you are a skilled mother, otherwise he wouldn't be presenting you a childlike behavior.
Client: Maybe.
Bradford Keeney: Yeah, so it's almost like he is saying, "I see that you are this great mother let me throw all this childish stuff at you and you mother me through it." Now the dilemma is that now that you know this is a mess . . .

Client: After you pointed it out, I can see it or maybe the reason why we're together is maybe as I will help him to straighten out and turn to a man . . .

Bradford Keeney: It's bizarre because he is complimenting you when he behaves this way, complimenting your skill as a mother, but it . . . it's a very crazy way of doing it. And I would say in some way since you are very bent on being a keen analyst of things, let's put our thinking detective hats on because I think that possibly this business of the drinking starting at that . . . at that funeral, like a "wake" in some way, it has signaled that he wants part of this childish behavior of his own to go away, to die, to pass.

Client: Yes, I think he does. I really do.

Bradford Keeney: So let's tie it together.

By predicting a characteristic pattern based on an understanding of the dynamics of a particular person's "logic" and past performance, the client is "challenged" by being exposed through Socratic questioning to other therapeutic possibilities. Such prognostications tend to dampen the impact of their occurrence—should they occur, that is. In the abstract, predictions can be used to predict an attitude, thought, feeling, behavior, and way of seeing things. In the concrete, it can be used to predict relapses, an unhappy weekend pass from the hospital, a quarrel with a family member between sessions, being late for appointments, and a disappointing vacation, but it can also be used to predict such things as loss of a job and being suspicious of new surroundings and/or people. It is paradoxical because it is absurd to predict (essentially, "bet on") what a client will do. In the example with Keeney, he predicts that she will continue to use her "mothering skills" with her husband, and he uses it to leverage a change in her behavior, by seeing the pattern or double-bind she is in (e.g., [1] Husband says: "I want you to take care of me." [2] He gets drunk and says (in effect): "I don't need anyone's help!" [3] He says: "How could you think of leaving me!"). That is, it can be used to predict any behavior with which a client is symptomatically involved. It becomes the closest thing to magic in therapy, and makes master therapists *look* like master sorcerers.

Master Example 5.3: But Don't Take Our Word for It!

In this transcript, master clinician and author *Michael Yapko* is interviewing a male client who is struggling with feeling inadequate (Alexander Street Press, 2012).

Mike: I can be whoever I wanna be. Or do whatever I wanna do, you know. Um—

Michael D. Yapko: There will always be people who tell you can't.

Mike: Yeah.

Michael D. Yapko: What're you gonna do?

Even in this brief example, Yapko is using a "gentle" prediction to stimulate the client's thinking and planning for when he might meet resistance from other people in his life. As an ending note, if a client does exactly as predicted, it can generate credibility in the therapist and the therapy so that more productive work can be accomplished. If the client is challenging in response to having succumbed to the prediction, the therapist can respond by stating that his behavior was predictable because he simply doesn't appear to be ready for the next step in the stages of change process. If the client doesn't behave as predicted, it demonstrates that he has the capacity to break a pattern of behavior and disengage. As Mozdzierz, Macchitelli, and Lisiecki (1976) stated,

> Viewed within this context, a paradoxical strategy employed by a therapist is a means of transforming the patient's symptomatic asocial uncooperative behavior into a cooperative venture between the patient and the therapist. . . . If the patient rebels against the therapist, he abandons the symptomatic behavior that was unconsciously designed to preclude cooperation, and he cooperatively participates in society. If the patient persists in the symptomatic behavior, he does so while cooperating with the therapist. *The patient wins* (cooperative participation) *either way.*
>
> (p. 173, emphasis added)

Either way the client wins, and *that's* nonlinear!

Positive Provocation

At first glance, it would appear that the term *positive provocation* is an oxymoron. How can something be positive and provocative at the same time? It is exactly in the *combination* of being *supportive, respectful, and genuine* and simultaneously *confrontational* that the paradoxical nature of both the intervention *and* therapeutic benefit lies (two truths that cannot simultaneously coexist, but do, etc.). We caution the reader with regard to the use of "confrontation" in treatment. In fact, it is probably more accurate to use the verb form ("confronting"). *Confronting is a process of directing someone's attention to something that she potentially avoids looking at (either deliberately or unconsciously).* The qualifier *potentially* is used because therapists of necessity have *limited certainty* about being accurate in their formulation of exactly what it is that a client may be avoiding. Confronting is often thought of as "holding up a mirror" to a client and *asking* her to look at or "bring to light" something that she appears to be avoiding. According to Hanna (2001),

> Confronting is the function of actively observing and closely scrutinizing a problem, issue, thought, behavior, emotion, person, situation, or relationship. The person uses his or her attention and powers of viewing to look into, through and even beyond a problem or issue . . . In terms of the actual change process, confronting involves an intentional, sustained, and deliberate directing of attention or awareness toward anything that is painful, intimidating, or stultifying. It involves continuing to

examine or investigate—"digging in one's heels"—in spite of fear, confusion, or the tendency toward avoiding or acting out. Almost anything at all can be confronted: mental images, memories, emotional pain, behaviors of all varieties, thoughts, thought patterns, beliefs, persons, places, objects, and relationships.

(p. 71)

The biggest concern about the use of *confronting* is practitioners' misunderstanding regarding its therapeutic meaning and intent. To begin with, *confronting* is mistaken for *confrontation*. Synonyms for *confrontation* are nouns such as *quarrel, argument, war of words,* and *conflict*. Unfortunately, all of these synonyms suggest pejorative and aggressive images of being "in your face." Therapist behaviors that suggest being *confrontational* (i.e., deliberately or unintentionally aggressive or hostile in nature) ultimately demonstrate that they are decidedly counterproductive, and born of ill-conceived therapist motivations (e.g., frustration or anger), or misguided intentions (e.g., attempting to "force change"). Being confrontational suggests therapist motivations whose purpose is most likely to prevail over a client (e.g., insisting to be "right") regarding an issue under discussion. This is counterproductive for any therapeutic endeavor (Horvath & Bedi, 2002). From the therapist's superior position of power and authority, confrontational behavior places a client in a "one-down" position—a place from which it is difficult to feel like cooperating. Thus, *extreme caution* is urged regarding practitioners' understanding and use of *confronting*.

To illustrate the care that must be taken regarding the difference between confronting and being confrontational, Miller, Benefield, and Tonigan (1993) found that

specific and observed therapist behaviors commonly associated with the term *confrontational* were found to predict poorer outcomes for problem drinkers. These findings are consistent with earlier reports that a directive-confrontational style evokes client resistance (Patterson & Forgatch, 1985) and is associated with unfavorable outcomes in treating alcohol problems (Miller et al., 1980; Valle, 1981). Indeed, the level of client resistance evoked during a treatment session appeared to be negatively related to long-term treatment success.

(p. 460)

In studying the differential effects of therapist style in treating problem drinkers, Miller et al. (1993) also noted, "Therapist styles did not differ in overall impact on drinking, but a single therapist behavior was predictive ($r = .65$) of 1-year outcome such that the more the therapist confronted, the more the client drank" (p. 455). Finally, Norcross and Wampold (2011) found that confrontation (as a style) has been demonstrated to have a negative effect on the therapeutic alliance and client outcome. Despite how this looks, however, these are not contradictory findings according to Hanna (2001), who notes that almost all modalities of psychotherapy confront clients in some way. Miller et al. (1993) appeared to have the most cogent rationale for understanding this exceptionally important issue: "confrontation literally means 'to bring face to face,' which does not necessarily mean going head to head. To confront is to help another person face the facts. In this sense, confrontation is a *goal* rather than a therapeutic procedure" (p. 460).

As might be suspected, intervening with positive provocation requires considerable reflection about the essential elements of any intervention. Where is the client stuck? What are the complaints? In light of the client's complaint, what objectives would the therapist like to accomplish to stimulate therapeutic movement? What does a therapist expect to accomplish by any therapeutic comment or other intervention? Engaging the client in a Socratic dialogue is a way to positively provoke them to see that their opinions or beliefs are not necessarily reflective of the reality of the situation. Advanced nonlinear listening is crucial in such instances, as the client will report that there are things that she is not doing that she wants to do or things that she should be doing but can't seem to get done. On the other hand, she may report she is doing things that she doesn't want to do. In addition, such clients often report that they can't control certain symptoms such as anxiety, depression, nervousness, insomnia, and so forth. These are the signature characteristics of ambivalence and the schema dynamics underlying that ambivalence. It sends the message, "I want this to stop. I want to get off!" but the client doesn't see how. Using advanced nonlinear thinking elements like clarifying values and using inductive reasoning can help positively "provoke" clients to take a different look at themselves.

Therapists frequently find themselves at a loss as to what to do about such complaints and impasses. At the same time, those complaints and impasses keep coming up. But, if the therapist begins to question how the complaint can be broached and not broached at the same time, certain "answers" typically arise as to how to stimulate therapeutic *movement* (i.e., not "cures") by being provocatively supportive. We hope to elaborate an understanding of this by the following examples.

Master Example 5.4: But Don't Take Our Word for It!

In this example, master clinician *Jon Carlson* works with a couple who are having relationship difficulties. In this brief segment, the couple discusses their ongoing conflict. Carlson introduces the idea of another motivation for the conflict (Alexander Street Press, 2012).

Jon Carlson: So how does that work for you, guys?
Leslie: It doesn't work.
Scott: No, it's not working at all.
Jon Carlson: Well, it works in some way, though. We usually do things that somehow work for us.
Scott: It's vented. It's venting on my part.
Jon Carlson: I mean, so how would, what would be different if, uhm, you know, this problem wasn't there anymore?
Scott: Like?
Leslie: On this new, this problem. (crosstalk)

Jon Carlson: No, no, no. I don't mean the one that you were talking about. But the way that you dealt with one another. So, if you were to wake up in the morning and his anger was gone or your attitude was gone, then what?

Leslie: Things would be very different.

Jon Carlson: How so?

Scott: Hmm. I'd be easier to live with.

Jon Carlson: Well?

Leslie: It's a mutual feeling. (laughter)

Jon Carlson: Huh?

Leslie: I said it's a mutual feeling. It's, it's hard living with somebody with a temper. (crosstalk)

Jon Carlson: Well, okay, so the advantage of this then is that you live in struggle? There's always a struggle that you, you don't have an easy life?

Scott: I wouldn't say always. But a lot of times, there's a struggle.

Jon Carlson: Uh-huh. So, that's why you do this? To keep life interesting?

Scott: No.

Leslie: No.

Scott: No. It's just, it's, it's kept interesting because this happens.

Leslie: I wish, I wish we could all change. That's what I want.

Jon Carlson: But, but then you'd have to be close together.

Leslie: What do you mean?

Jon Carlson: Well, if you weren't acting like this, wouldn't you be very close together with one another?

Leslie: We probably would be.

Jon Carlson: Would that be a good thing?

In this example, Carlson demonstrates several advanced nonlinear thinking elements that facilitate the positive provocation challenge paradoxical intervention. Specifically, he uses that Socratic method and inductive reasoning to work through the couple's interpretation and motivation for the current state of affairs. First he asks two "application questions" ("I mean, so how would, what would be different if, uhm, you know, this problem wasn't there anymore?" and "So, if you were to wake up in the morning and his anger was gone or your attitude was gone, then what?"). Then he followed with an interpretation question ("So, that's why you do this? To keep life interesting?"). Next, he asked them a synthesis question ("Well, if you weren't acting like this, wouldn't you be very close together with one another?"). Finally, when he asked an evaluation question ("Would that be a good thing?"), which helped to cement challenger paradoxical intervention and clarify the clients' values. This will help them to be able to address their conflict constructively and take a new perspective on it.

Next, consider this example from master practitioner Steve Andreas. See if you can identify the types of Socratic questioning that he uses to positively provoke the client to challenge her behavior and beliefs about her ex-boyfriend.

Master Example 5.5: But Don't Take Our Word for It!

In this example of a transcript with a master practitioner, *Steve Andreas* (creator of Neurolingusitic Programming, NLP), works with a woman who is dealing with her anger issues at everyone else, but herself (Alexander Street Press, 2012).

Steven Andreas: Now, how . . . how long did you know this person?
Melissa: Eight months.
Steven Andreas: Eight months! So you know him pretty well?
Melissa: I thought I did.
Steven Andreas: Well, now you know him better.
Melissa: Yeah!
Steven Andreas: Not in the way you wanted, but now you know him better. Usually in blame, there is a presupposition that he could have done differently.
Melissa: Yeah!
Steven Andreas: Now, I think maybe with some therapy or some knock alongside of the head or something like that, he could probably do differently?
Melissa: Probably.
Steven Andreas: But, at this time he was who he was, he did what he did and you needed to maintain your values, whatever went on violated your values, right? And you needed to, sorry, this is it. Can you understand that he couldn't have done any different than he did?
Melissa: No!
Steven Andreas: Okay! Can you think of sometime in the past when you harmed someone else? Maybe telling unintentionally or whatever and now looking back on it I assume you've some regret, alright?
Melissa: Hmm . . . hmm . . .
Steven Andreas: Now, at the moment that you harm them, could you've done anything different?
Melissa: Yeah!
Steven Andreas: I don't think so. This is for your self-forgiveness that . . . I have the idea, crazy or not, that everybody always does the best they can, given their knowledge, given their background, given their habits, their economics, and so on. People make the best choices they can at the time. Then I think that you made the best choice you could at that time, given what you knew at that moment, even though it resulted in harming someone?
Melissa: Yeah!

Again, Andreas (like Carlson) uses Socratic questioning to challenge the client via positive provocation. What is notable in *both* examples is how neither of them have to be *confrontational* in order to confront the clients! Yet, by using advanced nonlinear thinking and paradoxical interventions, they are both able to be successful in challenging the clients—who held some firmly entrenched ideas—that they needed to take another look at their beliefs. This kind of reappraisal is the first step to getting the client to make lasting, structural, second-order change.

Conclusion

The use of challengers is often considered when clients have taken entrenched, extreme, and oppositional positions toward life and others as a means of problem solving. As with all of the challengers, but especially with positive provocation, the client is in effect saying to the therapist, "No one (and you neither, Ms. Therapist) can make me give this up (i.e., a symptomatic behavior) or make me do this!" The "irritation" of provocation in particular and the challengers in general provide patients with strong medicine in the service of a need to help them to "disengage" themselves from very maladaptive entrenched behavioral, attitudinal, or emotional "solutions" when they are unable to do so. In the real world of seemingly impossible clients, therapists create conditions that stimulate change to occur with their clients, they burn out and clients terminate therapy prematurely, or therapy wanders somewhat aimlessly. This is why we believe that nonlinear paradoxical thinking is the essence of thinking like a master therapist and why it is a convergence factor and domain for all successful therapies across schools of psychotherapy. In the next chapter, we will extend this idea and incorporate one other, special case of paradoxical interventions: the use of humor in therapy.

Note

1. The curious reader may wonder, "What ever happened to the pee bucket?" Well, we might have responded that some things are simply better off left as is! Nevertheless, there was follow-up over a longer period of time with this woman. In fact, over the next 4 years, she would occasionally encounter the psychologist, who would ask about her son. When the young man turned 17 years of age, he enlisted in the military with his mother's permission. While serving his country, he completed his high school education with a GED and subsequently fulfilled his military service with distinction. *We can only assume that he had no further need for the bucket!*

6   Humor in Therapy

A Special Case of Paradoxical Intervention

Humor is reason gone mad.
—Groucho Marx

Humor: Linking the Tragic to the Comic

There may be no more enduring symbol in all of human history as the symbol for the-
atre: the twin masks. One mask is in the form of a frown or crying face—tragedy—while
the other one is smiling, or in the form of a laughing face—comedy. They symbolize the
relationship between the tragic and the comic. For many performers and writers, it is
not possible to have one without the other. In fact, in Greek mythology, Melpomene (the
muse of tragedy) and Thalia (the muse of comedy) are sisters—daughters of Zeus and
Mnemosyne (the goddess of memory). Thus, comedy and tragedy are intertwined and
at the same time rooted in memory! Literature and theater are full of allusions to this
relationship, from Paglicci the operatic clown who cries to modern-day comedians. In
fact, film critic Roger Ebert reflected this when he discussed actor and comedian Rodney
Dangerfield:

> Yet in Dangerfield, there has always been something else in addition to the come-
> dian. This is a man who has failed at everything, even comedy. Rodney Dangerfield
> is his third name in show business; he flopped under two earlier names as well as
> his real name. Who is really at home inside that red, sweating face and that know-
> ing leer? The most interesting thing about "Back to School," which is otherwise a
> pleasant but routine comedy, is the puzzle of Rodney Dangerfield. Here is a man
> who reminds us of some of the great comedians of the early days of the talkies—of
> Groucho Marx and W. C. Fields—because, like them, he projects a certain mystery.
> Marx and Fields were never just being funny. There was the sense that they were
> getting even for hurts so deep that all they could do was laugh about them. It's the
> same with Dangerfield.
>
> (Ebert, n.d.)

Some of the greatest comedians had a "dark side," and many of them suffered from
depression, addictions, and other mental illnesses. Often it is that contact with the pain
and suffering of life that allows the comedian to make humorous observations from it.

So it is no wonder that in a book devoted to teaching the advanced elements of counseling and psychotherapy, we would also discuss the use of humor. Not just because humor is healing in and of itself (which it is), or that it helps to build the therapeutic alliance (which it does), but because of its *structural* relationship to pain. In fact, the Greek word for pain and suffering—pathos—is at the heart of the term psycho*patho*logy (or mental illness). But, what you might not know is that pathos also refers to an appeal to an audience's emotions in order to persuade them. This is done in theatrical performances by actors' passion in delivering their lines in character (getting the audience to *feel* that they are the character). Pathos is also used in storytelling or narrative through the use of metaphors to relate an idea or concept that is being communicated to the audience or reader. In fact, Aristotle wrote that the purpose of pathos was to awaken emotion in the audience "so as to induce them to make the judgment desired." So, much like the process of "inception" (see Chapter 1), the use of inductive reasoning, and Socratic questioning, humor can be used to create pathos in clients as a form of advanced nonlinear thinking in order to help with psychopathology! It is why we believe that humor is a special case of paradoxical intervention, which we will detail later in this chapter. We will provide some examples of humor (jokes and riddles), and some clinical examples of humor in therapy throughout the chapter. But first, we wish to consider what *is* humor, and *how* it works.

Why and How Humor Works

> Humor can be dissected as a frog can, but the thing dies in the process and the innards are discouraging to any but the pure scientific mind.
> —E. B. White (White & White, 1941)

With E. B. White's quote in mind, we wish to present a brief "dissection" of humor (hopefully without the outcome he predicted, *or* without boring the reader in the process). The Oxford English Dictionary (2007, p. 1294) defines humor as "the faculty of perceiving and enjoying what is ludicrous or amusing." It differs from mockery or sarcasm, which are associated with a lack of caring, or outright contempt, for the person being mocked or belittled (Panichelli, 2013). Humor is also defined as the capacity to appreciate and derive some pleasure from things that are incongruous, ludicrous, ridiculous, absurd, or unexpected; in other words, anything that is funny and amusing. Humor and laughter are natural mechanisms that help one to confront the often harsh realities in daily life (Abrami, 2009). Humor is a universal human experience that is cross-cultural and can facilitate attachment relationships with other people (Gelkopf, 2011). It is also a tool for peeling back the absurdity of things by distorting or making absurd observations about them. Doing so often reveals a hidden truth that can provoke a person to reflect on the subject matter. However, for humor to work, it needs two crucial definitional elements: incongruity and timing.

Incongruity

How humor manages to create surprise and an alternative point of view is a subject that could fill volumes. We will try to succinctly discuss it here. One theory suggests that first, for humor to work, it requires some form of tension of a build-up. Then a resolution that is often unexpected or incongruous. Therefore, the theory of incongruity-resolution analyzes the processing of the "forced reinterpretation jokes" (Ritchie, 2006, p. 253): The audience hears the story of the joke up to the punch line, which contains an incongruity that forces it consider an unexpected interpretation of the beginning (p. 443). Take the following joke for example: *"I once bet on a horse that went off at twenty-to-one. He came in at half-past four!"* There is a violation of the internal logic of the joke. In the first statement (the setup to the joke), "twenty-to-one" refers to the odds of the bet (you'd win 20 dollars for every 1 dollar bet if the horse wins). The second statement (the punch line) suggests that the horse was so slow, it didn't finish the race until 4:30 pm ("half-past four"), which then forces a reevaluation of the original setup (twenty-to-one could also refer to time, or 12:40 pm), which then provides the humor (the horse that was bet on was *so* slow it took almost 4 hours to finish the race). The incongruity comes from the double meaning that is in the first line ("twenty-to-one" could refer to the time 12:40 pm *or* the odds 20:1), and the humor comes from the fact that it means *both at the same time!* This is called bisociation. Bisociation is defined as a collision and combination between two independent ideas in that thinking process (Makoto, 2011).

Take this common therapist joke: *How many psychotherapists does it take to change a light bulb?* The answer? *One, but the light bulb has to want to change!* The bisociation here is that, within the question, there are two ways to consider how to answer. The first way of thinking about it is in terms of the actual exchange of one burned-out bulb for a functioning bulb. Logically that should just take one person. However, the answer belies something else. It introduces the idea of change as in to change one's behavior, and forces a reinterpretation of the premise of the joke. The humor comes from the incongruity that (a) a psychotherapist would use therapeutic techniques to try to "change" a light bulb and that (b) the light bulb would have to *want* to change (which is absurd, since it is inanimate, that wouldn't happen). It is the ambiguity of language, in this case the word *change* that allows for the bisociation collision from two levels to occur (physically changing the bulb vs. psychotherapeutically changing the bulb). By the way, do you know what the best therapeutic approach is to take with light bulbs? Electro-shock therapy! (BA-DUM-BUM!)

On the other hand, there is also an emotional/affective component to humor. That is, we propose that *incongruity* is what makes things unique, different, unusual, and in effect, emotionally stimulating and appealing. As Dingfelter (2011) puts it,

> ... the idea that incongruity—when an idea or an object is out of place—is the heart of humor. . . . Truth plays an important role as well: *The juxtaposition of the two things often gives people a new insight into a familiar situation,* he notes. In fact, much of the enjoyment of humor may come from seeing familiar situations with new eyes.
>
> (p. 55, emphasis added)

Our human brain is addicted to novelty (McClure, Laibson, Loewenstein, & Cohen, 2004; Mikulciner & Shaver, 2005; Thornton, 2006). It draws our attention much like a magnet draws metal objects to itself. Such *differentness, incongruity, absurdity, uniqueness, etc. are attractive to the brain and its appraisal system*—especially given two contexts in which it can occur. The first context is that the differentness, incongruity, absurdity, etc. are *unexpected*. The second context is reciprocally related to the first. That is, the brain and human psyche are constantly being saturated with "normal" cognitive, logical repetitiveness of the physical world. The attractiveness of the absurd, incongruous, etc. (most often born of unexpectedness) becomes the essence of varying degrees of "amusing," interesting, and even exhilarating *emotional* stimulation for the brain (and in turn the troubled soul).[1] The amusement and exhilaration in something humorous, then, is that it doesn't follow logically the way the physical world logically operates, and therefore, it is different, unique, or unusual. It is that differentness that makes for the amusement that the brain is attracted to and enjoys as "humor" (we will discuss the role that the brain plays in humor later in this chapter). In turn, humor can be amusing, funny, or so outrageously or raucously funny as to defy description.

Timing

While understanding *how* humor works, knowing *when* humor will work is another matter altogether. This is the essence of *timing*. The ancient Greeks actually had two different meanings associated with the concept of time. Obviously, there is chronological time as measured in everyday use in nanoseconds, seconds, minutes, hours, etc. Chronological time stems from the Greek word *chronos* and also refers to our understanding of the past, present, and future. The second meaning that the Greeks had regarding the concept of time concerns the word *kairos,* which means the *right* or *supreme* moment. The meaning associated with the concept kairos approximates what it is that is involved in offering a client a new dialectical meaning to their troubling circumstances, complaint, thoughts, feelings, etc. Kairos refers to a moment of indeterminate time in which something special happens—it is qualitative in nature (White, 1987).

For professional comedians and amateurs, the concept of timing is crucial. If the delivery of a joke is too early or too late, the humor (no matter how incongruous or witty) will not make sense or could be in poor taste! Consider the following joke: A researcher looking into the sexual habits of airline pilots goes to the airport and interviews a pilot asking: "When was the last time you had intercourse?" The pilot replies: "Nineteen Fifty." The researcher is astonished and says: "You mean you haven't been with someone since then?" The pilot says, "Well, it's only 22:00 hours!" Now, at the right time, this joke may be funny. But suppose that just prior to telling the joke the person you were telling the joke told you that she had a family member die in a plane crash or that her husband was a pilot? The joke no longer seems funny because the timing is not right.

These conceptualizations of time are useful for clinicians in general. Clients in session operate and interface with the chronos definition of time when they tell their story, or recount events that have occurred to them. At the same time, when they have to make decisions about what they should do, or what they should *not* do, they operate within the definition of kairos. This seems to encapsulate significant aspects of what clients experience. The discomfort associated with a client being "stuck" with their dilemma and vacillating back and forth between wanting to be rid of something and at the same time holding on to it can be incredibly painful and totally absorbing. Clinicians must be aware of the twin meanings of time as well. The very *moment* (i.e., chronos) when a client is so absorbed, preoccupied, or feeling totally stuck with their quandary and its pain in many ways represents the "opportune moment" (i.e., kairos) for the therapist to suggest an alternative interpretation of the same set of facts. Sometimes, helping a client to see that part of their problem is that they are trying to make a decision when it is not yet time to make the decision can be liberating. Several of the tranquilizer paradoxical interventions are based on this idea (e.g., permission, prohibition, postponement, etc.). Suggesting an alternative *meaning* offers the client a way to relieve his or her agony by *reappraising* the meaning of what he or she originally believed. Humor can "soften" the blow of a reappraisal and provide the client with an easy interpretation (or reinterpretation) of their situation. However, there is a proper time and place for these kind of humorous reappraisals. If they are not done right, it could come off badly (as arrogant, sarcastic, or mocking). This would interfere with the therapeutic relationship and jeopardize the therapy altogether.

Brief Nonlinear Thinking Exercise

Speaking of time, here is a quick, nonlinear thinking exercise. We measure our time of day based on the rotation of the Earth, and the Sun's transit across the sky. Hours, minutes, and days are all measures that depend on it. So, consider the following statement: *What time is it on the surface of the Sun? How do you know when a day begins and ends? How would you be able to measure it?*

Benefits of Humor

A Short History of Medicine

Doctor, I have an ear ache.
bc 2000—"Here, eat this root."
bc 1000—"That root is heathen, say this prayer."
1850 ad—"That prayer is superstition, drink this potion."
1940 ad—"That potion is snake oil, swallow this pill."
1985 ad—"That pill is ineffective, take this antibiotic."
2000 ad—"That antibiotic is artificial. Here, eat this root!"

Although the scientific study of humor is not very old, or vast, research findings spanning the last 30 years have been interpreted to suggest that there is a linkage between humor and good health. Some of the specific benefits include pain relief, strengthened immune responses, improved positive emotional states, moderation of stress, and better interpersonal or social relationships (Gelkopf, 2011). The consensus on the general effects of humor on health is that "humor has a broad range of effects on perceptions, attitudes, judgments and emotions, which may mediate directly or indirectly to benefit the physical and psychological state" (Gelkopf, 2011, p. 6).

The Benefits of Laughter

Many researchers have indirectly studied the effect of humor by investigating one of the external responses to humor, namely, laughter. Laughter is the uncontrolled emotional expression that is the result of finding something humorous (Berk, Martin, Baird, & Nozik, 2008; Gelkopf, 2011). Laughter also coincides with a number of additional physical, emotional, social, and cognitive benefits as well (Martin, 2006, 2010). In terms of *physical* benefits, laughter triggers the release of endorphins, the body's natural painkillers, and produces a general sense of well-being. There is some evidence that mirthful laughter in response to humor reduces stress hormones while simultaneously increasing immune cell activity. It increases endorphins and dopamine, as well as blood flow. In turn, laughter is associated with increased relaxation and better sleep. Laughter is also associated with reduced pain sensitivity and reduced stress. In fact, in one study, people with diabetes had lower blood sugar levels after they watched a comedy compared to when they participated in a boring lecture (Abrami, 2009; Berk et al., 2008; Isen, 2003; Martin, 2006, 2010).

In terms of the *emotional* benefits, laughter was correlated with elevated mood and feelings of well-being, reduced depression, anxiety, and tension as well as an increase in self-esteem and resilience. People who laughed more were found to have increased hope, optimism, energy, and vigor. This translates into *social* and relational benefits, such as bonding with friends and family, reinforcement of group identity and cohesiveness, and social behaviors like increased friendliness and altruism. For people who laughed more, they were seen as being more attractive to other people and had happier marriages and close relationships (Berk et al., 2008; Gelkopf, 2011; Isen, 2003; Martin, 2006, 2010; Rust & Goldstein, 1989). Ultimately, it seems that laughter—whether it is laughing out loud, being quietly amused, anticipating something funny, or merely forcing a smile—can all lead to increased positive emotions (or at least neutralize negative emotions), which leads to an "upward spiral" to even greater happiness.

But perhaps most interesting are the *cognitive* benefits. Laughter actually impacts how we *think!* Indeed, laughter was associated with an increased capacity for creativity, improvements in problem-solving abilities, and better memory (especially for humorous material). In addition, laughter increased individuals' ability to cope with stressful situations by providing an alternative, less serious perspective on one's problems (Isen, 2003; Martin, 2002, 2010; Schmidt, 1994). In other words, laughter and humor increase the likelihood of being receptive to advanced nonlinear thinking techniques (for the client), as well as being able to utilize these techniques (as a therapist).

So while there are benefits to humor and laughter in general, what about laughter and humor in therapy? Mora-Ripoll (2010) suggests that

> Laughter has shown physiological, psychological, social, spiritual, and quality-of-life benefits. Adverse effects are very limited, and laughter is practically lacking in contraindications. Therapeutic efficacy of laughter is mainly derived from spontaneous laughter (triggered by external stimuli or positive emotions) and self-induced laughter (triggered by oneself at will), both occurring with or without humor. The brain is not able to distinguish between these types; therefore, it is assumed that similar

benefits may be achieved with one or the other. Although there is not enough data to demonstrate that laughter is an all-around healing agent, this review concludes that there exists sufficient evidence to suggest that laughter has some positive, quantifiable effects on certain aspects of health. In this era of evidence-based medicine, it would be appropriate for laughter to be used as a complementary/alternative medicine in the prevention and treatment of illnesses, although further well-designed research is warranted.

(p. 56)

Gelkopf (2011) agrees with this assessment, suggesting that

[h]umor or laughter is an easy-to-use, inexpensive . . . natural therapeutic modality that could be used within different therapeutic settings, with a multi-professional staff whose impact could, at the least, temporarily alleviate some of the daily distress experienced by the seriously mentally ill.

(p. 6)

However, neither training institutes nor academic departments have put forward a comprehensive method for imparting this information and studying its impact. We will discuss ways to do this therapeutically later in the text, but we wish to focus on the most important organ for humor (and it's not the funny bone!): The brain!

Our Nonlinear Brain: Neurobiology of Humor

They X-rayed my head, and found nothing!
—Yogi Berra (commenting after being hit by a pitch)

Obviously, the brain plays an important role in the understanding, appreciation, and creation of humor, so what have neuroscientists concluded thus far? Wild, Rodden, Grodd, and Ruch (2003) conclude that *expressing laughter as a result of encountering something humorous* seems to depend on two different brain pathways. One of the pathways involves the limbic system, that central location for the processing of emotions. They even refer to this system as "emotionally driven" (Wild et al., 2003, p. 2121). The second pathway seems to involve what they refer to as a "voluntary" system that has more to do with the premotor/frontal and motor areas. Further, they conclude that *for the perception of humor*, the right frontal cortex, ventral medial prefrontal cortex (i.e., the part of the brain responsible for "executive" functioning such as planning, decision making, etc.), and temporal lobe regions seem to be involved in varying degrees.

Bekinschtein, Davis, Rodd, and Owen (2011) compared which parts of the brain are active in jokes that involved ambiguous words compared with sentences containing not funny ambiguous words. They suggest that

. . . temporoparietal junction [TPJ] bilaterally is involved in processing humorous verbal jokes when compared with matched nonhumorous material. In addition, hearing jokes was associated with increased activity in a network of subcortical regions, including the amygdala, the ventral striatum, and the midbrain, that have been implicated in experiencing positive reward. Moreover, activity in these regions correlated with the subjective ratings of funniness of the presented material.

(p. 9665)

Kohn, Kellerman, Gur, Schneider, and Habel (2011) had similar results, as they describe an "integration hub" or "common network for different types of jokes [visual and language-dependent] comprising the ACC [anterior cingulate cortex] and temporo-parietal [junction, or TPJ]" (p. 888). So while there are certain brain structures that are important in processing humor, these areas also have roles to play in other cognitive and emotional processes that are important for therapy: empathy and ambivalence.

Empathy is the "interpersonal sharing of affect" (Jackson, Meltzoff, & Decety, 2005, p. 771). When subjects were asked to evaluate (from pictures) the pain level of people whose hands and feet were in situations likely to cause pain (a key element of empathy). Jackson et al. (2005) found that there were significant bilateral changes in the brain's electrical and metabolic activity in a number of areas, including the anterior cingulate, the anterior insula, the cerebellum, and to a somewhat lesser degree the thalamus. From previous research, it is known that these same regions of the brain participate significantly in pain processing. They also observed that the subjects' ratings of others' pain was strongly correlated with activity in the ACC. They concluded that there is an overlapping of areas in the brain that process perceptions of pain in others and experiences of our own pain. The brain is inherently sensitive to the differences between our own and someone else's pain. Both types of empathy yielded the activation of portions of the neural network that have been demonstrated in pain processing, including the parietal operculum, anterior cingulated cortex, and anterior insula.

In terms of ambivalence, new research has found that it is a much more complex neurobiological phenomenon, with interesting implications for clinicians, as well as for humor. Nohlen, van Harreveld, Rottveel, Lelieveld, and Crone (2013) used fMRI to study subjects in an ambivalence-provoking situation. They looked at regions of the brain that are associated with cognitive tasks (ACC), regions of the brain associated with emotional responses (limbic system), as well as areas of the brain associated with the social brain network (medial prefrontal cortex, posterior cingulate cortex [PCC], TPJ, and the insula region). Recall that these structures were also associated with humor and laughter. The so-called social-brain network is a relatively new discovery in neuroscience that is intriguing researchers, as it is associated with how a person interacts with others in a social context, takes on multiple perspectives, and is influenced by other people. It is not surprising that these regions would also be intricately involved with humor as well.

Finally, there is a "reward" for humor. McGhee (2010a), in summarizing results of the effects of humor, indicated that researchers have identified certain pleasure centers in the brain that are dopamine based. Dopamine is the "feel good" brain neurotransmitter that gives us that pleasurable feeling when we laugh to our hearts' content. McGhee also suggests that humor is but one part of building more positive emotions in our lives that neutralize and reduce feelings of anger and depression.

What does this mean for humor? Well, first you have to be able to imagine another person's plight, which requires empathy (and activation of the ACC). Then you have to be able to process ambiguous information that may be a part of the humorous stimuli. The nature of humor is the incongruity, and TPJ, is related to both the verbal nature of humorous stimuli, and in incongruity resolution that comes when the punch line is delivered and the humor is comprehended (Kohn et al., 2011). Finally, humor generally has a social component to it (even if you are alone, you have to imagine a social setting for most humor), and there is the reinforcement of pleasurable neurotransmitters.

It seems that there is, on a neuroanatomical level, a lot of similarity in these brain structures. It may be that the use of humor in therapy may activate these regions and have a "spillover" effect in changing clients' feelings about their circumstances, or adopting another person's perspective (viz. empathy), or even resolve their own ambivalence that has made it impossible for them to move forward on some area of their life. Therefore, humor may be a powerful, nonlinear tool that accomplishes many of the same things that master practitioners do with more traditional therapeutic interventions (such as paradoxical interventions).

History of Humor and Psychotherapy

> The future ain't what it used to be.
> —Yogi Berra

Laughter and humor have existed in all societies throughout the ages, but the first somewhat cohesive "modern" psychological analysis of it can be found in the work of Sigmund Freud (Gelkopf, 2011). While he (Freud, 1928, 1960) addressed humor as a topic to understand psychologically and not necessarily a behavior/attitude to introduce into treatment, his general observations form the foundation for concern about its use in treatment. As early as 1905, he proposed that humor was a reflection of unconscious emotions, such as underlying anxiety, bitterness, or unspoken hostility. Such unconscious hostile intent is, of course, one of the primary concerns expressed about using humor with troubled individuals whose sensitivities are often already elevated. On the other hand, he made some very careful distinctions between hostile or sexual jokes versus a humor untainted by such hostility or sexuality:

> Humor has in it a *liberating* element. But it has also something fine and elevating, which is lacking in the other two ways of deriving pleasure from intellectual activity. Obviously, what is fine about it is the triumph of narcissism, the ego's victorious assertion of its own vulnerability. It refuses to be hurt by the arrows of reality or to be compelled to suffer. It insists that it is impervious to wounds dealt by the outside world, in fact, that these are merely occasions for affording it pleasure. This last trait is a fundamental characteristic of humor.
>
> (1928, p. 2)

Following Freud's original thinking about humor, Kubie (1971) produced an "early" paper, often quoted, that advocated serious cautions regarding the "destructive potential" of the use of humor in psychotherapy. His concerns follow from a psycho-analytic theoretical frame of reference, but they can be considered the "clinical research" observations of a well-respected clinician. Among his concerns, Kubie cites three major things to worry about: (1) Especially in the hands of inexperienced therapists, humor can be damaging to the therapeutic relationship; (2) when humor is introduced too early in the therapy, it can block a more meaningful exploration of important topics/issues; and (3) humor can cause confusion in "patients" because they may not understand if a therapist is serious, denigrating, joking, or perhaps even covering up (i.e., "masking") his or her own hostilities. Kubie's observations are interesting and can be considered noteworthy at the time of their publication. Since Freud's original theoretical discussion of humor and Kubie's psychoanalytic critique of its use in treatment, numerous authors have attempted to review and consolidate research findings and the understanding of humor in counseling/psychotherapy treatment settings that those research findings reveal. For example, Fry and Salameh (1987) compiled a content rich "handbook" (i.e., a collection of papers) in which numerous authors provide their summaries of and perspectives on multiple aspects of humor, especially as it applies to psychotherapy. Shaughnessy and Wadsworth (1992) provided a "20-year retrospective" citing 67 annotated references on the development of research and theory relevant to the use of humor in psychotherapy beginning in 1970. Today, there are journals and professional organizations that are devoted to the use of humor in therapy. So while the scientific study, comprehensive understanding, and systematic training of clinicians still have a long way to go, the history and level of professional interest in the role of humor in therapy (as well as its reported benefits) indicate that the serious study of humor is no laughing matter! (BA-DUM-BUM!)

Humor and Other Domains

> You can see a lot just by observing.
> —Yogi Berra

A man goes to a therapist. He says he's depressed. He says life seems harsh and cruel. He says he feels all alone in a threatening world, where what lies ahead is vague and uncertain.

The therapist says the treatment is simple. The great clown Terrifini is in town tonight. Go and see him. That should pick you up.

The man bursts into tears: "But doctor . . . I *am* Terrifini!"

In the joke above, the therapist clearly doesn't understand his client, *literally!* He doesn't understand who his client is and doesn't understand how to help him. And that is the whole point of nonlinear thinking and the seven domains of competence: understanding who your client is and how to help them best (Mozdzierz, Peluso, & Lisiecki, 2014). In this text, we have tried to show how the seventh domain, using paradoxical interventions, encompasses all of the prior six domains. In this section, we will demonstrate how the proper use of humor in therapy incorporates many of the elements of the six domains (and later in this chapter, we will detail how it is a special case of the seventh domain).

Humor and Nonlinear Listening and Responding (Domain 1)

The nurturance and development of the use of humor in therapy lay in the sharpening and development of one's *nonlinear listening skills* and sensitivities. For example, *clients* often times introduce humor into the treatment process. The expression "nervous laughter" comes to mind in this regard. Clients perhaps demonstrate such nervous laughter in an effort to neutralize their stresses. It is a difficult process to tell the therapist, who is a stranger, about one's narrative, symptoms, stressors, dilemmas, shortcomings, failures, problems, or ambivalences. A client laughing and smiling about their imperfection can make the telling somewhat more tolerable. Listening and responding to the *presence* of these can be useful. A client may also demonstrate nervous laughter when discussing the fact that the "homework" assignment discussed in the last session was not completed. Humor and laughter can serve the purpose of masking anxiety, blunting its effects, and making one's failure to carry out a homework assignment more tolerable. It is the wise practitioner who recognizes a client's use of humor (either by listening for *congruence, absence, inference,* or *resistance*) as an adaptive coping mechanism even though it can mask other dynamics. When a therapist responds in kind, thus recognizing the client's attempts to cope with the stress of the treatment situation, it can bode well for the relationship. At the very same time, as mentioned earlier, therapists need to be mindful of and cautious in initiating the use of humor early in treatment because of possible client misinterpretation (i.e., perhaps feeling as though he or she is being mocked).

We emphasize that our discussion of humor bears a strong relationship to the essential domains and evidence-based principles described in our introductory text. *Nonlinear responding* is one of the principles emphasized. As a practitioner grows in their knowledge base, experience, and confidence, more and more opportunities for nonlinear responding will make themselves manifest. Of course, before anyone can *respond in a nonlinear way,* they have to be *listening in a nonlinear way!* In order to do so, the therapist has to be open to new ways of relating, being nondefensive, playful, while maintaining a professional context (Gelkopf, 2011; Panichelli, 2013).

Humor and Assessment (Domain 2)

"Humor" and "assessment" don't sound like two words that would naturally go together. However, within the domain of assessment, there *is* a place for humor. First, within the stages of change, while clients in the precontemplation stage may not appreciate humor, humor may be effective in moving a client from one stage to the next (i.e., from the contemplation to preparation stage, or the preparation to the action stage). For example, a therapist says to a client who describes all of the benefits of giving up smoking but can't commit to stopping: "I feel like a 'used car' salesman!" And saying in a salesman's tone: "What do I gotta do to get you to take this baby home!!" The client laughs and says: "How do I know it's not a lemon (or a bad car)!" In other words, through the use of humor and metaphor, the client can express his doubts about success *and* failure.

Humor can also be used to uncover hidden strengths or untapped resources. But perhaps the most powerful element of the domain of assessment is with the *theme* of the client's narrative (Gelkopf, 2011). For example, if a client with a condition that has caused liver damage that will eventually require a transplant (the theme of hopelessness), who is feeling depressed over his situation, also tells you that he is the coach of his son's baseball team, PTA secretary, and organizer of the local neighborhood watch, the therapist may say: "Hmm, I am not sure you *can* be depressed since that takes time. I wonder when you find the *time* to feel depressed?" As long as the relationship is strong between the therapist and client, this type of delivery might work to get the client to see that he is capable *despite* his condition.

Humor and the Therapeutic Relationship (Domain 3)

Humor can be used effectively to help deepen the therapeutic relationship. First, well-timed humor can build "rapport" if the client sees it as "You get me." For example, if a client comes into session and describes how she keeps getting into relationships where she wants to help and care for others (friends, relatives, romantic partners), but winds up getting hurt and betrayed by them. The therapist says "It sounds to me as if you are like 'Little Red Riding Hood' who is taking food to her sick grandma, only to have her be the 'big bad wolf' who devours her." The client laughed and said, "Yeah! It's almost like I should check to see if they have a tail and say, 'Oh my, what big teeth you have!'"

Another way that humor can help to deepen the relationship is through the use of self-deprecating humor. Self-deprecating humor (i.e., gently making fun of one's self) is effective in deepening the relationship because it communicates to the client that the therapist doesn't take himself too seriously. Showing the client that you can laugh at yourself may make it easier for the client to let down her guard and laugh at herself or her circumstances (Gelkopf, 2011). Self-deprecating humor can also be effective in asking questions in a nonthreatening or nonclinical (i.e., sterile) way. For example, a therapist may say "I know this might sound like a 'cheesy' counselor question, but how did that make you feel?" versus saying "And how did that make you feel?" Sometimes equalizing the power between the therapist and the client through the use of self-deprecating humor can really have a positive impact (i.e., like using the "car salesman" tone, etc.).

Humor and Schema Dynamics (Domain 4)

Humor can be used to work with schema dynamics, particularly in accommodating schemas and creating second-order change. In particular, the use of metaphors and inductive reasoning by analogy (part of the Socratic method) in a humorous or ironic way can help clients see the silliness in some of their ideas (Gelkopf, 2011). For example, recall the case of the mother in Chapter 5 who was disappointed that her young adult sons, who came home to visit, preferred going out to party with friends rather than have a "night in" with their mother. When the therapist jokingly "weighed" the options in an exaggerated manner with the palms of his hands illustrating the process of "weighing" the value of each alternative, the client was able to break out of her "one and only" way of viewing the situation. She was able to knowingly smile and relate to being young, carefree, and wanting to spend time with friends. As a result, she was able to be more flexible about the situation.

Humor and Emotions (Domain 5)

Humor can't be used to help with a client's emotional state. KIDDING! Of course it can! This chapter (and much of this book) has been devoted to this idea, so we will not dwell on it here. One area to consider, however, is how humor can be used to direct the session or the client toward being mindful (by pointing out some of the ironies of their life, see below), but it also can be used to *distract*. Sometimes the distractions might be bad (when the client wants to avoid a particular subject), while other times they may be good (when a client needs to be "neutralized" or "tranquilized" by a paradoxical intervention). Using sound clinical judgment and advanced nonlinear thinking are crucial to knowing the differences (Gelkopf, 2011).

Humor and Resolving Ambivalence (Domain 6)

Using humor to resolve client ambivalence, particularly double-binds, is extremely powerful. Just as with second-order change in schema dynamics above, humor can get a person who feels "trapped" by their circumstances and their schema dynamics to "take a second look" and instantly re-evaluate the logic of their problem (Gelkopf, 2011). For example, a client in the middle of a bitter divorce, and the mother of a 12-year-old boy, complained that her ex-husband gave their son some tools that she considered dangerous and had expressly forbidden. She was equally upset that her son had hidden them from her. She was angry at her ex-husband for defying her, and just as angry at her son. She was vacillating that she wanted to punish her son but didn't want to be the "bad guy" and that she wanted to confront her husband but knew that he would potentially delay his child support money that she depended on. She was very angry and upset that she was being forced into this position. The therapist had worked with her on managing these issues before, and she had been able to successfully negotiate her disagreements. However this time, while he empathized with her plight, he added: "And do you know who is the innocent victim here?" The client responded, was it her son, or herself? "No!" said the therapist. "The real victims here are the Ax, the Knife, and the Saw! I mean, what did THEY ever do to anybody, and now they are getting blamed!" The client laughed out loud at the absurdity of the comment, and agreed. She then began to brainstorm solutions that would be in line with her values. While the therapist could have tried to "reason" with the client, or dispute her cognitions, using humor to break away from the double-bind was a creative and healthy way to resolve her feelings of ambivalence.

Humor and Irony

A woman went to see a psychotherapist and said she was troubled by having no friends.

The therapist asked, "What do you think might be causing the problem?"

The woman said, "That's what I'm paying you to tell me, of course! What? Are you lazy and want me to do your job for you? If I knew already, I wouldn't be here, would I? You fat ugly slob!"

In Chapter 2, we discussed the corresponding clinician disposition for paradoxical interventions: irony. And just as humor is a special case of paradoxical intervention (see below), so too, does irony relate to the appreciation and use of humor. Irony is humor that occurs because the *opposite* of what you expect to happen, happens. For example, gunpowder was invented by Chinese alchemists who were looking for an "elixir of eternal life." Instead they invented one of the most potent instruments of death, responsible for warfare and killing throughout the ages (Kelley, 2009). If you were surprised or chuckled at that fact, then you have demonstrated an example of the appreciation of irony. It means understanding the sometimes cruel or painful parts of life and choosing to see the humor, or at least incongruity of it.

In fact, irony is often the product of a person's schema dynamics (view of self, view of others, or view of the world), especially if they are too rigidly and unrealistically applied. For example, a person who has a negative view of others and is suspicious may notice one week that his coworkers start to talk in hushed tones when he comes by. When he asks what is going on, nobody wants to say anything to him. Ultimately, he can't stand it and goes into his boss's office and threatens to file a hostile workplace complaint, only to find that his coworkers have been organizing a surprise party (which is now ruined). Or in the joke above, the irony (and the humor of the punch line) is that the client doesn't realize that *she* is the cause of her problem. In either case, the schema dynamics force a client to behave in a way that they *think* will help them but, in the end, will only hurt them.

Sometimes, however, clients come in with the sense of irony (sometimes thought of a "dark" or "gallows humor"). According to author Kurt Vonnegut (1971), gallows humor is a witticism in the face of—and in response to—a situation that seems hopeless (like death, war, etc.). While this may reflect extreme discouragement, there may also be an indication of some strength in the client to make a joke during such times. For example, a client who was preparing to get married for a third time (even after a very bitter divorce) wryly said: "What can I say, doc? I'm a romantic who wants to believe in marriage! Of course, I oughta start off by giving her the house and half my bank account, since that's how it usually ends up!" A nonlinear thinking therapist can use the humor to acknowledge the client's pain, sympathize with the seeming hopelessness of the circumstance, and align with the implied defiance to not let the situation defeat them (Casadei & Giordani, 2008). In several of the examples that have been presented in this book, and in several to follow, there have been expressions of "gallows" humor. Try to pick them out and see how clinicians may have used them to help the client understand their behavior or circumstance.

Nonlinear Thinking Exercise: Riddles!

A riddle is a type of puzzle to be solved that consists of a question or phrase that has a double meaning or a hidden meaning. Answering riddles requires the individual to come up with ingenious and often nonlinear answers (that is, they don't always logically flow from the literal meaning of the question), and/or a creative use of language (Hayden & Picard, 2009). Sometimes the answer is some form of pun in the question or the answer (e.g., "When is a door not a door? When it's ajar!"). While the link to nonlinear thinking should be obvious, what about the link between riddles and clinical work? Some master clinicians (i.e., Milton Erikson, Carl Whitiker) used riddles to get clients to see the error in their thinking. However, for the most part, understanding riddles is like understanding clients and their situations. It requires nonlinear listening and nonlinear thinking. It means really trying to appreciate the words that the client is using and the real meaning behind them. It also means slowing down and making sure that your understanding and your assumptions are correct before rushing to a solution. Just like answering riddles, with clients, things may not always seem to be how they appear at first. Sometimes taking a second look, or a step back, will help you to see a *better* answer!

Try these riddles to exercise your nonlinear thinking! (Answers are at the end of the chapter).

1. What five-letter word becomes shorter when you add two letters to it?
2. Johnny's mother had three children. The first child was named April. The second child was named May. What was the third child's name?
3. A clerk at a butcher shop stands 5' 10" inches tall and wears size 13 sneakers. What does he weigh?
4. If you were running a race and you passed the person in 2nd place, what place would you be in now?
5. What word in the English language is always spelled incorrectly?

Once you have answered these, look up the answers. How were these riddles good examples of nonlinear thinking?

Humor and Advanced Nonlinear Thinking

> Ninety percent of the game is mental. The other half is physical.
>
> —Yogi Berra

As we have presented in Chapter 1 and throughout this book, *advanced* nonlinear thinking includes sophisticated mental abilities like inductive reasoning, double-binds, Socratic questioning, and second-order change. It requires the master clinician to be creative, have an appreciation for the paradoxes of life, and be able to use these in order to help clients to change their perceptions of their problems and find new meaning for their life circumstances (just ask Yogi Berra). Closely tied into these creative and advanced thinking is humor. Casadei and Giordani (2008) linked the use of irony as a communication style with the use of the Socratic method. Indeed, self-deprecating humor can be used with the Socratic method to help pose difficult questions. Paolo and Gilli (2008) describe linkages between the work of Gregory Bateson (who helped to define double-binds) and his systems-based thinking with humor. Humor and double-binds share inherent incongruities that are required to make them work. With humor, there is a violation of the logic of the setup with the logic of the punch line, while with double-binds, there are the logical incongruities of the primary and secondary injunctions. Recall the vignette above of the mother with the innocent ax, knife, and saw? First she was in a double-bind. Her primary injunction was she should punish the husband and son for violating her wishes; otherwise, she was not standing up for herself. The secondary injunction was that she needed to protect her son from harming himself with the dangerous tools, but to do so, she would risk him lying again about them and conspiring more with his father. Then the tertiary injunction was on the financial level, where if she angered her ex-husband he could vaguely threaten to delay paying her child support. Then the humor of making the ax, saw, and knife the "innocent victims" (even though they were the objects of "offense") was used in a Socratic way to get her to reevaluate her situation and get out of the double-bind.

Advanced nonlinear thinking in general and humorous responses to a wide spectrum of therapeutic encounters require one to "think fast and carefully on your feet." Of course, part of creativity, humor, and advanced nonlinear thinking in order to "think fast" is *play*. Humor and play have much in common. According to Panichelli (2013),

> When the therapist succeeds in introducing a playful frame in a way that is accepted by the client, the therapy reaches a crucial point, a point where it becomes possible to answer *simultaneously* both levels of the auto-double-bind. Inside the playful frame, the therapist can actively use contradictory nonverbal communication to transmit two messages to the client at the same time. In the case of reframing a situation, while still sustaining joining, one message will be verbal, achieving either joining or reframing, and the second will be nonverbal, contradicting the first.
>
> (p. 444)

The playful frame is essential to appreciate humor. If a joke is told without noticing that it is a joke, the story will be heard and interpreted completely differently, and the amusement of humor can be totally missed. Play implies a relaxed atmosphere and a "safe" environment, both of which are crucial to a successful therapeutic relationship (Norcross, 2011). Well, the closest that can come to defining it is by describing it as the sort of thing done in improvisation. "Improv" as it is called in show business requires people to be courageous (i.e., risking with no guarantee of being funny), relaxed, open-minded (especially to *nonlinear* associations), freethinking, and willing to "bomb," as well as be playful. When comics do "bomb," they use *that* as an opportunity to garner laughter. For instance, a Level 1 practitioner is typically preoccupied with saying the "right" thing, not making a mistake, avoiding saying/doing something that will harm a client and so forth. Wanting to say the "right" thing and not wanting to make a "mistake" are very inhibitory in nature. Such preoccupations are unfortunately all too common, and usually do not allow for a person to get into a "playful" mindset (Panichelli, 2013). As such, it is not difficult to see how they interfere with "thinking fast and carefully on one's feet." Level 3 practitioners are not preoccupied with how they "look" but on using the information that the client presents to be most effective with their clients. Jokes and humor in general can be used to talk about the problem without talking about the problem, bringing it more safely into the interaction without disrupting the therapeutic relationship. The message is communicated in a disguised way that makes it more palatable to understand (Panichelli, 2013). Later in the chapter, we will discuss how this relates to paradoxical interventions, but next we wish to discuss how humor can help explain advanced nonlinear thinking processes.

Using Humor to Describe Advanced Nonlinear Thinking

There is a funny automobile insurance commercial where a man is outside of his apartment and his car has been involved in an accident. His neighbor comes up and asks him what he is doing. He tells her that he is documenting his accident on his insurance app right from his phone. The neighbor says "I heard they didn't have those apps." He asks, "Where did you hear that?" "On the Internet" she replies, "you know they can't put anything on there that isn't true." Dubious, he asks her, "Where did you hear that?" "On the Internet," she replies. A slightly nerdish guy walks up to them and she says, "Oh, here's my date. I met him on the Internet. He's a French model." To which the guys says "Uh . . . bon jour?" (in a decidedly *un*-French accent) as he gives the camera a knowing smirk and begins to walk away with the gullible neighbor. Of course, this is a funny example of the "Liar's Paradox" mentioned in Chapter 2, and an example of faulty deductive reasoning detailed in Chapter 1, because the audience is forced to oscillate between the literal meaning of verbal communication of the neighbor and the contradictory (and absurd) information (Panichelli, 2013). So the bottom line is don't believe everything you read (especially on the Internet) . . . unless it's in this book!

In addition to funny advertisements, many times cartoons (particularly political cartoons) can humorously point out the double-binds that many people find themselves in. Indeed, double-binds can be explained humorously by cartoons. For example, *The Far Side* by Gary Larson once featured a fishbowl with its castle inside on fire (which was strange because the castle was in the water as well). But with flames licking up out of the bowl, three fish are on the outside of the bowl discussing the situation. The caption summarizes the situation as one fish tells the others, "We got out of there just in time. Of course, now we are equally screwed!" In other words, the fish faced the primary injunction "Get out of the bowl or you will be burned alive (or boiled)!" and the secondary injunction "Outside of the bowl of water you can't breathe or survive." The fish realize that they are in trouble either way, and while they are taking a moment to congratulate themselves, they are still "in hot water." (BA-DUM-BUM!)

"Spitting in the Client's Soup" as a Way to Get Out of Double-Binds

Humor is not limited to the therapeutic hour, but also in the way we describe the processes that are employed in therapy! "Spitting in the soup" (albeit a distasteful metaphor) is a method from Adlerian therapy of confronting the client's behavior to reveal her underlying goals. Many times, the client either has difficulty with the interpretation or rejects it outright. This rejection occurs when the image that the therapist shares runs counter to his or her view of their circumstances and/or when the client's symptoms or behavior actually serve to help the client achieve his or her goals (e.g., a person who comes to help for depression, but doesn't actually want help since his or her depression allows them to deal with others). As Adler often stated, it is like when a waiter comes by and spits in your soup, you can continue to eat it, but it won't taste as good (Carlson, Watts, & Maniacci, 2006; Dreikurs, 1967). Once the underlying goal or secondary gain is revealed, the client can decide if they wish to continue to act in the same manner, even though the "payoff" will be diminished (since the real purpose has been brought to light). According to Driekurs (1967),

> Interpretation of goals is singularly effective in stimulating change. When the patient begins to recognize his (*sic*) goals, his own conscience becomes a motivating factor. Adler called this process "spitting in the patient's soup." However, insight into goals and intentions is not merely restrictive; *it makes the patient aware also of his power, of his ability to make decisions, of his freedom to choose his own direction.*
>
> (p. 12, italics added)

Master Example 6.1: But Don't Take Our Word for it!

In this example, master clinician *Marsha Linehan*, PhD (developer of DBT), works with a woman who became angry about being treated unfairly at work (Alexander Street Press, 2012).

Marsha Linehan: You're in a lot of trouble if that's true. You're in a world of trouble, if only anger works in your agency.

Client: Yeah.

Marsha Linehan: Okay. But if only, and a lot of people are in that situation where the only thing that works is angry behavior. But the trick to angry behavior is then to do it skillfully. In other words to be in control of angry behavior. Acting angry in other words can be useful but it's usually more useful if you can act angry and you're not angry.

Client: [Client laughs] and you can think more.

Marsha Linehan: You can be more strategic, yeah.

Linehan uses humor to break through the client's behavior and, essentially, "spits in the client's soup." The ultimate purpose of the technique is to help the client to see the futility of continuing her symptom or behavior and find that she has the power to adopt new, more healthy, and socially useful behaviors. This can be accomplished (and Adler often did) by using the Socratic method (Carlson et al., 2006). So if a client is in a double-bind and is continuing to play the role of the victim, pointing out to the client that the fear of damaging the relationship is the reason why she is continuing to be hurt and disappointed (i.e., "You're in a world of trouble, if only anger works in your agency"), and that only when she is ready to risk the relationship and confront the double-bind will she be able to change it. Humor can be employed in a "Socratic" fashion, as well as with paradoxical interventions. This is a particular combination or unity of all the principles that we have been discussing in this chapter, and we will demonstrate this next.

Humor: A Special Case of Paradoxical Intervention

> When you come to a fork in the road, take it!
> —Yogi Berra

By now the overlap between humor, advanced nonlinear thinking, and paradoxical interventions should be fairly clear. So we *really* don't need a special section making the argument that humor is a "special case" of paradoxical intervention, do we? Well, we think that we do! Actually, we feel that to fully appreciate the past four chapters on paradoxical intervention, and to truly understand how to utilize paradoxical interventions, an understanding of humor (as we have discussed in this chapter) is vital. First, let's go back to the definition of a paradox that we outlined in Chapter 2. A paradox is defined as "A statement or proposition seemingly self-contradictory or absurd, and yet explicable as expressing a truth" (*Random House American College Dictionary*, 2006, p. 878). At the same time, humor, as defined earlier in this chapter, is "the faculty of perceiving and enjoying what is ludicrous or amusing" (*Oxford English Dictionary*, 2007, p. 1294). With that in mind, we consider humor to be essentially nonlinear in nature. More specifically, we suggest that humor is based on irony, paradoxical meanings, absurdity, incongruity, exaggeration, etc.—in other words, the very principles of paradox that we have described in the previous chapters in this text. Abrami (2009) reported that both humor and paradoxical intervention allow recipients of them to distance themselves and take another perspective on a situation (kind of like coming to a fork in the road and taking it!).

To further illustrate this point, Mozdzierz (2011) described eight parallels between humor and paradoxical or nonlinear thinking. Briefly they are: a sudden shift in perspective, incongruity, ironic juxtaposition of two things that don't ordinarily go together, viewing the same situation from two different frames of reference, exaggeration, the activation of other, previously unseen or unaccessed schemas, incorporating multiple meanings and referents, and novelty. Each of these are summarized in Table 6.1. We will next describe how humor is incorporated into the four types of paradoxical interventions (neutralizers, tranquilizers, energizers, and challengers).

Humor and Neutralizers

Neutralizers are the class of paradoxical interventions that focus on the early development of the therapeutic relationship in order to "neutralize" any potentially negative or "acidic" comments and behaviors that can destroy any hope of therapeutic change. At the same time, it is precisely in the beginning phases of therapy when *appropriate* uses of humor can be very therapeutic, and paradoxical. First, in the beginning of therapy, clients may be expecting either a "fight" from the therapist (to change their behavior), or they may be expecting a staid, stoic, bland, or condescending figure who is stereotypical of a "therapist" that might be portrayed on TV. As a result, any therapist responses that would be incongruous with that stereotype can be neutralizing. According to Panichelli (2013), "[t]herapist's self-defeating humor can also be used at times to enlighten his/her modesty helping families solve their dilemmas, and maintain availability and expertise without being the expert responsible for family change" (p. 448). For example, in Case 3.1

Table 6.1 Parallels Between Humor and Therapeutic Nonlinear/Paradoxical Thinking

Common Elements Shared by Humor and Clinical Nonlinear/ Paradoxical Thinking	Humor	Paradoxical/Nonlinear Thinking
1. A sudden shift	Uses a sudden shift (i.e., "punch line") to deliver its impact.	Reframing (i.e., sudden shift) regarding the meaning of a client's behavior, feelings, beliefs, or situation frequently renders a powerful positive therapeutic impact (i.e., "I never looked at it that way!").
2. Incongruity	Incongruity: Larson's Far Side cartoons often have animals engrossed in human social endeavors/ interactions, which results in a powerfully funny impact. Other humor routinely employs the same dynamic in effecting comical impact.	Assigning a client to engage in symptomatic behavior within a benign context is completely incongruous: The client is instructed to do something that they are complaining about and want to stop doing or change.
3. Ironic juxtaposition of two things that don't ordinarily go together	Employs the combining of two things that don't ordinarily go together (i.e., are self-contradictory); are incompatible; and both of which can't be true at the same time but nevertheless provide a new amusing, comical, or absurd understanding that is unique.	The definition of paradox concerns a proposition that is "self-contradictory or absurd and yet explicable as expressing a truth."
4. Viewing the same situation from two different frames of reference	Requires simultaneously viewing the same situation from two different frames of reference (i.e., a literal frame and an implied frame).	Therapeutically reframing requires the therapist to understand and view the client's situation simultaneously from two different perspectives: the linear perspective (i.e., the client's "complaint and/or "problem"); and the nonlinear perspective, which the client does not see. The therapist points out a positive and adaptive dimension to the client's complaint and/or problem that the client does not see. The client "wins" if the complaint persists and if the client relinquishes it, "solves" his problem or changes his perspective.

(Continued)

Table 6.1 (Continued)

Common Elements Shared by Humor and Clinical Nonlinear/ Paradoxical Thinking	Humor	Paradoxical/Nonlinear Thinking
5. *Exaggeration*	*Exaggeration* of reality is often a key component in effecting a comedic outcome.	Therapist expands (i.e., enlarges) the meaning of a client's behavior, feelings, etc. through a nonlinear understanding of those phenomena that provides a new meaning.
6. *Allows for the activation of other, previously unseen or unaccessed schema*	*Activation* of unseen connections allows for a new humorous meaning to emerge.	Persistence in and repetitiousness of one "position" (i.e., a point of view or emotions that are self-defeating in certain circumstances) inhibits the activation of seeing other possibilities or feeling other emotions (e.g., an "angry" wife is "hurt" by her husband's actions, withdrawal, etc.); paradox facilitates the activation of other healthier possible meanings.
7. *Multiple meanings*	Humor "plays" on multiple meanings, dual entendres, word puns, etc.	Paradox develops alternative meanings.
8. *Provides novelty*	Humor provides a *different* understanding of realities that are incongruous, unexpected, original, etc. The human brain is intimately attracted to novelty, the unexpected, the previously unseen, etc.	Paradox encourages the development of an awareness of "I never looked at *it* that way!" That phrase is indicative of the surprise, delight, etc. of the novel, unexpected, the previously unseen, etc.

Based on Mozdzierz (2011).

(the "reluctant nun"), the therapist joked "Almost anyone can tolerate me for three sessions!" This showed the nun that the therapist was able to laugh at himself. In fact, if well-timed, the humor can surprise the client to begin to think, "Hey, this therapist doesn't take himself too seriously, he's a person, just like me. Maybe I *can* relate to him."

Neutralizing using humor can also convey the clinician's respect and esteem toward the client and his or her suffering. For example, using "gallows humor" (see above) when a client comes to therapy and has been the victim of another person's cruelty, "agreeing with a twist" and essentially saying "I'd probably want to give them a piece of my mind, but then I'd be hauled off to jail for violating confidentiality!" is a way to "lighten up" the sessions. Ultimately, the advantage of using humor as a neutralizer is to provide therapists with "the ability to provoke surprise and to stay unpredictable, and it offers the opportunity to inject creativity into the therapeutic system, providing a chance to enhance freedom and hope" (Panichelli, 2013, p. 447). Indeed, humor and neutralizing paradoxical interventions share many of the same qualities and serve the same purpose.

Humor and Tranquilizers

Tranquilizers are the types of paradoxical interventions that are focused on stopping a client's unproductive, frenetic behavior. This entails serious risk to the therapeutic relationship as it can often be taken as mocking, or putting down the client's behavior. For example, "To say to a patient anxious about microbes: 'You may be underestimating the dangers you take by continuing to breathe open air' may be a way to ridicule him by amplifying his problem to the absurd" (Bouaziz, 2007, p. 79, our translation). Therefore, using a tranquilizer (like permission, postponement, or persuasion) with humor should be done so cautiously.

At the same time, however, the absurdity of humor can help to point out the futility of some client's behavior, such as help-rejecting complaining, passive aggression, and reaction formation. For example, in Clinical Case Example 3.3, the therapist advises that the client audition for a musical job *just* for the experience, but *not* to take the job! This quirky and absurd suggestion is along the same lines of a riddle (i.e., "When is a door not a door . . .") by allowing the client to have his cake and eat it too. In fact, the intervention is most humorous when the client laughs at the suggestion (which is a release of tension but can also signal a willingness to consider alternative strategies), and the therapist maintains that he is serious and that the client should follow through. This enables the therapist to answer different paradoxes, such as those often present in psychiatric patients' symptoms. Inside its paradoxical frame, precisely because psychotherapy is *and simultaneously is not* like an everyday conversation, therapists can use humor to help clients consider alternative meanings, while still sustaining joining. Humor allows the therapist to answer both levels of the clients' paradoxical demand (double-bind), tranquilize the client's behavior, and also effectively utilize the therapeutic "auto double-bind" to the client's benefit. It is this kind of creativity that would allow master practitioners to "enjoy the paradox from the inside" instead of avoiding it (Elkaim, 1997).

Humor and Energizers

Energizers are the classification of paradoxical interventions that are designed to "kick-start" clients into action when they feel they cannot act. According to Milenković

(2007), therapy and humor are related precisely because they jolt clients into establishing new attitudes toward themselves and their circumstances. It implies the presence of the therapist's creativity and his sense of humor (the therapist as an artist), but it also involves awakening of the creativity in the patient/client (the patient/client as an artist), the awakening of which is brought about by encouraging and nourishing their sense of and response to humor. It is humor that enables the patient/client to have insight and initiates them to make new decisions, thus energizing them. For example, in Clinical Case Example 4.4, the "perfectionistic" client that was so worried about making a mistake that he was doing everyone else's work. He was advised to "screw up on purpose," so he wouldn't have to worry about doing it accidentally (a truly absurd and humorous thought, but one that the client actually liked). It used his need for control (being perfectionistic) to take control and "lose" control (by deliberately "screwing up"), thus creating the positive double-bind. According to Panichelli (2013), the goal is to

> bring the clients to a position where smiling or laughing at the problem becomes possible—not in order to avoid it, but to increase the capacity to face it—while always maintaining a strong therapeutic alliance. If the clients enter the playful frame, significant progress will be made in the therapeutic process, because "people are half over their emotional problems once they manage to laugh at their predicament."
>
> (p. 448)

To this point, recall Clinical Case Example 4.5 where the husband in a couple believed that he had a better way for his wife to manage the household and their children. The therapist suggested that he "design a plan and field test it!" He was pleased to be able to show the superiority, and then when he realized the folly of his hubris (thinking he could "tell" his wife what to do without really understanding her predicament), he was able to see the humor of his situation! The similarity between humor and a humorous paradoxical intervention in psychotherapy cannot be denied or underplayed (Milenković, 2007).

Humor and Challengers

Finally, challengers and humor are very closely linked. Humor is one of the ways that a therapist challenges clients with their old patterns of thought, feeling, and behavior. At the same time, it is a way in which the client can be moved from his or her old views and habits and directed toward searching for and creating new ones, which are healthier and more functional (Milenković, 2007). Humor can be inserted into the continuity of logic and thought by introducing unexpected and apparent nonsense (Gandino, Vesco, Benna, & Prastaro, 2010). This is the goal of the challenger paradoxical interventions. For example, in Clinical Case Example 5.1, the therapist used his hands to make gestures of a scale weighing the choices that the client's sons had ("hmmm . . . let's see, go out with friends and party, or stay at home with Mom"). In therapy, both humor and challengers are designed to unmask and disarm defenses and allow for gaining representations of the self and of reality, otherwise precluded or unknown. The humorous delivery, the use of gestures, and the absurdity all helped to gently challenge the client to rethink her stance. With humor and challengers, new horizons in meaning and consciousness open up and make unacceptable, difficult, and painful contents possible. Recall Clinical Case Example 5.2, with the mother and son who was "too weak" to use the bathroom at night (and had to use a "pee bucket"). The humor used was subtle, but the therapist was able to challenge the client to overcome his laziness and "dare" him to do better. By choosing to take his side of the argument (that he was unable), the therapist was able to motivate the client to show that he could accomplish the challenges he was avoiding (getting a job, growing up, etc.).

In therapeutic work, humor and paradoxical interventions are both "shortcuts" to deconstruct and reconstruct the meanings behind client beliefs and behaviors (usually by using a Socratic approach). This is especially true of challengers, which move clients to consider what is possible. The hilarious element can be expressed in the contents of communication or emerge from the paradoxical discrepancy between the verbal and the nonverbal levels (Gandino et al., 2010). For example, in Clinical Case Example 5.4, the therapist prescribed that the client, who claimed that she would get dizzy after a short exertion of effort (without a medical explanation), should interrupt *any* work she does after 10 minutes and lay down. The humor came in the form of the incongruity between the client's words and actions. The therapist was able to get her to see that she was not the victim of her "exhaustion," because her defiance of the "10 minute" injunction communicated that loudly. From that point, the client and therapist were able to move onto the real problem that she was coping with.

Ultimately, the essential point in making the observations about the concordance between humor and paradox is to demonstrate that there is more universality involved regarding *nonlinear thinking* in the counseling/psychotherapy process than the casual observer might ever imagine. It is for all of these reasons why we believe that humor is a special case of paradoxical intervention and a very potent and important tool for clinicians to understand. Next, we will demonstrate some of the ways that master practitioners utilize humor in a therapeutic context.

The Clinical Use of Humor

> Lose your mind and come to your senses!
> —Fritz Perls

It may be self-evident at this point in our discussion, but there are actually many different ways of describing humor in treatment. For example, Salameh (1987) has suggested, "Humor does not represent a theory of psychotherapeutic work. It is rather a *way of being* ... a ... tool which needs to be incorporated within the therapist's theoretical frame of reference" (p. 196, emphasis added). The editors of the *Handbook of Humor and Psychotherapy* define therapeutic humor as "constructive, empathic humor, which is totally unrelated to sarcasm, racist or sexist humor, deformations, put-downs and other abuses of humor" (Fry & Salameh 1987, p. xix). Gelkopf (2011) noted that interest in the topic of humor in therapy has also risen:

> Probably due to what seems to be the therapeutic potential inherent in humor and laughter, the noteworthy sense of humor observed in many of the "super-therapists," such as Ellis, Perls, Erickson, Satir, Rogers or Whitaker ... we have seen an increase in the use of humor in individual and group psychotherapy and in a number of humor

and laughter interventions within psychiatric institutions and with individuals with "serious mental illness" (SMI).

(p. 1)

Some clinicians find it easy to incorporate humor in their interactions with clients, while others might be intimidated by it. Nevertheless, with clinical experience, the development of confidence, and the development of their nonlinear thinking, the wide-ranging philosophical principles suggested here will hopefully become more natural when the opportunities for humor arise in therapy. Two things seem clear about laughter (and humor in general) in therapy: It does occur, and it can have either positive or negative effects on the therapeutic relationship (Nelson, 2008). In this section, we will discuss three additional ways that humor can be used in therapy (in addition to the paradoxical interventions above): to build rapport, to relieve tension, and to bring awareness.

Humor to Build Rapport

As we mentioned above in describing Domain 3, humor, jokes, and laughter at the beginning of the relationship help to create a working relationship with clients that is designed to minimize their anxiety and put them at ease. Using self-deprecating humor effectively, along with other relationship building techniques, can set the stage for the later development of the therapeutic alliance (Nelson, 2008; Panichelli, 2013). Consider the following from "The Case of Mike":

From the beginning of the session:

Mike: [WEARILY LOOKS OVER THE TOP OF MIRRORED SUNGLASSES] Alright . . . But look, when I was a teenager, I was forced to go to counseling, and it didn't do anything. The woman I went to see was all "touchy-feely" and had candles and incense . . . I thought she looked more like a gypsy or a fortune-teller! Anyway, I said enough of this and bolted.

Therapist: Yeah, I've known a few folks like that in my time. Sometimes people just don't mesh. Their styles don't match. So, if that starts to happen with us, you'll let me know before you bolt? [SILENCE] If you do, I promise no incense and candles . . .
[BOTH LAUGH]

Mike: OK.

And the therapist brings it back up again at the end of the session as an "inside joke":

Therapist: Our time is almost up right now. How was this session for you?

Mike: It was better than I had expected. It felt real.

Therapist: No incense or candles?

Mike: [LAUGHS]Yeah.

Using humor to build rapport by creating "inside jokes" is an effective way to be able to not only build and maintain the therapeutic relationship, but also to effectively repair it, if there are any therapeutic ruptures. In our previous text (Mozdzierz et al., 2014), we detailed some of the latest research on the impact of repairing (or failing to) therapeutic ruptures on clinical outcomes. The use of humor can be very facilitative in this process, as it creates a language for the therapist to admit that they might have been *wrong* in a particular instance, or reminds clients that they are human and can make mistakes.

Master Example 6.2: But Don't Take Our Word for It!

Consider this example from master practitioner *John Norcross* (chair of the American Psychological Association's Task Force on Empirically Supported Therapy Relationships and editor of the book *Psychotherapy Relationships that Work*) and how he demonstrates person empathy attunement to the client when he misspeaks in a way that builds their therapeutic relationship (Alexander Street Press, 2012).

John Norcross: And I want, I hope that we'll be able to find a place in which, uhm, I respect your awareness of the problem and I respect that you wanna change it. And then I can be direct with you about what I think we can do to help move you further along without you feeling I am being too pushy. You know therapists, we're kinda pushy.
Smith: Hmm.
John Norcross: You've had some therapist like that, huh?
Smith: Ah, I had some that was a little pushy.
John Norcross: So, if I get too pushy, you could say, "J.C., maybe back off a little"?
Smith: Sure.

. . .

Then Norcross comes back to it later in the session to repair a potential rupture:

John Norcross: Yes. Well, I just don't want to be one of those pushing people again. (laughs) You coming out of here with this long list of things to do. So, what's, what's top in your mind? Right now just to stay busy for a while . . . (crosstalk)
Smith: Well right. (crosstalk)
John Norcross: . . . with the painting?
Smith: Right now, right now, just the main thing I need to

. . .

And he makes light of it again, demonstrating that he is human and can make mistakes too:

John Norcross: I almost said that dreaded word "plan" again. (laughs) Let's, let's try to be concrete so, though our time is brief, that there'll be something memorable or lasting about this. Uhm, one thing is to decrease the amount of alcohol because if we push you anymore, it could backfire.

Both examples show how humor can build rapport, particularly in the early stages of therapy (as both cases were). Each clinician used a bit of self-deprecating humor. The "bisocation" of the humor allowed for an externalization of the problem, which increased the sense of shared "we-ness" through the use of an "inside joke." The effective management of the potential ruptures allowed for clients to relax their "guard" in therapy as well. The clients were able to "buy-in" to therapy just enough to begin to imagine a different way of being or interacting with their problem (Makoto, 2011).

Humor to Relieve Tension

As we mentioned previously (Mozdzierz et al., 2014), therapy is an anxiety-producing exercise, regardless of a client's motivation. This anxiety can often lead to tension in the therapeutic relationship, for which humor can often be a helpful antidote. Greenberg (2004) has clinically described using humor for dealing with troublesome negative emotions as "changing emotion with emotion" (p. 62). By doing so, it shifts attention and provides the ability to access strengths or direct attention toward a positive "goal." As an example, a somewhat overweight woman, tearfully sensitive to the fact that her waist and thighs were large and contributed to her being overweight, commented to her therapist that she had had a colonoscopy. When asked what the results of the test conveyed, she commented that her doctor told her that she had a very "slim" colon—a relevant fact for her medical condition. She spontaneously commented, "I may have fat thighs and a big waist, but I've got a really sexy-looking colon!" Her comment revealed the use of humor to transform sensitive and doleful emotions emanating from her general medical condition into something much more adaptive. While this was an example of "gallows humor" (see above), it also allowed her to address some of the issues without becoming overwhelmed by them.

Another example of humor being used to relieve tension in therapy is when clinicians suggest "homework" or activities for clients to try outside of session. Many times, lack of compliance is seen as "resistance," particularly by Level 1 or Level 2 clinicians. However, by creating a "playful" framework around the planning and implementation of the assigned tasks outside of therapy, it can increase the probability that clients will be willing to accept and complete them. Consider this excerpt from the "Case of Ashley:"

Therapist: But I guarantee that if you do let people know how overwhelmed you are, and let them help you, that you will find that they want to help you. You won't feel the need to control everything, and you won't feel that your life is so out of control. Now, with your husband, you are going to have to ask for him to help you get more connected to him. And since he is a gamesman, a fisher, you are going to have to make a game for him. He is going to have to "catch" you the same way he goes fishing on the weekends.

Therapist: I can see you like that idea.

Ashley: Yeah, it would be nice to be pursued. How do I do that, though?

Therapist: Well, first you have to let him know that you are available. This is where you have to "ask for help." Maybe suggest that you miss being with him and that you would like to spend time and go on a date together.

Ashley:	Oh, I have done that before. I've asked him and he never follows through.
Therapist:	I see. But remember the goal is to get you guys working together, not for him to do everything. If you want him to pursue you, you have to make it a game. You have to make it fun, and you can't make it too difficult. What if, in the spirit of collaboration, you told him you would handle the logistics of the babysitter, if he would agree to be in charge of the activities. Then let him know that at the end of the evening, if he does a good job, there is a prize for him: He "catches" you.
Ashley:	Oh?
Therapist:	Hey, I'm not going to tell you what to do, you have been married for 8 years and have two kids, I am sure you can figure that part out! [ASHLEY SMILES] The point is that there are three important elements: (1) You work together; (2) You get to feel connected and cared for; and (3) It is fun for the both of you. What do you think? If it all went successfully, do you think that would be a good start or at least a good evening?
Ashley:	Yes, I think so.

So in the example with Ashley, the therapist uses a playful and humorous approach to make the serious assignment of trying to get her and her husband to connect with one another into a "game." The paradox is that even though she is the nominal "prize" for the game, the real prize is in an emotional interaction with each other that is successful. "Homework" that is successfully completed represents a key "building block" for creating lasting second-order change (Frasier & Salovey, 2007; Norcross, 2011). Thus, using humor to help with this is like *Mary Poppins* famous quote: "Just a spoonful of sugar helps the medicine go down!"

Humor to Bring Awareness

Earlier, we discussed how humor can provide opportunities to direct client's attention toward or away from problems and invite them to be more mindful. Laughter at its best in the therapeutic relationship is a right-brain-to-right-brain bonding experience that is "in the moment." According to Nelson (2008), it says: "we are together, we are of one mind, we both get this and appreciate it viscerally—we don't have to put it into words" (p. 46). In fact, Gelkopf (2011) describes how using humor to bring awareness allows for themes to be brought up in therapy (via the Socratic method, inductive reason, or using paradoxical interventions) that can be explored in a nondefensive way. Consider this example from Steven Hayes:

Master Example 6.3: But Don't Take Our Word for It!

In this example of a transcript with a master practitioner, *Steven Hayes* (cocreator of ACT), works with a client who is working through issues of accepting her needs and problematic social behaviors (Alexander Street Press, 2012).

Steve Hayes: Now what I want you to do is see if you can get in touch with the amount of pain that she's in, and judgment that she's carrying. Wanting safety and not getting it. Getting criticism from Mom. And not even in a sense stepping up to honoring that violation that happened to her or acknowledging it. Is there something she wants form you that you can give her? You've got her here [holds air]. What does she want?

Client: To feel loved.

Steve Hayes: Okay. Do you love her?

Client: Maybe. I don't know. I mean. I'm annoyed at her a little bit.

Steve Hayes: Alright, she's coming back off your lap.

Client: [laughs, speaking to air] Sorry!

Steve Hayes: Now go in there. Don't answer this quickly but go inside this resistance. There's a place that you're sort of withholding, it's conditional? Yeah? With her? And I want you to open up to that, and see if there's some possibilities other than just getting stuck just there. But go there. Let's take a little time, and come on out; if you're going to stand there and just say that to her directly.

In the example, Hayes and the client share a playful moment (where he symbolically takes the "child" off the client's lap and she says "sorry!"), but then Hayes uses the positive momentum to get the client to go deeper and probe the feelings of conditionality to see if there are "possibilities" (or alternative explanations, second-order changes) that can be explored. From this, he is able to direct her attention mindfully to her ambivalent feelings and then connect that to her central issue and presenting concern. Finally, we present Clinical Case Example 6.1, which offers a relatively simple illustration of using humor to build rapport, relieve tension, *and* bring awareness to the client.

Clinical Case Example 6.1: Need for Female Companionship

A veteran who presented originally with severe anxiety and a drinking problem came for treatment. He had made a "mess" of his life after returning from the war and finally found his "bottom." He was hospitalized for detox, managed to work a 12-step program, and maintained sobriety. He was also in his final semester of college and realistically expected to graduate with a bachelor's degree from a large urban university. He actually had done very well academically. However, he was lonely and longed for the companionship of a woman who he could date. There was no one on the horizon. Alas, his expectations for what dating would represent to him were overwhelming. Medications were not an option to manage his anxiety for this man given his experiences with substance abuse. He was afraid that he would never find a companion to share his life with. "Who would ever want to be with me! I can't even *talk* to a girl without getting shaky. What hope do I have to make one fall in love with me?"

As a paradoxical measure, the therapist suggested that what this man needed was "practice." How could he get practice at talking to women and not encounter the paralyzing anxiety that he was likely to generate if he saw someone who he might want to date? When this was proposed to him, he simply didn't think it was possible. His therapist assured him that it was. The question was, would he be willing to agree to the "assignment"? He eagerly agreed.

The assignment was explained by first asking him if he could tell the married women on campus from the unmarried ones. He indicated that he thought he could because married women "almost always" wore wedding rings, and some of them were pregnant. The therapist agreed and further offered that pregnant women were also a "fair," although not foolproof, indication that a woman was married. He was to approach only the married and/or pregnant women, strike up conversations with them, and *avoid at all costs engaging any single woman* in conversation. Obviously, married women (less of a threat and sometimes difficult to discern) were automatically excluded from being eligible to date. He eagerly delighted in this proposed assignment and reported in therapy that he soon found himself becoming not only desensitized to the fear of talking to women but also soon talking to even single women.

In the case example, the client was clearly in a double-bind. He had developed an avoidance response to interacting with women while at the same time feeling lonely and desiring female companionship but knowing that he was not ready to date! The therapist's assignment provided the client an opportunity to engage in his avoidant behavior (i.e., interacting with women) and simultaneously not put himself in danger of encountering a woman who might want to go out with him. Presumably, married and/or pregnant women were "safe"; the client would not be threatened with the prospect of approaching women ineligible for dating. This represented a fundamental "shift" in his thinking, or an accommodation to his schema from, "No woman will accept me the way I am" to, "Some women will accept me the way I am." This prompted an emotional response that allowed him to reappraise his circumstance and altered his subjective view of women. This also altered his interpretation of their intention (i.e., context), which led to his being able to approach women (". . . from a certain point of view"). The alteration of his context allowed him to both address his loneliness for female companionship and not date (something he admittedly was unprepared for). This fulfills the definition of a paradoxical intervention (i.e., two truths that cannot coexist).

Of course, there are very many different ways to describe and define a *playful manner* of relating. Some might be emotionally healthy and some not so healthy. Besides the therapeutic context, humor can help clinicians deal with frustrating sessions, and difficult-to-treat chronic patients that may affect burnout (Gelkopf, 2011). Thus, while humor as a "way of being" and relating in the world can be very emotionally healthy, it is not always appropriate; but when it is, it can be very stress relieving, emotionally positive and invigorating, contribute to building a therapeutic relationship, and generally constructive. Hopefully this discussion will develop what represents an appropriate use of humor.

Warnings/Caveats About Humor

How do you go about implementing humor in treatment? The very first thing we encourage regarding the "how to" of humor in therapy is quite paradoxical. Do *not* use humor if you have any hesitation that it isn't appropriate or natural to your personality. The objective is to nurture that which is already there, to be aware of what is not necessarily there, and to discover your potential for using humor in treatment. Correspondingly, the objective is also not to convert you into something that you are not.

In addition, while the bulk of this chapter has been devoted to the use of humor in therapy, how it relates to the domains of competence, advanced nonlinear thinking, and is a special case of paradoxical interventions, there are also some limits to its use (no matter how witty or humorous you might be). Some of them we have mentioned above (e.g., not recommended with "precontemplators"). However, there are several instances where we urge caution, if not discourage the use of humor outright.

In the Early Stages of Therapy

Typically, it may be ill-advised to use humor in the very earliest stages of treatment. (The true master may be the exception here because such a practitioner is exceptionally skilled at "reading" clients, confident regarding the limits, pros and cons of humor, and the wide range of humor interactions that can be employed.) The main reason is because the early phase of humor is when the client is trying to get comfortable in treatment, the therapeutic relationship/alliance has not been established; the therapist is an unknown quantity to the client; trust has not been established; and the client may misinterpret the practitioner's remarks. If any humor is used, it is best for it to be self-deprecating humor, and even that should be used sparingly!

Loss and Uncertainty

Under dour, tragic circumstances such as the death of a loved one, unexpected loss of a job, development of a life-threatening illness, circumstances whose outcome is grave but uncertain, humor cannot be advocated. The client may feel that the therapist is not appreciating the potential and/or actually dreadful consequences of their circumstances, or their circumstances are even being mocked. While the client may employ "gallows humor" (see above) to cope with the situation, attempting to invoke humor on the therapist's part may be seen as entirely *unempathic*.

Possibility of Self-Injury and Violence

When threats of self-injury or violence toward others are being expressed and it is clear that the client is under extreme duress (especially if the client has a history of attempted self-injury, etc.). This becomes a serious ethical obligation for the therapist, where direct, clear communication is important for understanding the severity of the threat. A close examination of the client's potential for violence must be undertaken. The potential for gross misinterpretation of attempts at humor can be catastrophic.

Dire/Desperate Client Circumstances

When a client's options for shelter, protecting children, need for surgery, the diagnosis of a life threatening illness, etc. are extremely limited and possibly calamitous. In these circumstances, what is needed is not taking circumstances lightly but rather concrete problem-solving measures such as shelter, protection of children, and in general, helping clients increase their options. Again, the client may use "gallows humor" to deflect some of the pain, but therapists should be very wary of using humor themselves, but rather pick up on the strengths that may belie client attempts at humor.

In addition, humor should never be used in a mocking, overt, or subtly insulting, sarcastic, or self-aggrandizing way. It should also never be used to create a power differential with a client, or to make a client feel humiliated. These are all contrary to the best research on therapeutic effectiveness (Norcross & Wampold, 2011), as well as to all ethical codes and obligations (see Chapter 7). Put bluntly, *misusing humor is simply no laughing matter!*

Conclusion

A therapist was walking along a Hawaiian beach when he kicked a bottle poking up through the sand. Opening it, he was astonished to see a cloud of smoke and a genie smiling at him.

"For your kindness," the genie said, "I will grant you one wish!" The therapist paused, laughed, and replied, "I have always wanted a road from Hawaii to California."

The genie grimaced, thought for a few minutes and said, "Listen, I'm sorry, but I can't do that! Think of all the pilings needed to hold up the highway and how long they'd have to be to reach the bottom of the ocean. Think of all the pavement that would be needed, and the maintenance that would be required after it was built. That's just too much to ask."

"OK," the therapist said, not wanting to be unreasonable. "I'm a psychotherapist. Make me understand my patients. What makes them laugh and cry, why are they temperamental, why are they so difficult to get along with, what do they really want? Basically, teach me to understand what makes them tick!"

The genie paused, and then sighed, "Did you want two lanes or four?"

In the joke above, the truth of the difficulty of working with clients is evident. At times, it can seem overwhelming and daunting. However, in this chapter, we have attempted to show how humor can be used to create powerful change in clients. We have described how humor in therapy can be woven through each of the domains of competence, requires the use of advanced nonlinear thinking, and is a special case of paradoxical intervention. Finally, we described ways that humor can be used appropriately in session to build rapport, relieve tension, and bring awareness (among other things). Finally, we provided some guidance for when humor should *not* be used. In the next chapter, we will summarize the essential points of this book, and the seventh domain, as well as address some of the professional and ethical issues related to using paradoxical interventions.

However, we leave you with one last witty "gift" for you to ponder. It is a list of "Rules for the Therapist" developed by noted family therapist Carl Whitaker (1989), who was known for his often humorous, sometimes bombastic, and decidedly nonlinear way of working! See if you can appreciate the irony, humor, paradoxical absurdity, and embedded wisdom of his comments.

1. Relegate every significant other to second place.
2. Learn how to love. Flirt with any infant available. (Unconditional positive regard probably isn't present after 3 years old.)
3. Develop reverence for your own impulses and be suspicious of your behavior sequences.
4. Enjoy your mate more than your kids, and be childish with your mate.
5. Fracture role structures at will and repeatedly.
6. Learn to retreat and advance from every position that you take.
7. Guard your impotence as one of your most valuable weapons.
8. Build long-term relationships so your can be free to hate safely.
9. Face the fact that you must grow until you die. Develop a sense of the benign absurdity of life—yours and those around you—and thus learn to transcend the world of experience. If we can abandon our missionary zeal, we have less chance of being eaten by cannibals.
10. Develop your primary process living. Evolve a joint craziness with someone you are safe with. Structure a professional cuddle group so you won't abuse your mate with the garbage left over from the day's work.
11. As Plato said, "Practice dying."

Answers to Nonlinear Thinking Exercise: Riddles: (1) Short. (2) Johnny. (3) Meat. (4) Second place. (5) Incorrectly.

Note

1. For the purposes of our discussion (i.e., humor and counseling/psychotherapy), we are excluding the physiology of tickling and the fact that it also produces laughter, as do things involved in the humor of jokes, gags, one-liners, etc.

7 Final Thoughts

Back to the Movies

"In a world . . ." With these three words, viewers of movie trailers have been transported into stories of drama, comedy, wonder, and impossibility. By following with our imagination what comes *after* those three words, moviegoers may find themselves in the gritty streets of a crime-ridden city, in the sun-bathed parlors of Victorian aristocracy, trapped in a child's animated video game, or on a bizarre planet with blue-skinned inhabitants. Following those three words into a story is essentially what clinicians *have* to do when they work with clients: They listen to what the client says and *follow* them into *their* world. At the same time (and here is the nonlinear part!), that is also essentially what we ask our clients to do. We ask them to consider a world where their problem is solved, where their relationships are not toxic, and where their *lives* are better.

So perhaps it is because of this natural connection between films and therapy (or perhaps it is because we spend WAY too much time watching movies) that movie scenarios provided us with an easy method to describe complex therapeutic concepts. But as we thought of ways to summarize the system of understanding the essential domains and nonlinear thinking of master practitioners, we thought that we would go back and review using all of the movie references that we have employed across two books, in order to describe seven domains and three levels of therapeutic mastery. So grab some popcorn: It's about to start!

In a world where a magical book was able to teach the therapeutic secrets and nonlinear thinking to the profession's next generation of great experts . . .

Interestingly, *both* books start with movie references to sorcerers. In Mozdzierz, Peluso, and Lisiecki (2014), we started with Mickey Mouse in the role of the sorcerer's apprentice from the Disney film *Fantasia* as a metaphor for novice clinicians trying to mimic the "magic" of a master practitioner without properly understanding the *thinking* behind it. This was the departure point for our journey as we introduced the nonlinear thinking of master practitioners. As we began *this* volume, we referenced Yoda's final exhortation to Luke Skywalker in *Return of the Jedi* where he tells him to "pass on what you have learned." Unlike Mickey, at this point, Luke is on the cusp of becoming a Jedi Master, and has learned how to *think* like one. This text has been dedicated to passing on the advanced "secrets" (i.e., the advanced nonlinear thinking behind paradoxical interventions) to the next group of master practitioners: YOU!

Table 7.1 presents the movie references in each of the first six domains. In addition, you can see how each movie reference describes unique elements of each of the domains, from illustrating nonlinear listening and responding to understanding and resolving ambivalence.

Table 7.1 Summary of Movie References in Domains 1 through 6

Domain	Movie	Purpose
1	*Analyze This*	Nonlinear listening and responding, connecting and engaging the client for therapy
	Columbo*	"Not knowing" stance. Responding to congruence
	Alice in Wonderland	Going "down the rabbit hole." Listening for absence
2	*Deadliest Catch**	Every story has a beginning, middle, and end
3	*The King's Speech*	The power of the therapeutic relationship to heal and overcome adversity
	Don Juan De Marco	Relating to clients from their frame of reference, without losing one's own
4	*The Shawshank Redemption*	The subtle power of a person's schema dynamics to keep them "imprisoned" in an old way of thinking
	50 First Dates/Memento	How the loss of schema dynamics (viz. the plot device of anterograde amnesia) would impact a person's life
	Mythbusters*	How we rigidly cling to decisions we make based on schema dynamics even when it would be better to abandon the decision (called "The Monty Hall Paradox")
	Green Eggs and Ham*	The difference between assimilation and accommodation of schema dynamics
	House*	Use of metaphor to create accommodation in schema dynamics
	Gone With the Wind	"Scarlett O'Hara moment." How experiences shape schema dynamics: "*As God as my witness, I'll never . . .*"
5	*Good Will Hunting*	The power of emotions, the role of attachment injury, and the healing nature of the therapeutic relationship
	Dr. Jekyll and Mr. Hyde/ The Incredible Hulk	How emotions are commonly (mistakenly) feared as being disruptive, and thus must be "controlled"
6	*The Odyssey*	Ambivalence—Being stuck between a rock and a hard place, and wanting to "have one's cake and eat it too." Creatively solving the problem/dilemma
	2001: A Space Odyssey	Resolving ambivalence/double-bind by changing the circumstances
	Star Trek (2009)	Resolving ambivalence/double-bind by changing the rules (getting out of the "no-win" scenario)

* Technically NOT movies, but close enough!

Table 7.2 presents the movie references that have been used in this text. Here, you can see how these movie references describe elements of advanced nonlinear thinking (including inductive reasoning and double-binds), as well as aspects of paradoxical interventions.

In addition to these movie references, we have included numerous examples and transcripts of counseling sessions, as well as examples using master practitioners demonstrating the use of the Socratic method that addresses double-binds and creates neutralizer, tranquilizer, energizer, or challenger paradoxical interventions.

We pose a question: Are we *ever really done* with the learning process? Then again, why would we want to be? Of course, we are really never done learning as human beings or practitioners. Given that, one objective of this chapter is to address the question, What sort of summary can be presented that adds to the reader's clinical knowledge base in a utilitarian way after an already very extensive ride up the learning curve? It is admittedly an assumption that all practitioners strive for excellence no matter what their level of development. It is hoped that the Level 3 practitioner striving toward mastery will find some measure of focus from the observations, discourse, and summary aspects of this chapter. According to Ericsson, Chamness, Feltovich, and Hoffman (2006),

> Deliberate practice is therefore designed to improve specific aspects of performance in a manner that assures that attained changes can be successfully measured and integrated into representative performance. Research on deliberate practice in music and sports show that continued attempts for mastery require that the performer always try, by stretching performance beyond its current capabilities, to correct some specific weakness, while preserving other successful aspects of function. This type of deliberate practice requires full attention and concentration, but even with that extreme effort, some kind of failure is likely to arise and gradual improvements

Table 7.2 Summary of Movie References in *Advanced Principles* Text

Topic	Movie	Purpose
Advanced Nonlinear Thinking	*Inception*	Therapeutically altering the client's perspective and having *them* develop the insight
	Sherlock Holmes	Deductive reasoning vs. inductive reasoning. The power of observation
	Tangled	The nature and subtlety of double-binds
	The Matrix	Second-order change
Paradoxical Interventions	*The Avengers*	Paradoxicality—How doing the opposite of what is expected can produce the desired results
	Star Wars/Return of the Jedi	Reframing—Changing one's point of view changes one's perspective about previous beliefs
	Good Will Hunting	Neutralizing disparaging comments from precontemplators

with corrections and repetitions are necessary. With increased skill in monitoring, skilled performers . . . focus on mastering new challenges by goal-directed deliberate practice involving problem solving and specialized training techniques.

(p. 698)

Clinical Exercise 7.1 gives you one more opportunity to practice creating paradoxical interventions and using advanced nonlinear thinking.

Clinical Exercise 7.1: Summary Exercise on Paradoxical Interventions

1. A young client in his mid-20s who had been diagnosed with schizophrenia came to his therapy situation looking very tired and "washed out." When asked if he had been sleeping well, the patient responded that he had spent a "terrible night." He explained that he was having difficulty falling asleep because he had been paying increasing attention to the sound of airplanes on their way to landing at O'Hare Airport. The more preoccupied he became with these thoughts, the more anxious he became. He then became convinced that one of the planes could very well crash into the trailer in which he was living. Soon, he found himself even more unable to sleep, pacing intermittently through the nights and bizarrely turning his house-trailer lights on and off in an effort to "warn" approaching aircraft of his presence. It was usually morning before he was able to fall asleep.

2. A man comes to therapy to address his anxiety, especially around his supervisor at an accounting firm. At the end of the initial session, you and the client agreed to some specific homework tasks that included speaking up at a staff meeting, setting up an appointment to speak with the supervisor, and inquiring if a female coworker who he has been interested in is dating anyone. When he returns, he says that he didn't accomplish any of the tasks because "the meeting went too long, the secretary was never at her desk to make the appointment, and I just didn't get around to it" (i.e., asking about the coworker). He states that he intends to do it at the beginning of the next week.

3. The client is a 29-year-old man who works as an attorney for a prestigious law firm in a major metropolitan city. The client has come to therapy to address his struggle with depression that has plagued him since his adolescent years and all throughout college and law school. He tells you that he often feels so bad that he cannot get out of bed. He reports, however, that he had never missed a day of work or a court date due to his depression.

4. A patient with a litigious paranoid personality was bitterly complaining about and arguing with his young teenage daughter, whose boyfriends and girl friends constantly invaded the privacy and sanctity of his home—raiding the refrigerator,

dancing "crazily," etc. He expressed the wish that he would be rid of them so he wouldn't have to fight with them and his wife over the issue all the time.

5. An elderly gentleman in his late 70s was diagnosed as having congestive heart failure. Although there were clearly cardiac medications available that would have decreased the severity of his symptoms and made him both more comfortable and more functional, he adamantly refused to take such medications. His reasoning was that such medications were "chemicals," and "chemicals" are bad for the body. He just couldn't get himself to use a "new way" of treating his heart condition but instead wanted to rely on herbal medicine to treat himself (often a very dangerous practice). But he was competent to make such decisions and knew the risks of not taking his doctor's advice.

6. A client who had become depressed due to a recent divorce was having casual sexual relationships with numerous women. His parents (with whom he was living) were putting pressure on him to stop his promiscuity and to settle down with a "decent" woman. The client, however, was in no way prepared to get involved in any kind of intimate and enduring relationship at this point and continued to date three and four women in a single week. But, he strongly felt he should begin to "settle down."

7. A middle-aged man who elected to enroll in a night college course in general psychology. He hoped this would be an opportunity not only to expand his social life but also to enhance his knowledge of other people as he was being promoted to a supervisory position at work. The client was an "action-oriented" man who had poor academic experiences in his youth, even dropping out of school from time to time. About a third of the way into the course, he expressed having the "same old feelings" of once again wanting to quit. This was particularly distressing because it only served to reinforce and remind him of what he considered past failures to improve himself. In fact, he felt these feelings were evidence of an eventual relapse. Although fellow group members encouraged him to "stick it out," the client listened politely but remained discouraged.

Questions for Each Case

- What is the client's dilemma in the scenario above?
- What is the behavior that needs a paradoxical intervention?
- What advanced nonlinear thinking elements would you consider using?
- What kind of paradoxical intervention would you use (neutralizer, tranquilizer, energizer, or challenger)?
- Discuss the paradoxical nature of the intervention for the client (i.e., two elements that were mutually incompatible, yet both are true) and the counselor (i.e., an absurd or contradictory statement that contains an element of truth).

Mastery? There's an App for That!

While we hypothesize that there is but one psychotherapy, and the delivery of that therapy is as infinite and diverse as the practitioners that conduct it. Furthermore, those practitioners work with an unimaginable number of clients in a wide spectrum of settings with an immense diversity in their cultural backgrounds, ethnicity, assets, personal circumstances, pathology and its breadth, depth, and longevity. The interface between these disparate realities has to be reconciled, but how?

This entire text has been developed to enhance the Level 3 practitioner's awareness of and skill at employing nonlinear thinking, not as an end but as a means—a means of facilitating a client's movement toward goal attainment and disengagement. This is an imperfect world inhabited by imperfect people who struggle with life. In a world filled with very complex, painful, and disruptive circumstances, it is difficult to imagine a linear solution to most human problems in living. In essence, that is a very cogent rationale for developing nonlinear thinking skills in a treatment setting. Such thinking should *not* be seen as an end in itself but rather as a means of responding to client's inability to manage life complexities, painful circumstances at the moment. This text has emphasized nonlinear paradoxical thinking as a powerful ubiquitous resource and method of understanding troubled clients. It has also described and identified advanced nonlinear thinking (i.e., inductive reasoning, the Socratic method, double-binds, second-order change, humor) as a way of creatively responding to clients in an encouraging manner and a powerful method of facilitating therapeutic movement so that clients are able to go positively forward with their lives.

We have identified seven domains in our model that all master practitioners pay attention to. Paying attention to these domains is literally inescapable in clinical practice. In turn, each of those seven domains contains a wealth of material to be understood and learned thoroughly. At a Level 3 of professional development, a practitioner may be very skilled at each individual domain. But, the more complex a particular case, is the more difficult it may be for such a practitioner to therapeutically respond with maximal effectiveness. What, then, is the "secret" that the masters carry within them in the clinical setting so that they make what it is that they do appear so effortless and most often so on target?

We maintain that master practitioners have so thoroughly committed themselves to linear and nonlinear listening and thinking/understanding that they engage clients while maintaining a seamless access to all of the domains at will, in addition to having access to their vast "data base" of clinical experience. If this is difficult to understand, think about it like running an "app" on your iPhone or smartphone. When you are running a particular app on your iPhone, many other apps may still be turned on but not visible. Any of those apps can be activated instantaneously with a single tap or slide of a finger. In many respects, that is exactly how master practitioners operate. With intense linear and nonlinear focus on a particular client in the here and now, any of the seven domain apps can be activated in a linear or nonlinear response to a client.

Reexamine Figure 7.1 (reprinted from the Introduction). Those are the apps that a master practitioner is attending to and/or using at any given time. What makes them master practitioners is that they have practiced and practiced and practiced their craft so thoroughly, with such reflection and study and with such joy that they make accessing and running those apps seem effortless, seamless, and even magical. They glide through

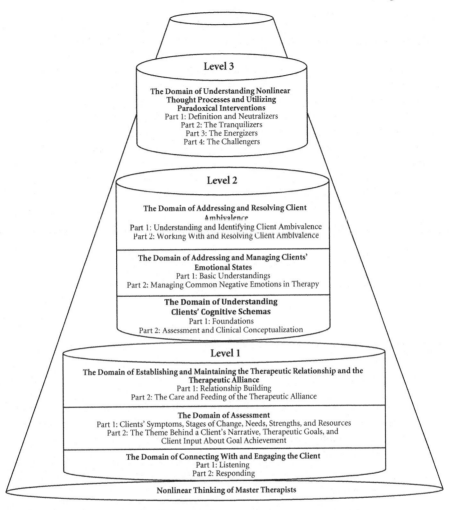

Figure 7.1 The Seven Domains that Master Practitioners Attend to and Emphasize

sessions with clients who may be confused, or anxious, or depressed, or exhausted, etc., and they know what app needs to be activated in response to what a client's complaint or state of being might be. That seamlessness is what we observe in a variety of video "demonstrations" by those experts. That's what accounts for the "WOW" we experience when we see a master working with a client.

The seven domains to which all master practitioners attend are represented in Figure 7.1, which was first introduced in our introductory text. These are the substantive areas to which master practitioners pay attention and use in their work. They review their work, obtain feedback from clients on their satisfaction with therapy sessions, study, practice, etc. until their use of the domains is smooth, seamless, and so functional as to be automatic. But what else do we know about these "master therapists"?

Personal Characteristics of Master Therapists

Research findings of "expertise" in therapy have potentially shed light on the processes of highly effective practitioners. Understanding the processes and practices of highly effective practitioners, in turn, may provide valuable clues as to how to solve the problem of the sorcerer's apprentice. Skovholt and Jennings (2004; Jennings & Skoholt, 1999) pursued the question of expertise by qualitatively researching the traits of expert therapists. Through extensive interviews with 10 master therapists, they defined the personal characteristics that were common to these practitioners and created a model of characteristics that may be useful in addressing the problem of the sorcerer's apprentice. The researchers found that there were specific *personal characteristics* that allowed certain therapists to "use both experience and intelligence to increase their confidence and comfort when dealing with complexity and ambiguity" (Jennings & Skovholt, 1999, p. 9). Their model of these characteristics has three broad domains—cognitive, emotional, and relational—and nine specific categories within those domains (see Table 7.3).

The Cognitive Domain

Skovholt and Jennings (2004) identified what they call the cognitive characteristics of master therapists:

- They are voracious learners
- Their accumulated experience has become a continually accessed, major resource for them
- They value cognitive complexity and the ambiguities inherent in the human condition

In other words, master therapists delight in the pursuit of knowledge; have a healthy sense of curiosity; possess the intellectual sophistication to handle complex situations; and understand that ambiguity in human beings attempting to solve their problems is normative, not aberrant.

The Emotional Domain

According to Jennings and Skovholt (1999), expert therapists access and use the following behaviors:

- They appear to have emotional receptivity, defined as being self-aware, reflective, nondefensive, and open to feedback
- They seem to be mentally healthy and mature individuals who attend to their own emotional well-being
- They are aware of how their emotional health affects the quality of their work

Hence, master therapists are nonreactive (e.g., nondefensive, calm, etc.) in the face of a client's strong emotional reactions, can appropriately use their emotional impulses to illuminate the therapeutic discourse, and have sufficient capacity to soothe themselves in the moment when their own emotions are aroused.

Table 7.3 The Cognitive, Emotional, and Relational Characteristics of Expert Therapists

DOMAINS	CATEGORIES	DESCRIPTION
Cognitive	1. Expert therapists are voracious learners.	Demonstrate a love for learning, and continuously seek out professional development.
	2. Accumulated experiences have become a major resource for master therapists.	Experience is reflected upon and enriches the practice of therapy.
	3. Expert therapists value cognitive complexity and the ambiguity of the human condition.	Complexity is welcomed as a part of the dynamic makeup of clients' thinking and of therapy itself.
Emotional	1. Master therapists appear to have emotional receptivity defined as being self-aware, reflective, nondefensive, and open to feedback.	Need for continuous self-reflection and feedback in order to learn more about themselves and their work.
	2. Master therapists seem to be mentally healthy and mature individuals who attend to their own emotional well-being.	See themselves as congruent, authentic, and honest, and strive to act in congruence with their personal and professional lives.
	3. Master therapists are aware of how their emotional health affects the quality of their work.	See the benefit of appropriately utilizing transference and countertransference reactions in session.
Relational	1. Master therapists possess strong relationship skills.	Developed, many times, out of family-of-origin dynamics, caring for the welfare of others, or a wounded past.
	2. Master therapists believe that the foundation for therapeutic change is a strong working alliance.	Have a deep respect for client's right to self-determination, and power of self-directed change. Value the client's struggle to discover answers over supplying the solution.
	3. Master therapists appear to be experts at using their exceptional relationship skills in therapy.	Therapeutic relationship provides the safe environment where challenges can be issued and accepted and where tough issues can be brought up.

Source: From Jennings and Skovholt (1999).

The Relational Domain

Last, in terms of how they relate to others, expert therapists are characterized as follows:

• They possess strong relationship skills
• They believe that the foundation for therapeutic change is a strong working alliance
• They appear to be experts at using their exceptional relationship skills in therapy

Briefly, this means that master therapists are keenly attuned to the relationship dimension with a client and have the ability to perceive how much change they can expect the client to tolerate before there is a rupture in the therapeutic alliance. Clearly, all of these are crucial in being effective with clients.

In our model, "connecting with and engaging a client" is at the bottom of our inverted cone (in Figure 7.1)—a precursor to establishing a positive therapeutic relationship and an effective therapeutic alliance. *Nonlinear/paradoxical thinking (along with humor) is at the top of the pyramid because it requires the integration of the other domains and thinking differently. It represents a vehicle for understanding how to develop an effective therapeutic relationship and alliance in a variety of circumstances.* Therapists must often use nonlinear thinking in order to connect with clients in the process of developing a therapeutic relationship.

Wampold (2010) forcefully argues for this, saying:

> Missing from these attempts to list then categorize the common factors is that the common factors are not analogues of specific ingredients that can be added and removed singularly. . . . One often reads that the most prominent common factor is the relationship with an empathic healer, but quite obviously this ingredient cannot be removed from psychotherapy and still have a practice that would be classified as psychotherapy. Consequently, the common factors cannot be experimentally manipulated in the same manner as specific ingredients but this does not suggest logically that such factors cannot be responsible for the benefits of psychotherapy.
>
> (p. 67)

Following from the suggestion of Wampold and others, we put together a list of clinician "dispositions" that correspond to each of the seven domains. These are seven traits that all master therapists share. In fact, we believe that if you watch *any* master practitioner, you will see examples of them demonstrating: curiosity, collaboration, optimism and hope, pattern recognition, self-soothing, mindfulness, and irony. Many of these have been empirically linked with effective therapeutic relationships (Norcross & Wampold, 2011). We recommend that you, the reader, consider the degree to which *you* demonstrate these characteristics and encourage you to develop these in yourself.

Clinical Case Example 7.1: Redefining a Horrible Set of Work Conditions

A broad-shouldered, burly 6'5" tall, brawny 53-year-old man appeared for treatment complaining of anxiety and depression. A college-educated, happily married for many years with three children, he had been successfully employed and supportive of his children throughout his life. When asked what his anxiety and depression were all about, he replied, "It's my job . . . I hate it . . . can't stand it . . . my boss is constantly demeaning and belittling . . ."

As he elaborated, after the "crash" of 2008, he lost a job in an industry related to the housing crisis that he had held for over 20 years. Then, after 2 years on unemployment benefits, he found a job with a very small company that seemed to be ideal because it took advantage of his broad knowledge of the housing industry. Hired for roughly half of the salary that he used to make, he was glad to be able to return to work; unfortunately the owner of his new company became a source of unrelenting distress to him.

According to the client, she was an avaricious, oppressive, micro-managing, belittling, and "terrible" person to work for. She was publicly demeaning of her employees, continuously negative about her employees' job performance, and seemed to have no sense of respect or fairness regarding the treatment of others. She regularly demanded overtime hours without compensation, no vacation with pay for the first year of work, on-call responses 24/7; weekends at the office without pay to catch up on accumulated "paper work," among other things. According to the client, "no one" liked her, neither customers with whom she occasionally had contact or employees. It seemed to him that she was especially harsh and humiliating toward him:

> She's constantly on me . . . it's been horrid! No matter what I do she always gives the same comment . . . "You could have done better." She'll berate me for 2 hours over something minor that could take a few minutes. She is constantly fault finding, critical in her tone, and doesn't even allow for any vacation time. I get so worked up I've even had the dry heaves some mornings before having to go to work. I ask myself, "What could be worse?" but how would I pay the bills? I need to have this weight lifted from me but I'm in a trap.

The client described himself as a nonconfrontational person despite his prodigious size and in fact his self-schema was that of a "scared little boy." When asked what he thought that was all about, he replied that he and his brothers and sisters lost their father quite prematurely when the client was only 12 years old; then just 2 years later, their mother also died unexpectedly. As a result of losing their parents, he and his siblings had to go and live with a bachelor uncle whom he described as being alcoholic and emotionally and verbally abusive. He had no difficulty in relating the psychological profile of his current employer to his uncle and indicated that they were "cut from the same cloth." Nevertheless, despite the uncle's abusiveness, he took in his four nieces and nephews and "kept the family together." In other words, just as his uncle provided something desirable (i.e., keeping the brothers and sisters together), his current boss also provided something desirable (i.e., a "pay check" that was allowing him to send his children to college).

He was *adamant* about "family" being the most important thing in life and was deeply committed to helping his children finish college. Given his feelings of being disempowered and literally helpless to influence the behavior of his employer, during the course of the third session the client was asked when in his life he felt most empowered. Without hesitation, he replied that he felt the most empowered when, ". . . being in charge of taking care of my family, caring about them. I always want to give them the best or more than I take for myself."

His ambivalence toward his situation is quite straightforward: To stay in his current job is personally intolerable and to leave his job in a terrible job market would be to "abandon" his children. When all was said and done, he felt "trapped." In summing up his circumstances, the client indicated that, "I stay there for the pay check but I'm miserable."

Knowing of his early background, and thus how important it was for the client to maintain family integrity, it occurred to the therapist that there were in actuality *two* realities that prompted his client to stay at his current job. The first "reality" was straightforward: He stayed there for a "pay check." A second reality, equally plausible (i.e., an element of truth) but perhaps not quite as obvious to the client, was that *he stayed in his intolerable circumstances out of love of family.* When the therapist related those two realities to the client, his eyes immediately swelled with tears, and he replied, "I think you've got something there."

Staying in intolerable circumstances motivated by *love of family* rather than simply a "pay check" made working under extremely difficult conditions much more acceptable. His attitude turned brighter, less depressed, he felt more optimistic, more inoculated from the daily stresses his boss imposed, and redoubled his efforts to search for a job commensurate with his skills and interests. He finally decided to resign and devote full time to a job search. Within about 2 months of leaving the job he so detested, the client found another job in his field of expertise.

Applying Linear and Nonlinear Thinking to Ethical Practice

Although ethics is rarely thought of as a *common factor* in treatment, it can be looked at as *an essential,* common, transtheoretical, and universal factor in all therapy. Ethics is a complex subject that stands at the interface between theory and practice, reality/practicality, the law, and clinical circumstances. All of these interfaces can and do collide to create worrisome and sleepless difficulties for practitioners, and there are volumes of texts written about ethics in therapy (see Koocher & Keith-Spiegel, 2008; Pope & Vasquez, 2010; Sperry, 2007). But a practitioner may spend his or her entire career and never have to invoke major guiding principles such as "a duty to warn." On the other hand, depending upon the law and clinical setting in which someone works, another practitioner may have to regularly invoke guidelines regarding child (or elder) abuse in order to protect those who are most vulnerable. Given that this text advocates nonlinear thinking and paradoxical intervention, it is important to briefly discuss how these "interface" with an ethical mindset.

The cautious reader will note what is being advocated: *Everything* a practitioner does has implications for ethical practice, even returning phone calls when promised, and yet a practitioner may not feel like returning a phone call to a particularly upset borderline personality disordered client. Such issues can be interpreted by clients as an issue involving trust, the essential ingredient in establishing/nurturing/maintaining a therapeutic relationship and the therapeutic alliance. While phone calls may be considered as peripheral or given little attention, they are actually integral to ethical clinical practice. Considering ethics as infused in everything a practitioner does is essential for practitioners to maintain an *ethical mindset.*

Ethical Practice and the Disengagement/Engagement Hypothesis

The disengagement/engagement (change) hypothesis suggests that an overarching goal of treatment is for a client/patient to *disengage* from nonproductive thoughts, affective reactions, and maladaptive behaviors as a prelude to being able to engage in much more prosocial, adaptive thoughts, affective reactions, and behaviors. Of course, this is a paradoxical phenomenon: Disengagement most often takes place in a gradual way as clients' apprehensions, concerns, feelings of life being out of control, etc. As their symptoms, concerns, etc. are allayed and clients feel safer, less anxious, less depressed, etc., the gateway to more adaptive engagement with life becomes possible. As discussed above, there are a variety of ways in which such disengagement/engagement can be facilitated as clients do the difficult "working through" of self-examination, exploring new ways of coping, taking risks, assuming responsibility, etc. There are other ways in which such disengagement can be facilitated, as elaborated in our advanced text.

Do no harm is the primary rule of ethics in medicine, and it can be considered an equally appropriate caution for all of health care, including psychological and counseling services across the spectrum of approaches. All disciplines, regardless of theoretical orientation, share a fundamental starting point regarding the practice of therapy with their clients: All practitioners of psychotherapy and counseling have a *fiduciary* relationship to their clients. There is a *relationship of trust* that exists between the practitioner and the client. As a fiduciary, the practitioner *must* put the interests of the client above his or her own interests. A good, ethically sensitive relationship cannot be exploitative, by definition, as it is derived out of a sense of maturity, care, and responsibility to the client. Of all things, clients seeking therapy are vulnerable. Vulnerable to what? Clients are vulnerable to a number of things: any comment, suggestion, behavior, gesture, etc. of the practitioner; being taken advantage of or exploited; being diminished in any way; etc.

In this brief section, we present the major ethical principles described in the literature for which professional individuals are responsible in rendering care to their clients/patients. There are five principles of ethics to which all psychotherapists and counselors aspire to adhere: autonomy, fidelity, nonmaleficence, justice, and beneficence. Although initially elements of biomedical ethics, they have been adopted and expanded by all of the therapeutic helping professions (see Peluso, 2006).

Autonomy: Respect for the Individual

Respect for autonomy is one of the ethical principles that is relevant to our discussion.

The principle of respect for autonomy demands that patients who consult us are esteemed as autonomous rational agents whose consent to treatment must be elicited. Furthermore, their consent to treatment must be freely voluntary, without controlling coercion, as well as based on a full understanding of what the treatment entails. This can be especially challenging for practitioners because many clients enter treatment under duress from a spouse, an attorney representing the client, employer, court, etc. Sensitivity to such therapeutic contingencies and how to navigate the fact that the client may not want to be in treatment is exceptionally important.

Competent patients, that is, those individuals who are capable of making informed, intentional medical decisions in their best interests on their own behalf, have a right to refuse *any* treatment, even life-sustaining medical treatments. The courts have upheld those rights for many years now (see *Cruzon v Missouri Department of Health, 1990*). That right to refuse even a life-sustaining treatment is a guarantee stemming from the "right to privacy" that is protected by the U.S. Constitution. The psychotherapy/counseling experience offers a client additional choices that can be made within the context of a safe and trustworthy relationship. The client can accept or reject those choices, but once presented, they can be considered even if rejected. In that brief moment of consideration, the client is open to a new possibility, even a new reality that had not been considered previously. It is crucial that information is not forced upon a client, which would be a violation of the principle of autonomy. Indeed, such additional choices simultaneously enhance the disengagement/engagement process by providing clients different choices than they perhaps had before entering treatment.

Fidelity: Respect for the Truth

A respect for the "truth" can be challenging for practitioners. Clients can ask their therapist many questions that the answers to which can be discouraging. The issue that arises as to exactly what the "truth" really is. Thinking through very tough questions posed by clients and coming up with truthful answers that are not discouraging is challenging and demanding. It is practice, supervision, and thinking in nonlinear ways that allows master practitioners to be truthful while at the same time not discouraging their clients/patients in a way that impedes recovery from their episode of crisis.

Nonmaleficence: "Do No Harm"

The biomedical ethical principle of nonmaleficence requires that we do not intentionally, needlessly harm or injure someone we are treating by either an act of commission or an act of omission. An act of omission—not doing something we should have done as part of our professional obligation to a patient, which causes harm—can be the basis for a malpractice suit based on negligence. Causing someone harm intentionally (other than the harm, for example, inflicted by the basic nature of a surgical procedure, i.e., cutting someone open) would be a violation of the principle of nonmaleficence.

The processes of psychotherapy and counseling are fraught with painful memories, losses, failures, sad realizations, fears, anxieties, confrontations no matter how gently they may be presented, and the like. Such experiences are endemic to the process of therapy and the human condition. In addition, most clients have the expectation that therapy or counseling is going to "hurt" in some way, but in the long run, it is going to "help"; it's the paradoxical nature of the therapeutic process. By facilitating the patient's disengagement from symptomatic preoccupation, healthier processes become possible, and that is the purpose for which clients come for help.

It is extremely important for the therapeutic enterprise to establish and maintain a strong working alliance. To be cavalier or to take the relationship for granted is negligent and runs the risk of violating the nonmaleficence principle.

Justice: Doing What Is Right

Proper assessment, and thorough understanding of the client's schema dynamics, his emotional system, and the nature of his ambivalence must also be taken into consideration. Therapists are responsible for maintaining the therapeutic alliance and attending to therapeutic ruptures (see Chapter 7). As a result, they must act in ways that are fair as well as beneficial to the client. Coale (1998) commented about the issues of therapeutic relationships and what transpires in them, which is relevant to our consideration of justice:

> Establishing therapeutic relationships based on mutual interconnectedness involves working within therapeutic paradoxes—establishing equality in a hierarchical relationship, mutuality in a nonmutual relationship, empowerment in a power-imbalanced relationship, and respect for *client* meaning and belief within a frame of therapy theories and beliefs. . . . Setting boundaries in the context of such therapeutic paradoxes is a joint process between therapist and client. It is not just something that the therapist can do *to* the client but rather something that, in interaction, the client and the therapist do together. The client must agree to respect the boundaries that he and the therapist set together. He must be open to what the therapist has to give.
>
> (p. 97)

Beneficence: Doing What Is Good

The ethical principle of beneficence is to do good. If anything is clear about the work of counseling and psychotherapy, it is that their foundations are at best based on theories, highly poetic metaphors, and beliefs about the way things work, which are supported by ongoing research. It is an aspirational field, and the best practitioners are ones who believe that the best is possible for each person. To do this often (paradoxically) means taking clients where they may not want to go in order to explore their ambivalence or dilemma. Beier's (1966) therapeutic concept of "beneficial uncertainty," in addition to being a part of nonlinear thinking, is relevant to the concept of beneficence:

> The patient, within the experience of a permissive atmosphere, has to be challenged to experience and tolerate uncertainty; but as such a challenge does occur within the framework of a permissive atmosphere, the sense of uncertainty experienced by the patient is likely to beneficial—one which leads to an exploration rather than defense.
>
> (p. 57)

Beier (1966) noted, however, that simply creating uncertainty is not sufficient in clinical activity. He emphasized that it must be beneficial, meaning *it is created nonjudgmentally with a sense of concern for the client's well-being:*

> The presence of concern and the freedom from having judgment imposed permit the patient to interpret the responses to his messages as beneficial rather than threatening. The messages of the therapist are, in a true sense, persuasion; they are designed to give the patient both hope and courage to dare into the unknown.
>
> (p. 9)

This is similar to a physician showing concern regarding the serious nature of a medical condition and the need for surgery. All clients bring problems, concerns, anxieties, and uncertainty to therapy. In practice, "beneficial" uncertainty frequently involves a clinician saying the unthinkable, which brings the client's worst fears into the open (Beier, 1966). Beier cautioned, however, that these interventions can be dangerous and must be delivered free of countertransference, free from being entertained by the client, and free of an urge to retaliate, harm, punish, or reject the client.

Advanced Nonlinear Thinking, Paradoxical Interventions, and Resolving Ethical Dilemmas

Of course, there are many times when the above ethical principles are in conflict with one another, and the clinician finds herself in the position of not being able to resolve one ethical dilemma without violating the other. For example, if a client says that they are determined to go into his boss's office and quit his job, and has not prepared himself financially or otherwise for being without a job (which will surely trigger depression, which is his presenting concern, and which you have spent the last 6 months helping him with), then you have a dilemma. Do you let him go ahead with his plan or do you try to dissuade him (and how heavily do you try to dissuade him)? If you value the ethical principle of autonomy, then you have to let him make his own decision. However, if you value the ethical principle of beneficence, then you cannot let him do this action. So, both principles are at odds with each other. If you advocate for one you are violating the other, hence you are in a double-bind. All too often, this is what most practitioners find themselves wrestling with when they have an ethical dilemma. Fortunately, *advanced nonlinear thinking* elements that are used to help clients get out of double-binds can be used here. Again, with the example above, a practitioner can use the Socratic method to question their logic (beliefs vs. facts) and inductive reasoning to create universal definitions and ultimately clarify values. The clinician (or perhaps the clinician's supervisor or peer) can help identify the "injunctions" (in this case the competing ethical values) that create the double-bind. Finally, paradoxical interventions (tranquillizers, energizers, or challengers) can be constructed to find creative ways to resolve the ethical dilemma. Ultimately, humor can be employed to help break through some of the stress and develop an absurd framework where a creative solution can be found. Indeed, advanced nonlinear thinking and paradoxical interventions can offer many benefits to master practitioners in their professional peer and supervisory relationships.

Conclusion: "Think Different . . ."

In 1997, after over a decade of "exile" from the company that he created, Steve Jobs returned as CEO of the technology company Apple. During his time away, the company went from being an innovative and influential leader in the computer field to being marginalized and a "has been" company about to be bought out and dismantled. Jobs was a visionary and charismatic leader, and he returned to the company to return it to its former glory. In order to signal a new beginning for the company, Apple created a new marketing campaign called "Think Different" that included a television commercial with the following text:

> Here's to the crazy ones.
> The misfits. The rebels. The troublemakers.
> The round pegs in the square holes.
> The ones who see things differently.
> They're not fond of rules. And they have no respect for the status quo.
> You can quote them, disagree with them, glorify or vilify them.
> About the only thing you can't do is ignore them.
> Because they change things.
> They push the human race forward.
> While some may see them as the crazy ones, we see genius.
> Because the people who are crazy enough to think they can change the world . . . are the ones who do.

The commercial featured video of great visionary individuals of the 20th century such as Albert Einstein, Bob Dylan, Martin Luther King, Jr., John Lennon, Thomas Edison, Mahatma Gandhi, Amelia Earhart, Alfred Hitchcock, Jim Henson (with Kermit the Frog), and Pablo Picasso. History, of course, records that in the decade that followed, Apple went on to introduce revolutionary technology to the world, including the iPod, iPhone, and iPad, creating the digital music revolution, usher in the smartphone era, and redefine the tablet computer. All of these remarkable inventions were spearheaded by Steve Jobs, himself. In many ways, like the luminaries in the commercial, he embodied the "Think Different" spirit of Apple.

We would like to think that what we have done, over the course of two texts, is to create a system of training that (1) illustrates how the best therapists indeed *think differently* and get superior results for clients, and (2) presents an easy to understand method for learning this sophisticated way of thinking (and practicing) in order to achieve expertise in the field and get the same results as the masters. In the end, what makes us *all* nonlinear thinkers is that we want to be *change agents,* we want to change the world. As therapists, we want to do this one person at a time, or one family at a time, or maybe even one community at a time, but we want to change it for the better. The ancient Jewish religious text the Talmud states: "He who saves one life, saves the world entire." We can't think of a better exhortation, or inspiration, to begin the work of employing the advanced nonlinear thinking of paradoxical interventions. Again, "because the people who are crazy enough to think they can change the world, are the ones who do."

References

Abrami, L. M. (2009). The healing power of humor in logotherapy. *International Forum for Logotherapy, 32*(1), 7–12.

Alexander Street Press. (2012). *Principles of counseling and psychotherapy: The essential domains and non-linear thinking of master practitioners* [Motion picture]. Alexandria, VA: Author.

American heritage dictionary of the English language, 5th ed. (2011). New York, NY: Houghton Mifflin.

Bateson, G. (1969). The position of humor in human communication. In J. Levine (Ed.), *Motivation in humor* (pp. 159–178). New Brunswick, NJ: Aldine Transaction.

Beck, A. T., Rush, A. J., Shaw, B. F., & Emery, G. (1979). *Cognitive therapy of depression.* New York, NY: Guilford Press.

Beck, A. T., Wright, F. D., Newman, C. F., & Liese, B. S. (1993). *Cognitive therapy of substance abuse.* New York, NY: Guilford Press.

Bekinschtein, T. A., Davis, M. H., Rodd, J. M., & Owen, A. M. (2011). Why clowns taste funny: The relationship between humor and semantic ambiguity. *Journal of Neuroscience, 31*(26), 9665–9671.

Beier, E. (1966). *The silent language of psychotherapy: Social reinforcement of unconscious processes.* Chicago, IL: Aldine.

Berk, R., Martin, R., Baird, D., & Nozik, B. (2008). *What everyone should know about humor & laughter.* Baltimore, MD: Johns Hopkins.

Betrando, P., & Gilli, G. (2008). Collapsing frames: Humor and psychotherapy in a Batesonian perspective. *International Journal of Psychotherapy, 12*(3), 12–22.

Beutler, L. E., Moleiro, C. M., & Talebi, H. (2002). Resistance. In J. C. Norcross (Ed.), *Psychotherapy relationships that work: Therapist contributions and responsiveness to patient needs.* New York, NY: Oxford University Press.

Bohart, A. C., & Tallman, K. (2010). Clients: The neglected common factor in psychotherapy. In B. L. Duncan, S. D. Miller, B. E. Wampold, & M. A. Hubble (Eds.), *The heart and soul of change* (2nd ed.). Washington, DC: American Psychological Association.

Bouaziz, I. (2007). Laugh or not laugh, this is not the question: Humor and paradox in psychotherapy. *Cahiers critiques de thérapie familiale, 39*(2), 73–81.

Burns, D. D. (2010, October 15). Workshop on "Paradoxical agenda setting: How to dramatically boost your effectiveness in the treatment of: Depression, anxiety, relationship problems, eating disorders, and drug/alcohol abuse." Personal Communication.

Carey, T. A., & Mullan, R. J. (2004). What is Socratic questioning? *Psychotherapy: Theory, Research, Practice, Training, 41*(3), 217–226.

Carlson, J., Watts, R. E., & Maniacci, M. (2006). *Adlerian therapy: Theory and practice.* Washington, DC: American Psychological Association.

Casadei, A., & Giordani, A. (2008). Irony and psychotherapy. *International Journal of Psychotherapy, 12*(3), 5–11.

Chi, M. T. H. (2006). Laboratory methods for assessing experts' and novices' knowledge. In K. A. Ericsson, N. Charness, P. J. Feltovich, & R. R. Hoffman (Eds.), *The Cambridge handbook of expertise and expert performance* (pp. 167–184). New York, NY: Cambridge University Press.

Coale, H. W. (1998). *The vulnerable therapist: Practicing psychotherapy in an age of anxiety.* New York, NY: Haworth.

Copi, I. M., Cohen, C., & Flage, D. E. (2007). *Essentials of logic* (2nd ed.). Upper Saddle River, NJ: Pearson Education.

Davey, M., Duncan, T., Kissil, K., & Fish, L. S. (2011). Second-order change in marriage and family therapy: A Web-based modified Delphi Study. *The American Journal of Family Therapy, 39,* 100–111.

Davidson, J. E., & Sternberg, R. J. (1998). Smart problem solving: How metacognition helps. In D. J. Hacker, J. Dunolsky, & A. C. Graesser (Eds.), *Metacognition in educational theory and practice* (pp. 47–68). Mahwah, NJ: Lawrence Erlbaum Associates Publishers.

Dingfelter, S. F. (2011). The formula for funny. *Monitor on Psychology, 37,* 54–55.

Doyle, A. C. (1892/1986). *Sherlock Holmes: The complete novels and stories.* New York, NY: Bantam.

Dreikurs, R. (1967). *Psychodynamics, psychotherapy and counseling.* Chicago, IL: Alfred Adler Institute of Chicago.

Duncan, B. L. (2010). Prologue: Saul Rosenzweig: The founder of common factors. In B. L. Duncan, S. D. Miller, B. E. Wampold, & M. A. Hubble (Eds.), *The heart and soul of change: Delivering what works in therapy* (2nd ed., pp. i–xxii). Washington, DC: American Psychological Association.

Duncan, B. L., Hubble, M. A., & Miller, S. D. (2000). *The heroic client.* San Francisco, CA: Jossey-Bass.

Ebert, R. (n.d.). Review of "Back to School." Retrieved from www.rogerebert.com/reviews/back-to-school-1986

Ekman, P. (2007). *Recognizing faces and feelings to improve communication and emotional life.* New York, NY: Holt Paper Backs.

Elkaim, M. (1997). *If you love me, don't love me: Undoing reciprocal double-binds and other methods of change in couple and family therapy.* New York: NY: Jason Aronson.

Ellis, A., & Dryden, W. (2007). *The practice of rational-emotive therapy* (2nd ed.). New York, NY: Springer.

Ericsson, K. A., Chamness, N., Feltovich, P. J., & Hoffman, R. R. (Eds.). (2006). *The Cambridge handbook of expertise and expert performance.* Cambridge Handbooks in Performance. London, UK: Cambridge University Press.

Fielder, F. E. (1950). A comparison of therapeutic relationships in psychoanalytic, nondirective and Adlerian therapy. *Journal of Consulting Psychology, 14*(6), 436–445. doi: 10.1037/h0054624

Fraser, J. S., & Solovey, A. D. (2007). *Second-order change in psychotherapy: The golden thread that unifies effective treatments.* Washington, DC: American Psychological Association.

Freud, S. (1928). Humor. *International Journal of Psychoanalysis, 9,* 1–6.

Freud, S. (1960). *Jokes and their relation to the unconscious* (J. Strachey, Trans.). New York, NY: Norton.

Fry, W. H., & Salameh, W. A. (Eds.). (1987). *Handbook of humor and psychotherapy: Advances in the clinical use of humor.* Sarasota, FL: Professional Resource Exchange.

Gandino, G., Vesco, M., Benna, S. R., & Prastaro, M. (2010). Whiplash for the mind: Humor in therapeutic conversation. *International Journal of Psychotherapy, 14*(1), 13–24.

Gelkopf, M. (2011). The use of humor in serious mental illness: A review. *Evidence-Based Complementary and Alternative Medicine,* 1–8.

Gibney, P. (2006). The double bind theory: Still crazy-making after all these years. *Psychotherapy in Australia, 12*(3), 48–55.

Gladwell, M. (2005). *Blink: The power of thinking without thinking.* New York, NY: Little Brown.

Goldberg, C. (1980). The utilization and limitations of paradoxical intervention in group psychotherapy. *International Journal of Group Psychotherapy, 30,* 287–297.

Greenberg, L. S. (2004). *Emotion-focused therapy: Coaching clients to work through their feelings.* Washington, DC: American Psychological Association.

Hanna, F. J. (2001). *Therapy with difficult clients: Using the precursors model to awaken change.* Washington, DC: American Psychological Association.

Hayden, G., & Picard, M. (2009). *This book does not exist: Adventures in the paradoxical.* New York, NY: Fall River Press.

Horn H., & Masunaga, J., (2006). A merging theory of expertise and intelligence. In K. A. Ericsson, N. Chamness, P. J. Feltovich, & R. R. Hoffman (Eds.), *The Cambridge handbook of expertise and expert performance* (p. 601). Cambridge Handbooks in Performance. London, UK: Cambridge University Press.

Horvath, A. O., & Bedi, R. P. (2002). The alliance. In J. C. Norcross (Ed.), *Psychotherapy relationships that work: Therapist contributions and responsiveness to patient needs.* New York, NY: Oxford University Press.

Hsu, M., Bhatt, M., Adolphs, R., Tranel, D., & Camerer, C. F. (2005). Neural mechanisms responding to degrees of uncertainty in human decision-making. *Science, 310,* 1680–1683.

Hsu, M., Bhatt, M., Adolphs, R., Tranel, D., & Camerer, C. (2005). Neural systems responding to degrees of uncertainty in human decision making. *Science, 310,* 1680–1683.

Hubble, M. A., Duncan, B. L., & Miller, S. D. (1999). *The heart and soul of change: What works in therapy.* Washington, DC: American Psychological Association.

Hughes, P., & Brecht, G. (1979). *Vicious circles and infinity.* New York, NY: Penguin Books.

Isen, A. M. (2003). *Positive affect as a source of human strength.* In L. G. Aspinwall & U. M. Staudinger (Eds.), *A psychology of human strengths: Fundamental questions and future directions for a positive psychology* (pp. 179–195). Washington, DC: American Psychological Association.

Jackson, P. L., Meltzoff, A. N., & Decety, J. (2005). How do we perceive the pain of others: A window into the neural processes involved in empathy. *NeuroImage, 24,* 771–779.

Jennings, L., & Skovholt, T. M. (1999). The cognitive, emotional, and relational characteristics of master therapists. *Journal of Counseling Psychology, 46*(1), 3–11.

Johnson-Laird, P., & Byrne, R. M. (1991). *Deduction.* New York, NY: Lawrence Erlbaum Associates.

Kahneman, D. (2011). *Thinking, fast and slow.* New York, NY: Farrar, Straus and Giroux.

Kelley, J. (2009). *Gunpowder: Alchemy, bombards, and pyrotechnics. The history of the explosive.* New York, NY: Basic Books.

Kohn, N., Kellerman, T., Gur, R. C., Schneider, F., & Habel, U. (2011). Gender differences in the neural correlates of humor processing: Implications for different processing modes. *Neuropsychologia, 49,* 888–897.

Koocher, G. P., & Keith-Spiegel, P. (2008). *Ethics in psychology and mental health: Standards and cases.* New York, NY: Oxford University Press.

Kubie, L. (1971). The destructive potential of humor in psychotherapy. *American Journal of Psychiatry, 127,* 861–866.

Lambert, M. (2010). "Yes, it is time for clinicians to routinely monitor treatment outcome M. A. Hubble, B. L. Duncan, & S. D. Miller (Eds.), *The heart and soul of change: What work therapy* (pp. 239–266). Washington, DC: American Psychological Association.

Lambert, M. J., & Barley, D. E. (2002). Research summary on the therapeutic relations psychotherapy outcomes. In J. C. Norcross (Ed.), *Psychotherapy relationships th Therapist contributions and responsiveness to patient needs.* New York, NY: Oxford Press.

Lambert, M. J., & Shimokawa, K. (2011). Collecting client feedback. *Psychotherapy, 4*

Luborsky, L., Diguer, L., Seligman, D. A., Rosenthal, R., Krause, E. D., Johnson, S., . . . Schweizer, E. (1999). The researcher's own therapy allegiances: A "wild card" in comparisons of treatment efficacy. *Clinical Psychology: Science and Practice, 6,* 95–106.

Makoto, S. (2011). Effects of humor elicited by bisociation in narrative approach. *Japanese Journal of Counseling Science, 44*(1), 60–68.

Marshall, R. J. (1972, Summer). The treatment of resistances in psychotherapy of children and adolescents. *Psychotherapy: Theory, Research and Practice, 9,* 143–148.

Marshall, R. J. (1974). Meeting the resistances of delinquents. *Psychoanalytic Review, 61,* 295–304.

Marshall, R. J. (1976). "Joining techniques" in the treatment of resistant children and adolescents: A learning theory rationale. *American Journal of Psychotherapy, 30,* 73–84.

Martin, R. A. (2006). *The psychology of humor: An integrative approach.* Burlington, MA: Elsevier Academic Press.

Martin, R. A. (2010). *The psychology of humor: An integrative approach.* Burlington, MA: Elsevier.

Masters, W. H., & Johnson, V. E. (1966). *Human sexual response.* Oxford, UK: Little, Brown.

McClure, S. M., Laibson, D. I., Loewenstein, G., & Cohen, J. D. (2004). Separate neural systems value immediate and delayed monetary rewards. *Science, 306,* 503–507.

McGhee, P. (2010a). *Humor as a survival training for a stressed out world.* Bloomington, IN: AuthorHouse.

McGhee, P. (2010b). *Humor: The lighter path to resilience and health.* Bloomington, IN: AuthorHouse.

Mikulincer, M., & Shaver, P. R. (2005). Attachment security, compassion, and altruism. *Current Directions in Psychological Science, 14*(1), 34–38.

Milenković, S. (2007). Humor as a paradoxical intervention in psychotherapy. *International Journal of Psychotherapy, 11*(3), 56–65.

Miller, S. D., Duncan, B. L., & Hubble, M. A. (1997). *Escape from Babel.* New York, NY: Norton.

Miller, S. D., Duncan, B. L., Brown, J., Sparks, J. A., & Claud, D. A. (2003). The outcome rating scale: A preliminary study of the reliability, validity, and feasibility of a brief visual analog measure. *Journal of Brief Therapy, 2,* 91–100.

Miller, S., Hubble, M., Duncan, B., & Wampold, B. (2010). Delivering what works. In *The heart and soul of change, Second Edition: Delivering what works* (pp. 421–429). Washington, DC: American Psychological Association.

Miller, W. R., Benefield, R. G., & Tonigan, J. S. (1993). Enhancing motivation for change in problem drinking: A controlled comparison of two therapist styles. *Journal of Consulting and Clinical Psychology, 61,* 455–461.

'ler, W. R., & Rollnick, S. (2002). *Motivational interviewing: Preparing people for change* (2nd '. New York, NY: Guilford.

V. R., & Rollnick, S. (2012). *Motivational Interviewing 3rd edition: Helping people change 'ions of Motivational Interviewing).* New York, NY: Guilford.

& Rose, G. S. (2009). Toward a theory of Motivational Interviewing. *American Psy- '27–537.

r, C. A., & West, J. C. (1980). Focused versus broad-spectrum behavior therapy 's. *Journal of Consulting and Clinical Psychology, 48,* 590–601.

The therapeutic value of laughter in medicine. *Alternative Therapies* 56–64.

'related structural and operational characteristics of motivational 'adoxical/nonlinear thinking. Unpublished manuscript, Western

'lli, F. (1989). The mandala of psychotherapy: The universal 'nd more confusion. *Psychotherapy: Theory, Research and*

Mozdzierz, G., Macchitelli, F., & Lisiecki, J. (1976). The paradox in psychotherapy: An Adlerian perspective. *Journal of Individual Psychology, 32*, 169–184.

Mozdzierz, G. J., Peluso, P., & Lisiecki, J. (2014). *Principles of counseling and psychotherapy: Learning the essential domains and nonlinear thinking of master practitioners* (2nd ed.). New York, NY: Routledge.

Murray, R. (2002). The phenomenon of psychotherapeutic change: Second-order change in one's experience of self. *Journal of Contemporary Psychotherapy, 32*(2/3), 167–177.

Nelson, J. K. (2008). Laugh and the world laughs with you: An attachment perspective on the meaning of laughter in psychotherapy. *Clinical Social Work Journal, 36*, 41–49.

Nohlen, H. U., van Harreveld, F., Rotteveel, M., Lelieveld, G. J., & Crone, E. A. (2013). Evaluating ambivalence: Social-cognitive and affective brain regions associated with ambivalent decision-making. *Social Cognitive Affective Neuroscience*. doi: 10.1093/scan/nst074.

Norcross, J. C. (Ed.). (2002). *Psychotherapy relationships that work: Therapist contributions and responsiveness to patient needs*. New York, NY: Oxford University Press.

Norcross, J. (2010). The therapeutic relationship. In M. A. Hubble, B. L. Duncan, & S. D. Miller (Eds.), *The heart and soul of change: What works in therapy* (pp. 113–141). Washington, DC: American Psychological Association.

Norcross, J. C. (2011). *Psychotherapy relationships that work: Evidence-based responsiveness* (2nd ed.). New York, NY: Oxford University Press.

Norcross, J. C., & Wampold, B. E. (2011). Evidence-based therapy relationships: Research conclusions and clinical practices. *Psychotherapy, 48*(1), 98–102.

Olson, D. H. (1972). Empirically unbinding the double bind: Review of research and conceptual reformulations. *Family Process, 11*(1), 69–94.

Omer, H. (1981). Paradoxical treatments: A unified concept. *Psychotherapy: Theory, Research and Practice, 18*, 320–324.

Omer, H. (1991). Dialectical interventions and the structure of strategy. *Psychotherapy, 28*, 563–571.

Omer, H. (1994). *Critical interventions in psychotherapy*. New York, NY: Norton.

Overholser, J. C. (1993a). Elements of the Socratic method: I. Systematic questioning. *Psychotherapy, 30*(1), 67–74.

Overholser, J. C. (1993b). Elements of the Socratic method: II. Inductive reasoning. *Psychotherapy, 30*(1), 75–85.

Overholser, J. C. (1994). Elements of the Socratic method: III. Universal definitions. *Psychotherapy, 31*(2), 286–293.

Overholser, J. C. (1995). Elements of the Socratic method: IV. Disavowal of knowledge. *Psychotherapy, 32*(2), 283–292.

Overholser, J. C. (1996). Elements of the Socratic method: V. Self-improvement. *Psychotherapy, 33*(4), 549–559.

Overholser, J. C. (1999). Elements of the Socratic method: VI. Promoting virtue in everyday life. *Psychotherapy, 36*(2), 137–145.

Overholser, J. C. (2010). Psychotherapy according to the Socratic method: Integrating ancient philosophy with contemporary cognitive therapy. *Journal of Cognitive Psychotherapy: An International Quarterly, 24*(4), 354–363.

Oxford English Dictionary. (2007). New York, NY: Oxford University Press.

Panichelli, C. (2013). Humor, joining, and reframing in psychotherapy: Resolving the auto-double bind. *The American Journal of Family Therapy, 41*, 437–451.

Paolo, B., & Gilli, G. (2008). Emotional dances: Therapeutic dialogues as embodied systems. *Journal of Family Therapy, 30*, 362–373.

Patterson, G. R., & Forgatch, M. S. (1985). Therapist behavior as a determinant for client noncompliance: A paradox for the behavior modifier. *Journal of Consulting and Clinical Psychology, 53*, 846–851.

Peluso, P. R. (2007). The ethical and professional practice of couples and family counseling. In L. Sperry (Ed.), *The ethical and professional practice of counseling and psychotherapy* (pp. 285–351). Boston, MA: Allyn & Bacon.

Pope, K., & Vasquez, M. J. T. (2010). *Ethics in psychotherapy and counseling.* New York, NY: Wiley.

Prochaska, J. O. (1999). How do people change, and how can we change to help many more people? In M. A. Hubble, B. L. Duncan, & S. D. Miller (Eds.), *The heart and soul of change: What works in therapy* (pp. 227–255). Washington, DC: American Psychological Association.

Prochaska, J. O., & DiClemente, C. C. (1982). Transtheoretical therapy: Toward a more integrative model of change. *Psychotherapy: Theory, Research and Practice, 20,* 161–173.

Prochaska, J. O., & DiClemente, C. C. (1984). *The transtheoretical approach: Crossing traditional boundaries of change.* Homewood, IL: Dorsey.

Prochaska, J. O., & DiClemente, C. C. (2005). The transtheoretical approach. In J. C. Norcross & M. R. Goldfried (Eds.), *Handbook of psychotherapy integration . Oxford series in clinical psychology* (2nd ed., pp. 147–171). New York, NY: Oxford University Press.

Psychotherapy.net. (2006). *The legacy of unresolved loss: A family systems approach* [Motion Picture]. Alexandria, VA: Alexander Street Press.

Random House American College Dictionary. (2006). New York, NY: Random House.

Ritchie, G. (2006). Reinterpretation and viewpoints. *Humor: International Journal of Humor Research, 19*(3), 251–270.

Rogers, R., & Reinhardt, V. R. (1998). Conceptualization and assessment of secondary gain. In G. Koocher, J. C. Norcross, & C. E. Hill (Eds.), *Psychologists' desk reference* (pp. 57–62). New York, NY: Oxford University Press.

Rust, J., & Goldstein, J. (1989). Humor in marital adjustment. *Humor: International Journal of Humor Research, 2*(3), 211–223.

Salameh, W. A. (1987). Humor in Integrative Short-Term Psychotherapy (ISTP). In W. H. Fry & W. A. Salameh (Eds.), *Handbook of humor and psychotherapy: Advances in the clinical use of humor.* Sarasota, FL: Professional Resource Exchange.

Schmidt, S. R. (1994). Effects of humor on sentence memory. *Journal of Experimental Psychology: Learning, Memory, & Cognition, 20*(4), 953–967.

Shaughnessy, M. F., & Wadsworth, T. M. (1992). Humor in counseling and psychotherapy: A 20-year retrospective. *Psychological Reports, 70,* 755–762. doi: 10.2466/pr0.1992.70.3.755

Skovholt, T. M., & Jennings, L. (2004). *Master therapists: Exploring expertise in therapy and counseling.* Boston, MA: Allyn & Bacon.

Skovholt, T. M., & Rivers, D. (2004). *Skills and strategies for the helping professions.* Denver, CO: Love.

Sperry, L. (2007). *The ethical and professional practice of counseling and psychotherapy.* Boston, MA: Allyn & Bacon.

Stoltenberg, C. D. (1993). Supervising consultants in training: An application of a model of supervision. *Journal of Counseling and Development, 72,* 131–138.

Stoltenberg, C. D. (1997). The integrated developmental model of supervision: Supervision across levels. *Psychotherapy in Private Practice, 16*(2), 59–69.

Stoltenberg, C. D., & Delworth, U. (1987). *Supervising counselors and therapists: A developmental approach.* San Francisco, CA: Jossey-Bass.

Stoltenberg, C. D., & McNeill, B. (2009). *IDM supervision: An integrated developmental model for supervising counselors and therapists.* New York, NY: Routledge.

Taylor, J. (2011). Common sense is neither common or sense. *Psychology Today: The power of prime.* Retrieved from www.psychologytoday.com/blog/the-power-prime/201107/common-sense-is-neither-common-nor-sense

Thornton, J. (2006, July/August). A new path to change. *Men's Health,* pp. 156–159.

Valle, S. K. (1981). Interpersonal functioning of alcoholism counselors and treatment outcome. *Journal of Studies on Alcohol, 42,* 783–790.

Van Sant, G. (Dir.). (1997). *Good Will Hunting* [Motion picture]. Los Angeles, CA: Be Gentlemen Limited Partnership.

Vonnegut, K. (1971) Running experiments off: An interview. In W. R. Allen, *Conversations with Kurt Vonnegut.* Jackson: University Press of Mississippi.

Walt, J. (2005). An interview with Scott Miller. *The Milton H. Erickson Foundation Newsletter, 25,* 1–20.

Wampold, B. E. (2005). What should be validated? The psychotherapist. In J. C. Norcross, L. E. Beutler, & R. F. Levant (Eds.), *Evidence-based practices in mental health: Debate and dialogue on the fundamental questions* (pp. 200–208, 236–238). Washington, DC: American Psychological Association.

Wampold, B. E. (2010). The research evidence for common factors models: A historically situated perspective. In B. L. Duncan, S. D. Miller, B. E. Wampold, & M. A. Hubble (Eds.), *The heart and soul of change: Delivering what works in therapy* (2nd ed., pp. 49–81). Washington, DC: American Psychological Association.

Wampold, B. E., & Brown, G. S. (2005). Estimating therapist variability: A naturalistic study of outcomes in managed care. *Journal of Consulting and Clinical Psychology, 73,* 914–923.

Watzlawick, P. (1976a). *How real is real?* New York, NY: Random House.

Watzlawick, P. (1976b). *The situation is hopeless but not serious (The pursuit of unhappiness).* New York, NY: Norton.

Watzlawick, P., Beavin, J. J., & Jackson, D. D. (1967). *Pragmatics of human communication: A study of interactional patterns, pathologies and paradoxes.* New York, NY: Norton.

Watzlawick, P., Weakland, J., & Fisch, R. (1974). *Change: Principles of problem formulation and problem resolution.* New York, NY: Norton.

Weisberg, R. L. (2006). Modes of expertise in creative thinking: Evidence from case studies. In K. A. Ericsson, N. Charness, R. R. Hoffman, & P. J. Feltovich (Eds.), *The Cambridge handbook of expertise and expert performance* (pp. 761–787). New York, NY: Cambridge University Press.

Whitaker, C. A. (1989). *Midnight musings of a family therapist.* New York, NY: WW Norton.

White, E. B., & White, K. S. (1941). *A subtreasury of American humor.* New York, NY: Coward-McCann.

White, E. C. (1987). *Kaironomia: On the will to invent.* Ithaca, NY & London: Cornell University Press.

Whitehead, A. N., & Russell, B. (1910–1913). *Principia mathematica.* Ann Arbor: University of Michigan Press.

Wild, B., Rodden, F. A., Grodd, W., & Ruch, W. (2003). Neural correlates of laughter and humour. *Brain, 126,* 2121–2138.

Wright, J. C. (1960). *Problem solving and search behavior under noncontingent rewards.* Unpublished dissertation, Stanford University.

Wright, J. C. (1962). Consistency and complexity of response sequences as a function of schedules of noncontingent reward. *Journal of Experimental Psychology, 63,* 601–609.

Index

Note: Page numbers in *italic* format indicate figures and tables.

Made in the USA
Middletown, DE
20 January 2022

59209943R00119